Vagrant Lives in Colonial Australasia

Empire's Other Histories

Empire's Other Histories is an innovative series devoted to the shared and diverse experiences of the marginalized, dispossessed and disenfranchized in modern imperial and colonial histories. It responds to an ever-growing academic and popular interest in the histories of those erased, dismissed, or ignored in traditional historiographies of empire. It will elaborate on and analyse new questions of perspective, identity, agency, mobilities, intersectionality and power relations.

Published:

Unhomely Empire: Whiteness and Belonging, c.1760–1830, Onni Gust
Extreme Violence and the 'British Way': Colonial Warfare in Perak, Sierra Leone and Sudan, Michelle Gordon
Unexpected Voices in Imperial Parliaments, ed. by José María Portillo, Josep M. Fradera and Teresa Segura-Garcia
The Making and Remaking of 'Australasia': Southern Circulations, ed. by Tony Ballantyne
Across Colonial Lines: Commodities, Networks and Empire Building, ed. by Devyani Gupta and Purba Hossain
Imperial Gallows: Murder, Violence and the Death Penalty in British Colonial Africa, c.1915–60, Stacey Hynd
Arctic Circles and Imperial Knowledge: The Franklin Family, Indigenous Intermediaries, and the Politics of Truth, Annaliese Jacobs Claydon
Early Capitalism in Colonial Missions: Moravian Household Economies in the Global Eighteenth Century, Christina Petterson

Forthcoming:

Dwelling on the Margins of Empire, ed by. Katherine Crooks and Lisa Binkley
Biocultural Empire, ed. by Antoinette Burton, Samantha Frost and Renisa Mawani
Challenging the British Empire in India, Andrea Major
Extreme Penalties, David M. Anderson and Katherine Bruce-Lockhart
Children of the Cape Colony, Rebecca Swartz

Vagrant Lives in Colonial Australasia

Regulating Mobility, 1840–1910

Catharine Coleborne

BLOOMSBURY ACADEMIC
LONDON • NEW YORK • OXFORD • NEW DELHI • SYDNEY

BLOOMSBURY ACADEMIC
Bloomsbury Publishing Plc, 50 Bedford Square, London, WC1B 3DP, UK
Bloomsbury Publishing Inc, 1359 Broadway, New York, NY 10018, USA
Bloomsbury Publishing Ireland, 29 Earlsfort Terrace, Dublin 2, D02 AY28, Ireland

BLOOMSBURY, BLOOMSBURY ACADEMIC and the Diana logo are trademarks of Bloomsbury Publishing Plc

First published in Great Britain 2024
This paperback edition published 2025

Series design by Tjaša Krivec
Cover image © Michael Kirwan, a clerk who had fallen on hard times, photographed at Lyttelton Gaol on 24 January 1902. Archives New Zealand Te Rua Mahara o te Kawanatanga

A catalogue record for this book is available from the British Library.

Library of Congress Cataloging-in-Publication Data
Names: Coleborne, Catharine, author.
Title: Vagrant lives in colonial Australasia :
regulating mobility and movement 1840–1920 / Catharine Coleborne.
Description: London, UK ; New York, NY, USA : Bloomsbury Academic, 2024. |
Series: Empire's other histories | Includes bibliographical references and index.
Identifiers: LCCN 2023042598 (print) | LCCN 2023042599 (ebook) |
ISBN 9781350252691 (hardback) | ISBN 9781350252721 (paperback) |
ISBN 9781350252714 (epub) | ISBN 9781350252707 (ebook)
Subjects: LCSH: Vagrancy–Australia–History. | Vagrancy–New Zealand–History.
Classification: LCC HV4630.A3 C654 2024 (print) | LCC HV4630.A3 (ebook) |
DDC 364.1/48099409034–dc23/eng/20231220
LC record available at https://lccn.loc.gov/2023042598
LC ebook record available at https://lccn.loc.gov/2023042599

ISBN:	HB:	978-1-3502-5269-1
	PB:	978-1-3502-5272-1
	ePDF:	978-1-3502-5270-7
	eBook:	978-1-3502-5271-4

Series: Empire's Other Histories

Typeset by Integra Software Services Pvt. Ltd.

For product safety related questions contact productsafety@bloomsbury.com.

To find out more about our authors and books visit www.bloomsbury.com and sign up for our newsletters.

Contents

Figures

Acknowledgements

This book marks my return to a prevailing interest in the intersections between law and history. It also continues the conversation between my different pieces of research and writing about 'outsiders', a preoccupation that started with my interest in social histories of the status and experience of the widow in early modern England many years ago as an undergraduate student at the University of Melbourne and kept going with my work on the social and cultural histories of mental illness. It now also finds expression in this study about mobility and vagrancy. I am delighted that these mobile ideas have made a home in this 'Empire's Other Histories' series.

This book brings together several strands of my historical research into colonial policing, vulnerable populations, legislation and social formation, and the ways in which gender, class and ethnicity played out in the politics of culture across places in the colonial world. It also draws on new forms of digital scholarship. I remain grateful that my career as a researcher was shaped by historian Diane Kirkby at La Trobe University, currently Adjunct Professor at the University of Technology Sydney. Diane introduced me to the Australian and New Zealand Society for Law and History which has been a warm and welcoming scholarly environment for many years.

At the University of Waikato in Aotearoa/New Zealand, Peter Gibbons and I co-taught the history of 'Travellers, Settlers and Outlaws: Oceania 1800 to 1900', where many of the ideas about the many mobile peoples who moved around the colonies started to fascinate me. Postgraduate students and research assistants worked to produce bibliographies and locate primary sources used in this book, especially Debra Powell, Heather Duff and Chelsie Foley. Although an earlier planned 'sourcebook' about Oceanian histories was abandoned, the ideas about 'regulating bodies' made their way into my various pieces of writing over the years. Later, Nan Seuffert, Tahu Kukutai and I contributed to different faculty-funded editing projects and research about mobile peoples in the Pacific. These were interdisciplinary experiments involving legal, demographic and historical research and led to my interactions with the New Zealand mobilities research network. Participating in co-supervision teams with the Māori and Psychology Research Unit also inspired new thinking and reading around understandings of 'homelessness'.

In 2015, I was awarded a Centre for Mobilities Research (CeMoRe) Visiting Fellowship at the University of Lancaster, where the late John Urry kindly shared his ideas and contacts with me, and where Lynne Pearce was a wonderfully kind host, also organizing a half-day event. Each of these colleagues came from disciplines other than history, making me aware of the rich potential of the mobilities framework for historical research and writing. Colin Pooley has proved to be an excellent, insightful and generous mentor. My time at CeMoRe was critical at this juncture in my development as a scholar, and especially for my thinking about mobilities research as I move into new projects and fresh thinking. The interdisciplinary environment is very important to help extend and to challenge scholarship across boundaries. I'd like to sincerely thank CeMoRe staff for the financial support to enable me to visit the Centre. Thanks also to Pennie Drinkhall, Monika Buscher, Lynne Pearce of course, and a good many other people for their company, conversations and assistance, and for the very warm welcome to Lancaster that year.

Later in 2015 a small team of us held a mobilities conference at the University of Waikato, and I owe thanks to Holly Thorpe and Gail Adams-Hutcheson for their collaborative and inventive work. The ideas in this book were much earlier rehearsed as papers presented to different audiences between 2012 and 2016, including departmental seminars at the Universities of Auckland and Canterbury in Christchurch; invited talks at the former Colonialism and its Aftermath (CAIA) at the University of Tasmania, Hobart; an invited talk as part of a plenary panel at the Australian Historical Association Conference at Wollongong, as well as a short plenary paper to the ANZLHS conference held at UTS; my paper presented to the Dangerous Mobilities Conference at the University of Waikato; and papers presented at national workshops, and the International Conference of Historical Geographers held at the Royal Geographical Society, London, England in 2015. I offer particular thanks to David Lambert and Peter Merriman for inviting me to be part of what became impressive two impressive panels on mobility and empire during that meeting, now published as a collection for Manchester University Press.

Researchers and colleagues in Australia and New Zealand have provided support, read draft material and shared practical research assistance. The research for this book has not been funded by one project, and it has taken place over a long period of time, and across locations. Thanks to Nancy Cushing, Penny Edmonds, Rachel Franks, Jesper Gulddal, Kristyn Harman, Victoria Haskins, Andrew May, Julie McIntyre, Jan McLeod, Georgia McWhinney, Victoria Nagy, Rebecca Read, Lyndall Ryan, Kate Senior and Christina Twomey who offered help, expertise and ideas. Hugh Craig read draft material for the first introductory chapter and also invited me to bring my data, and ideas about vagrancy and mobility, into the Time-Layered Cultural Map (TLCMap) project funded by the Australian Research Council's Linkage Infrastructure, Equipment and Facilities program in 2023. Colleagues in the social sciences at the University of Newcastle offered me ideas about precarity and vulnerability: thanks to Hedda Askland, Julia Coffey, Julia Cook, Duncan McDuie-Ra and Steve Threadgold. A short period as a Fellow at the Humanities Research Centre for their theme of 'Mobilities' at the Australian National University was restorative and productive in the final quarter of 2022, and I appreciated comments from participants at a work-in-progress seminar who offered insightful feedback on my paper. Hamish Maxwell-Stewart provided me with additional data sets produced from his research into crime and punishment over several years. These data sets include cases of vagrancy prosecutions in Victoria, Tasmania and New South Wales listed in *Police Gazettes* shared as part of the 'Dataverse' described at the end of this book. Robyn Dunlop assisted with some editing work towards the end of the process of manuscript production, and always adds immense value to the historical work she conducts.

Finally, thank you to my colleagues at the University of Newcastle and beyond for their encouragement to produce this work, and to my family and close friends for their ongoing intellectual companionship, support and interest.

1

Approaching the colonial histories of vagrancy

An introduction

In his 2013 novel *Harvest,* Jim Crace writes about a changing world: a place that I imagine as being around the time of the Enclosure Acts in Britain.[1] Through his representation of the three dangerous vagrant outsiders who infiltrate the precariously 'settled' world of the gleaners, Crace tells the story of the central character, Walter Thirsk, who comes to realize that his own community is made up of those who had themselves once been people on the move.

Through Thirsk's eyes we see that the real danger in the small village is not the newly arrived vagrants, but the presence of new landowners accompanied by officials and notaries. These officials are planning to move the gleaners off the land, an act that would turn them into the dispossessed, despite their self-proclaimed 'settled' community. There is a new threat: a shift from that posed by 'the other within', or the figure of the vagrant, to the changes being enacted through land management and bureaucracy. This novel has continually captivated me as I have examined the histories and representations of vagrancy in the colonial world of Australasia. In its fictional account of an undefined historical moment – but redolent with descriptions of landscapes, people and beliefs shaping a world transitioning into the industrial era – Crace shows us how we might deepen and enhance our historical understanding of vagrancy as mobility and its multiple meanings.

In this book I want to tell the stories of some of those who people the historical record as I write this history of 'vagrancy from below'.[2] Vagrants were everywhere in the colonial world. From Margaret Kegan, with 'no home to go to, and no means of living' who pleaded guilty to vagrancy in 1902, and asked to be 'locked up' in New Zealand's North Island, to Christina Lawson, who had almost 200 convictions by 1907 for vagrancy and drunkenness, women and men endured poverty and life on the streets until they attracted police attention and pecuniary fines or short custodial sentences which gave them shelter and food for periods of time.[3] Vagrants held in gaols for periods of a week or three to six months were likely often protected from further crisis, but the evidence suggests few of them welcomed the respite, given prison conditions in the period. Judges also determined that recidivists, especially women with records of drunk and disorderly charges, needed to spend time in welfare institutions run by the Samaritans for their own safety. Some people charged with vagrancy wanted to keep moving, cheerfully pledging to 'clear out' from the places where they had been identified as a threat. These people included men like Francis Priestly, who 'made his living by begging' in Auckland, but who claimed to have lived all over the world without ever being called a 'rogue and a vagabond'.[4]

Francis Priestly presented in court with an air of insouciance. Newspaper court reports in the colonies reproduced these court proceedings, with thorough descriptions of events that appealed to the news reading public. The audience for vagrancy prosecutions was a mix of concerned citizens hoping to offer welfare or representing charitable organizations; journalists and writers who wanted to explain the human condition of the colonial criminal; and an assortment of actors who played their part in the courtroom drama of prosecutions including police, lawyers and outraged complainants. In each of the vagrancy cases described in mostly scant detail there is a consistent story of mobility stopped: embodying the paradox inherent in the policing of unwanted or unauthorized movement, and transgression of local 'fixed' spaces by the person 'on the move'.

The sheer scope of any study of people who were lived as 'vagrants' in the colonies means that writing about vagrancy is an enormous undertaking: it needs to be limited and shaped by the available evidence and approaches to it. To tell the stories of vagrants' lives, this book rests on an array of legal and social historical evidence including legislation, prosecution data, newspaper reports, contemporary accounts and representations of vagrancy, and the records of courtrooms and prisons. It takes the themes of law, policing, everyday lives, poverty, age and illness, and finally, wandering and adventure, to organize the material. I present some narratives of people arrested as vagrants, or living lives described as vagrant, to allow for our historical imagination of the people, their times, and their lives.

The book seeks to examine both mobility and vagrancy within a socio-legal history. The constant policing and sentencing of vagrants throughout the nineteenth century was part of a wider problem of 'social order' facing lawmakers and the criminal justice system, with vagrancy one of the most common crimes.[5] Historians show that the development of a 'new criminology' in the later decades of the century revealed the way that 'habitual criminals' in the Australian colonies were mostly arrested on minor charges including vagrancy, drunkenness and other minor offences, leading to 'a distraction and an irritant to the main business of criminal-justice'.[6] Vagrancy has been described as a 'crime of social status', which further explains these challenges for the policing of people using vagrancy laws.[7]

The regulation of mobility across the colonies of south-eastern Australia and New Zealand started with the surveillance and monitoring of convicts and their movement in New South Wales and Van Diemen's Land (VDL, later Tasmania) in the 1830s, and continued with the introduction of vagrancy laws in Victoria and New Zealand in the 1860s.[8] Indigenous peoples – from many displaced Aboriginal clans and Māori iwi – were made subject to other, more severe interventions than mere surveillance: mostly violence, dislocation and land alienation, as well as specific and harsh legal controls such as 'protection' policies and segregation from Europeans from the 1860s until well into the twentieth century. Their relationship to European-style vagrancy laws is an interesting aspect of this story and is captured here throughout this book.[9] Most of the vagrants caught up in this regulation of mobility were Europeans, both men and women, as the records of policing and prosecution show. However, a small number of Aboriginal and Māori people were prosecuted using vagrancy laws, as explained by the available prosecution data used in this book. Other mobile people including the Chinese men who came to the colonies as part of the rush for gold, some from the 1850s and others in the 1870s, also feature in vagrancy prosecution records. This study looks more closely at the way vagrancy was felt and lived, but along the way, the differences between vagrants as shown in the prosecution data can tell us more about the way police observed ethnic difference and whether it became a focus for the use of the laws of vagrancy.

By the late nineteenth century, economic conditions across the colonies created a 'nomadic tribe' of workers, itinerant populations of men looking for seasonal work in rural areas.[10] There was a growing number of impoverished families and single people in the cities. Not all of these men on the move, poor families, or urban people alone were charged as vagrants, but some fell into extremely harsh life conditions and were identified as vagrant or arrested as vagrants, as I go onto show. In the first two decades of the twentieth century, vagrancy had become a part of the landscape, with cultural meanings attached to the vagrant, who was mostly viewed as masculine. Despite a tinge of sentimentality about the adventures of men 'on the swag', evinced by poetry and fiction, there was little about the hardship of mobility that could be said to be romantic.[11]

Using mobility as a frame to examine these questions about vagrancy also links the vagrant to empire, and to imperial world processes. There is now a large historical literature about vagrancy including cultural, social and legal histories of vagrants in Britain, the United States, parts of Europe and in colonial contexts.[12] These histories remind us of the widespread attitude towards unauthorized movement, as well as the spread of legal models and approaches to regulating unwanted mobility in the context of a mobile world undergoing a vast 'demographic transition'.[13] Scholars writing about the circulation of ideas around the British Empire find multiple connecting points and explanatory power in the concept of mobility: 'excessive freedom and a social threat led to its association with criminality'.[14] In his introductory chapter for the wide-ranging edited collection *Cast Out*, Paul Ocobock also points to the connection between changing forms of labour and the regulation and criminalization of idleness in the nineteenth century. Although that book only refers to Australia and New Zealand in passing, the global experiences of a 'massive, disposed population of men' following war and conflict in the United States and Europe – demobilized, and affected by economic change and downturn – have both resonance and material outcomes in the Australasian colonies.[15] The records of prosecution reveal that there were sailors and seamen abandoned at ports around the colonies who were charged as vagrants. The colonies were part of a vast transportation system – an 'arc' of transportation of peoples from the 'old world' to new worlds – suggesting that understanding vagrancy's history in Britain in the early modern period also sheds light on convict transportation to Australia.[16] Convict mobility was the basis of imperial growth and the construction of empire through convict workers' labour.[17]

The aims of this book

My book has three aims. First, it views the world of the settler-colonial mobile populations across four colonies through the figure of the vagrant to illustrate the impulse to regulate and criminalize forms of movement. Second, the book provides new insights into the socio-legal meanings of vagrancy over time in historical context. What were the local and human stories of vagrancy that highlight the experiences and processes of this mobile population across places? By uncovering sources of archival knowledge from the broadly defined 'legal archive', this book highlights the unsettled and complex world of people on the move. Third, this book adopts ideas about mobility in an exploration of the 'mobility turn' from the point of view of academic history. This turn to an attentiveness to forms of mobility as a mode of analysis is useful because it asks us to look at evidence through forms of movement itself. There is a role for the mobility turn in historical research that uncovers the uneven access to mobility for people in the past. Mobility exists in the archives through accounts of travel, escape, convict transportation, institutional transfers, and free settler movement and migration. It also surfaces in the communication of legal ideas and practices, and in legality and control. Criminal records, for instance, can tell us much about mobility in the past: the way people moved around, why they moved, how their movement was constrained or restricted, whether that was gendered or shaped by identities and expectations of social groups.[18]

Vagrancy laws in the colonies were established to capture and fix unwanted movement.[19] In contrast to the example of the populations of North America and Europe, where people were moving with industrializing economies to urban environments, in the colonies, new populations were forming with waves of migration from the 1850s, with the high point of immigration to Australia and New Zealand in the 1870s. The end of penal transportation to the south-eastern colonies of Australia in 1852 made way for free settlers, but convicts and ex-convicts (some of whom became vagrants) remained in the population. The social histories of the people who were perceived as vulnerable groups in the highly mobile population of the colonies have received little attention in separate studies of vagrants, crime and criminality, prostitution and those hospitalized as mentally ill.[20] There is a strong connection between histories of social institutions in the colonies and fears about people who were perceived as unproductive, but who were also 'out of place'.[21] As I show in my earlier work, institutions including asylums and prisons devoted much energy to categorizing people who 'passed through' them, unless they died inside asylums.[22]

Yet vagrancy has not been a focus for a study across these places in a way that brings out the connections between law, policing, social formation and cultures of mobility. Therefore, this book also points to the potential significance of this study of vagrants in the colonies of Victoria, New South Wales, Tasmania and New Zealand to a much broader context. India, South Africa and Canada all have histories of the regulation of vagrancy that were similarly defined by the politics of mobility, and by the different framing of class, gender, and 'race' or ethnicity inside an imperial world.[23] While a close study of other jurisdictions lies beyond the scope of this book, it does pay attention to these places and their approaches to vagrancy.

Detailed studies of the institutions of the period also reveal social circumstances including poverty and homelessness that have not been the subject of sustained research. In particular, earlier work on the histories of insanity and institutions points to a productive strand of evidence about 'wandering' peoples and institutional confinement in India, South Africa and parts of the Pacific that can expand our view of the vagrant as a person.[24] Interpretations of motility and the liminal status of wanderers in nomadic societies with Indigenous populations – as well as histories of their vulnerability to policing – are central to knowing how vagrancy was understood in specific places and periods, and also makes other identities more visible, such as homeless family groups and people whose affinity with Aboriginal or Māori societies made them 'guilty by association' with those people deemed as outsiders to settler formation.[25] In his thinking about the role of the law in shaping early Australian society in the 1820s and 1830s, legal historian Bruce Kercher reflects that law 'stories' found in the records of the court help us understand the operation and meaning of the law. He considers distinct types of 'legal outsiders', focusing on women as wives, convicts and Aboriginal people.[26] My work conceives of another group of outsiders through law stories, those who were mobile through poverty and creative survival, and were made subject to the criminalization of their movement.

Allied to this theme, this book presents new ideas about the way that humanities scholars might engage with the mobilities research paradigm.[27] Sociologist John Urry argued for a 'post-disciplinary' scholarship in his thinking about mobilities, privileging the conceptualization of mobility over the fixity of places or objects. What was novel here was that movement itself was the subject of analysis. The vagrant, then, was of interest, along with the 'pilgrim', the 'nomad', or people with complex mobility patterns where destinations and itineraries were less important than their movement through spaces and across boundaries.[28] Scholars following Urry, including Tim Cresswell, have developed these ideas to apply them to social change, recognizing the need for a 'politics of mobility' that can be grounded in time and space, and made relevant to historical thinking about the figure of the tramp or the immigrant.[29] Using mobility allows me to connect people, places and movement to what Tony Ballantyne describes as the 'extended domains created by empire' including the use of law, police practices and technologies, colonial social formation, the writings of contemporaries, and ways of seeing the vagrant in Australia and New Zealand.[30]

Temporal and geographical contours of this study

The book focuses on mobility in different places during the several decades between 1840 and 1910. During this period the south-eastern Australian colonies, 'settled' from the late 1780s, and Aotearoa/New Zealand, settled in 1840, saw waves of immigration from Britain and other countries. Both New South Wales and VDL had early histories of convict settlement before 1840. European surveyors, land seekers and squatters moved south from New South Wales to Port Philip (later Victoria) from the 1830s, as well as north from VDL. The colonies of New South Wales, Victoria, Tasmania and New Zealand together comprised part of the 'Australasian' world traversed by mobile peoples.[31] This was, as some historians have suggested, a restless world of 'nomads', sojourners and migrants. Some people travelled for commercial gain, others to seek home and new adventures.[32] By 1840, there was already a history of mobility between the different colonies and across the Tasman Sea. This world constitutes what I describe as a coastal and overland belt of mobility, of the 'other' histories of empire. It was an 'Oceanian world' inside the British world of empire with the cultures and connections forged in the regional colonial world and its intersecting histories.[33] Historian Alan Atkinson has described the 'restlessness' of people in this colonial world, writing that relationships and notions of 'place' were easily 'disassembled' and 'dissolved', themes I have pursued in my writing about mental illness in the colonies.[34]

Relationships between places in this study were instrumental in the development of local approaches to vagrancy. The Australian and New Zealand colonies were quick to urbanize. Regulating spaces – the uses of public streets and parks, for example – fell to municipal authorities, and affected the people who occupied and moved through these spaces, such as the vagrant person.[35] Colonial peoples were learning to live together in public spaces, experimenting with ideas about sociality and togetherness, a process also marked by social division and class divides. Not only were the 'slums' a subject for contemporary scrutiny, but also parks, gardens, ports and wharves, street corners, alleys and lanes, and the places of authority like court houses and police stations.[36] The spread of these institutions and their proximity played a role in the many vagrancy prosecutions in the period. In rural areas, barns and outhouses, roads, transportation and shared spaces like hotels and boarding houses all featured in discussions of fairness, morality and shared ideas about occupancy. In all of this, the vagrant was able to transgress the limitations of space, even while she or he was held responsible for those incursions. The vagrant was also a signifier of places beyond the settled and occupied spaces that she or he entered; as Tim Cresswell suggests, the 'wayward travels' of the 'vagabond' suggested 'traces of elsewhere' which disturbed peoples' settled existence and 'threatened to undo the comforts of place'.[37]

The study ends around 1910 to show a world in transition before the First World War and before the Commonwealth introduced legislation providing an old age pension across the states (formerly colonies) of Australia in 1909, and around the time of the introduction of New Zealand's old age pension in 1908.[38] The parameters here allow me to venture into the world of debates about welfare and support but without fully developing the theme; the scope of the study and its emphasis on several jurisdictions and themes is already vast.

Different studies of vagrancy in each place signal the trajectories of historical scholarship over time. In the 1980s and early 1990s, historians including Miles Fairburn, writing about New Zealand, and Susanne Davies, writing about Victoria, shaped the field by looking at the socio-economic circumstances of vagrancy. Fairburn's analysis of the vagrant as a symptom of the lack of social connections in the atomistic, 'bondless' society of colonial New Zealand posited that the shaming language of the period points to long 'moral panic' about the problem of vagrancy in that context.[39] The 'othering' of the stranger – someone who did not settle but moved and wandered – is important in this interpretation of vagrancy. Davies' doctoral research explicitly examined the 'social construction' of vagrancy through laws, policing, trials and punishment in Melbourne between 1880 and 1907.[40] Both Fairburn and Davies were influenced by the strong social history modes of the 1980s including accounts of vagrancy in histories of Britain. Fairburn's work remains powerful in its conception of the vagrant as a signifier of social change, and especially the relevance of the very transience of the person moving from place to place.

Histories of criminality and policing also emerged in this era of histories of social control. Fairburn noted that in New Zealand, the police and courts were agents of the 'public degradation' of the vagrant.[41] Davies based her research on large samples of arrests and imprisonment of vagrants but also set these inside the story of Melbourne's urban development and the life of the city, while Fairburn was interested in rural frontiers and the development of surveillance and controls in New Zealand's provincial communities. Charlotte Macdonald's study of crime and punishment in New Zealand argues that women were policed and prosecuted for vagrancy, and that many but not all of these cases related to prostitution. Women were also destitute and drunk, like men, on the streets of nineteenth-century New Zealand cities and towns.[42] These findings are supported by the historical research of Australian feminist scholars Kay Daniels and Judith Allen, among others, who carved out important histories of women, prostitution and convict experience in the colonies, writing about the utterly desperate situations of some women, as well as about their agency and strength in the context of poverty and brute struggles to survive.[43] So many women in urban and rural colonial worlds very quickly became destitute and dependent on forms of social welfare and charity; their stories also appear in the numerous appearances of vagrants in the colonial archives.[44]

More recent historical-legal scholarship adds depth to the earlier historical scholarship about vagrancy in Australia and New Zealand, placing it inside the social and legal historiography, and showing the role played by the laws of vagrancy in modulating poverty in the colonies, and in creating both 'social policy and criminal sanction' around destitution and houselessness.[45] Histories of policing show that vagrancy has re-emerged as a focus of inquiry in studies of large data and prosecutions. Work by Alana Piper and Victoria Nagy examines women as offenders between 1860 and the 1920s using prosecution statistics and prison records.[46] Piper and Nagy look closely at the colonies of Victoria and Tasmania. Their analysis of patterns of prosecution for women offers useful points of intersection with themes in this book including the interaction between gender and age in police arrests.[47]

This book touches on the intertwined histories of social institutions such as asylums, benevolent homes, immigrants' homes, and homes for the aged in the context of economic depression and social change, themes documented by historians in Australia and New Zealand. Welfare and medical institutions also served the colonial populations with positive intent but could be experienced as 'punitive' given contemporary formulations of 'deserving poor'. Both Stephen Garton's study of people in poverty and their access to social welfare in Australia and Margaret Tennant's history of charitable aid in New Zealand touch on the precarity of life for people seeking work, dependent on handouts, and unmoored from social and familial networks in the colonies.[48] The evidence used in this book also shows that vagrants moved between these social institutions, sometimes in never-ending cycles of reliance on welfare of different types, also caught in systems of policing and institutional confinement.

Approaches

The idea of 'vagrancy from below' helps to signal that this book seeks to place the stories of people who became vagrants at the centre of the narrative about colonial mobility, among them the stories of Mary Anne Ward, Sarah Jones, John Spurridge, Christina Lawson, Maurice Jeffrey and many others.[49] Examining their lives – insofar as it is possible to do – allows us to understand vagrancy from the point of view of those people who occupied the position of 'vagrant'. Along the way, by using prosecution data, I also point to the many intersections between gender, 'race'/ethnicity, class, age, and sexuality which are now deeply ingrained in social and cultural historical analysis; these categories both inform and shape our thinking about vagrancy and its prosecution.

Writing about a much earlier period in England, A. L. Beier described vagrants as 'masterless men', hinting at a new rising 'class' of people who no longer remained fixed in places and bound by older ways of life confined by social stratification, and found themselves moving around for employment.[50] Beier also examined 'fragmented families', such as the 'unstable' family groups on the road in the early modern period.[51] Vagrancy is most often individualized because of the nature of prosecutions, but there are hints of homeless families in the colonies, children without parents left to fend for themselves, and also 'dangerous liaisons' and loose collectives of associates, all of which remind us of the array of possible vagrant identities.[52]

Colonial societies were fearful of downward mobility.[53] It was the problem of the poverty among Europeans, or the circulation of a concern about the weaknesses of the settler-colonial population – whiteness under threat – that challenged the vision of the healthy and productive new world for migrants and future citizens. The stories of people who were making their way in colonial society as 'unmoored' from the fixity of colonial expectations of settling tell us more about colonial power relations and place making, as this book shows; transgressive, subversive acts of identity making, evasion of control, and of life on the move remind us of the multiple modes for the personal exercise of power in the colonial world. Yet it was not only the poor, unemployed, or socially 'outcast' who were caught up in the fears about vagrancy: Davies has described the fate of political activists in the colony of Victoria in the 1890s and their imprisonment under vagrancy law.[54]

Vulnerability to the mechanisms of social control is often implied within social histories of policing and prosecution for vagrancy. Yet what does it really mean to say that someone might be in a 'vulnerable category'? Legal scholar Martha Fineman, writing about 'the vulnerable subject' in law, worries that categorizing some populations as vulnerable to 'poor health' or other social inequalities reinforces the structural inequality wrought by the modern State. She argues instead that everyone is vulnerable and therefore equal, reclaiming the idea of vulnerability as core to 'humanity'.[55] Reflecting on whether vulnerability can examined in relation to agency and power, as well as identity, forms part of the analysis of vagrancy in this book. Vulnerability could shift and change in the way it was conceptualized by policy and lawmakers, or by people with power and status in specific social and political settings. In our present we think of 'precarity' as a better term for that ever-broadening social group more vulnerable to economic change and the uncertain nature of employment in the future, as social science scholars argue.[56] This points to suggestive evidence for the articulation of 'class' in colonial society and allows me to put forward a bolder theorization and history of vulnerability to bring together my various strands of work about people who were caught in a web of social institutions, and other health and welfare responses to social formation over time. As I aim to show, some of the people prosecuted as vagrants were also the recipients of welfare assistance, benevolence and charity.

Sources and methodologies

Historians are already accomplished in their use of different repositories, archives and data sets, but they more rarely signal the highly contingent and tenuous nature of their sources as traces of mobility in the past.[57] These sources remind us that people in the past also came into contact with different institutions that collected information about them and about their movements. In this book I examine courtrooms and prison cells as 'transfer points' in the experience of mobility, with the records of vagrants who came into contact with legal systems evidence of this monitoring of movement.[58] Mobility studies offers us a new lens through which to view the laws regulating vagrancy in settler-colonial settings. By combining interpretations of legislation, *Police Gazettes*, newspaper reports, court cases, criminal trials and institutional records we can find out more about the 'registers' of mobility and vagrancy in the past.[59] These include physical reminders of encounters with the law; representations of the vagrant experience in the media of the period; speech, behaviours and interactions between people in the past, including violence; and finally, movement itself in the form of journeys and places traversed, providing both metaphorical and literal maps of the vagrant lives described in this book.[60] The mobility of vagrants also presents a challenge in terms of research and methodology, with different modes of inquiry such as socio-legal histories informed by digital scholarship that offers the potential to uncover vagrancy's meanings in the past.[61]

The 'legal archive' might include more than explicitly legal records such as court records, laws and policing. It might also include social histories of peoples' brushes with the law, newspaper narratives of crime and punishment, and other representations including travel writing, visual imagery and personal accounts.[62] Legal records, as Alecia Simmonds writes, can sound like 'a jumble of voices, a collaborative, slightly fictive enterprise undertaken by litigants, court clerks, lawyers and scribes'.[63] The urge to reconstruct the stories of the lives of people who appear in these records in the micro-historical mode is made slightly easier by legal formalities: dates of arrest, notations of offence, physical descriptions of criminals, and sometimes the proximity of other cases and offending, which tell us more about the landscape of policing or social conditions. Legal archival sources offer us narrative shape in a way that other primary sources do not, allowing us to plot the sometimes-curious experiences of criminals in the past.[64]

Sitting at the heart of this book are the copious records of the *Police Gazettes* of each colony. *Police Gazettes* were produced in Sydney from 1854 but were first published as New South Wales Reports of Crime, becoming *Police Gazettes* in 1862. These appeared several times a week and went out from the Office of the Inspector General of Police to all police stations. The Reports included details of crimes committed, descriptions of people to be apprehended and of stolen property and rewards offered, and other police notices. From the 1860s, the *New South Wales Police Gazette and Weekly Record of Crime* was published weekly. These publications were similar across the colonies, and aided police in their work to locate offenders in different places: in this way they were a technology of policing. In Tasmania, the Reports of Crime were published from 1861, and became the *Tasmania Police Gazette* after 1883. A variety of mobile people were surveilled in the gazettes, including street hawkers and people who worked in similar occupations. In Victoria, the *Victoria Police Gazette* was published from late in 1853, and went out weekly to city police stations, to police in rural towns and to government offices and newspapers. In New Zealand, the provincial centres had produced police gazettes in the 1860s but these were replaced by the *New Zealand Police Gazette* in 1877. It was published in Wellington but had a wide distribution and remained a weekly publication until 1904.

The *Police Gazettes* are important to this study because they provide access to the numbers, names and descriptions of vagrants charged with vagrancy offences.[65] Historians agree it is difficult to 'count' instances of vagrancy, with uncertainty about the numbers of people who lived as vagrants.[66] 'Vagrants' wrote Margaret Crowther, 'did not wait to be counted'.[67] In the British context – where much historical scholarship has looked at the tramp and the vagrant – different social responses to vagrancy prosecution including the use of the workhouse means that deriving statistics for vagrancy is fraught.[68] This book collects the stories of vagrancy as it was prosecuted. It reveals some suggestive patterns of policing and the vagrant populations of the colonies by highlighting aspects of the prosecution data reported in each colony's *Police Gazettes*, read alongside government and police offences reports, newspaper accounts and cultural evidence.[69] In exploring the policing of vagrancy the book draws connections between places, delving into some of the characteristics of the prosecutions. Each of the colonial gazettes included a table of 'discharged prisoners' each week, detailing names, offences, where the person was tried, sentences handed down and places of confinement. Material from the different colonial gazettes appeared in each place, including reprinted material from across the Tasman, showing the work of police extended beyond their own locale and involved transcolonial communication. For instance, the *Otago Police Gazettes* published in the 1860s included reports of missing persons, offenders wanted for rape and assault, escaped prisoners, ticket-of-leave identities, bushrangers and deserters, suggesting the volume of traffic and mobility across the Tasman, especially involving men.[70]

Police Gazette prosecution data, described in this broad manner, provides a context for the individual stories elaborated in more detail in each chapter. Read alongside the cultural representations of the figure of the vagrant, the prosecution data derived from the *Police Gazettes* helps to provide insights into the world of police and their monitoring of mobility across the colonies. The textual portraits of vagrants preceded the photographic images of criminals that appear later in the period under investigation; the words used to describe vagrants give us a sense of the people themselves as they lived and moved in the community but also need to be used with caution as they were descriptions recorded as a way of monitoring so-called 'criminality' in the period. As historian David Hitchcock suggests, writing about the 'literature-driven typologies of "rogues" and "vagabonds" … the literary, visualised vagabond still has much to tell us', and scholarship needs to take 'interdisciplinary' approaches to the study of the 'mobile' in the past, especially people who might be classed as the 'mobile poor'.[71]

The lives of people in the past appear and disappear as shadowy portraits in histories of crime and punishment, seeming to peep around the side of the edifices of the legal system or stare at us from prison photographs. Some archives, libraries and repositories have started to showcase nineteenth- and twentieth-century police mugshots and prison photographs in accessible online collections, and the digitization of records including criminal records now expands our visual sense of the people in the past.[72] The use of these sources helps us to round out the textual portraits and also to amplify the use of prosecution data, allowing historians to humanize, contextualize and understand the figure of the vagrant.[73] The available data sets embed assumptions about birthplace, ethnicity, gender, age and other characteristics belonging to individuals; these attributes mean that individuals are rendered as generalized populations in data used to count people prosecuted as vagrants. While such approaches offer empirical 'certainty', surfacing identities, they also obscure people inside categories. For this reason, the book draws out a number of stories and also focuses on rare first-person accounts of being vagrant which tell us about the darker experiences of precarious existences, including the effects of endless walking, hunger, thirst, rough sleeping and encounters with people along the way.[74] The physical body is especially important in the study of mobilities: the smallest of 'embodied movements … [such as] looks, gestures' offer the potential for interpretation, as chapters in this book demonstrate.[75]

This book deploys these approaches to find the different traces of vagrants in the past, and to discover the meanings of mobility among vagrants. By piecing together broad historical evidence about vagrancy prosecutions with the accounts of a few people's lives, we can get closer illustrating the great challenges and also the creative possibilities of life in the colonies for 'the vagrant'. This process forces us to scrutinize the legal-historical sources produced in the colonial world, contemporary meanings made from information that was – in its own time – at the cutting edge of technology and communication, making us hyper aware of the role played by the historical imagination. Even more rare are the first-hand accounts penned by people who themselves lived lives as mobile or vagrant people. Where possible, I draw upon such accounts to offer insight into precarious mobile lives. Most of the individuals who are described in more detail appear in one of the sets of data underpinning this study but also left a larger footprint in terms of the evidence surrounding their lives and experiences of vagrancy. My hope is that this book challenges us to 'see' and revisit the rich social histories of previous decades: work by historians invested in telling stories about people who appeared in the social record. The fact that 'mobility remained central to the life of [the] new frontier of settlement' through the 'structures' of social regulation such as law, police and welfare acts as a reminder of the way we can 'locate' mobility as historians.[76]

Digital scholarship has changed the way I set out to write this history of mobility and vagrancy during the lifetime of the project's research. Other research projects with accessible data sets have appeared over time, such as an interactive map of Australian prisons, and indicative data held by some archives that highlight one specific jurisdiction.[77] Therefore, this book is not based on one definitive data set but draws upon several separate collections of material related to vagrancy prosecutions in the colonies, set out and explained in the Annotated guide to data and digital sources used in this research which is appended to the main body of the text. This is suggestive of the new reality for historical research in our present. Put positively, the digital tools we now have allow us to enter into some of the worlds of peoples who occupied the past despite their liminality as historical subjects.

In this book

Chapter 2 explains the laws of vagrancy including local discussions about the introduction of legislation in the 1850s and 1860s in separate colonies. The new vagrancy laws across New South Wales (1835, 1851), Victoria (1852), Tasmania (Police Act, 1865) and New Zealand (1866) each derived from the British Vagrancy Act of 1824. The separate acts of colonies influenced each other, and also referred to laws in other parts of the British Empire. Laws were perceived by some contemporaries to be too broad in their criminalization of citizens, revealing the politics at work in the imagining of forms of regulation of people. Law in the colonial world was central to the formation of power for colonists over the colonized peoples whose lives had been disrupted so severely by imperial projects to create new colonies over time, but also over the wandering poor, or those migrants whose mobility presented challenges to expectations of settler stability. The uneven impact of change can be plotted through legislative changes wrought at different moments and affecting specific jurisdictions. The shared understandings of what was at stake for colonial society – the reasons for monitoring and regulating populations, such as bushrangers in early New South Wales and Tasmania – point to the way imperial law found expression in new places and brought to life older notions of 'settlement' and order, such as practices from Britain in the eighteenth and nineteenth centuries.[78] Historians explain that people convicted as vagrants in the sixteenth century were treated harshly: they were whipped, and burned through the ear, as reminders of the dangers of being mobile and wandering away from one's parish or place of residence.[79] These ideas travelled as memories as the imperial world was forged.

The focus of Chapter 3 is on the policing of vagrancy and the use of the laws described in the second chapter. This chapter expands the knowledge about colonial vagrancy through the policing of the law. It pays attention to the way more detailed accounts of those vagrants who challenged attempts to control them in place as fixed subjects might tell us about their reliance on mobile practices. The chapter gives an overview of the rates and locations of arrest, addresses the theme of recidivism and describes the common uses of vagrancy legislation by police. Another focus is on police and their work and how they became agents of law seeking to curtail mobility in the case of the vagrant.

The everyday lives of vagrants also reflected laws and local policing practices and become symbolic of the politics of mobility in settler-colonial environments. People who were arrested for vagrancy, sometimes multiple times, were finding spaces to exist and carving identities and lives that were often forced outdoors or into poverty. It was when the vagrant stopped for any length of time, attracting suspicion about their habits or intentions, that police could make an arrest. Chapter 4 looks at several stories pieced together from the many different sources we have to offer a glimpse of what it was like to live on the streets or on the move, and it shares stories of survival as well as hardship.

Although some vagrants sought freedom from social restrictions, many – if not most – were forced into mobility and were therefore living precarious lives of subsistence and fear. These were people made vulnerable to the vagaries of social formation in new colonies. The unpredictable experiences of work, family, housing, weather, and welfare or support for good health and sustenance made vagrancy highly contingent and variable as a path for people seeking freedom. Chapter 5 is concerned with understanding who became vulnerable in the colonial world, and why. It examines the processes that shaped vagrant mobility and reactions to vagrancy from more settled society. To understand the mobile life as well as evidence of its hardship it focuses on an extremely rare individual account of that experience, that of James Cox in New Zealand in the 1890s.[80] Examining vulnerability allows us to uncover and consider social structures created as models for the colonies – meaning the assumption of poverty and illness was inscribed from the beginning, despite hopes for 'equality' in society. Evidence suggests that 'technologies' of the State, such as the census, helped to create meanings of different forms of disability in this period.[81] By uncovering stories about people surviving, exposed to violence, suffering old age and disability, the chapter sets out a new formulation of historical ideas about 'being vulnerable' that help point to the formation of class and identity in the colonies in the light of concerns about settling and mobility. The mobility of people living with physical disability in the colonial urban setting also made them visible to public scrutiny, with forms of disability viewed as a potential advantage to those begging for survival, as colonial newspaper cartoons show.[82]

The vagrancy concept was changing by the early twentieth century. A finely grained distinction was being drawn by contemporaries who saw forms of the vagrant lifestyle as an evasion of social networks and a refusal to contribute to labour and the social fabric. The idea of 'the vagrant' in Australia and New Zealand was being situated in a wider world framework of labour and productivity, and a context in which welfare was also being formed and contested. The new 'modern vagrant' was a type whose identity was being articulated by governments and their instruments of population management.[83]

Overall, this book is concerned with understanding vagrancy through the experiences of people who lived as vagrants in the colonies: mobile people who were part of an imperial world that was itself highly mobile. It is not a history about migration but many of its subjects were immigrants. Whether they made criminal threats to safety, or were people seeking adventures, or those who remained mobile wanderers and persisted as outsiders to settled society, their movement was significant.[84] The waning of prosecutions in some jurisdictions over time demonstrates a changing sensibility about the crime of vagrancy but also the practicalities of policing.

To conclude the book, Chapter 6 draws our attention back to the concept of the 'mobility turn'. I argue that the stories of vagrant lives sitting at the centre of this book remind us of the outlier experience in social and cultural histories, highlighting the possibility of using mobility as a way of refracting historical evidence. The final chapter offers an explanatory frame for understanding regulating mobility – legality and the legal apparatus, textual surveillance through the *Police Gazette*, and narrative typology and representation – and briefly examines the themes of adventure, wandering and predation in turn as metanarratives of vagrancy that informed the vagrant identity which helped to shape fears and myths about 'the vagrant' in colonial society. It uses mobility as theoretical tool to look closely at these themes and to suggest the interpretive power of the complex of mobility, criminality and otherness brought together as one frame for understanding the history of vagrancy.

2

Vagrancy laws in the colonial world

Convict Uriah Smith was sentenced to seven years imprisonment following his trial at Middlesex Gaol and transported to New South Wales on the convict ship *Mangles*. The ship arrived in August 1820 after sailing in March that year. Uriah Smith was one of around 190 convicts on the transport, most of whom had received longer sentences.[1] By 1878 he was described as a 'vagrant of long standing' in the newspaper report of his arrest in Sydney.[2] Born in 1798, he was by then an old man. There were many convicts who appeared in colonial accounts of vagrancy, with 'poverty ... compounded by the aftermath of the convict system'.[3] Their movements – forced, as well as acts of freedom – have become a valuable source of historical information about mobility in the imperial and colonial world itself. The policing of this mobility came to define the world of the colonies for Europeans, and like tracing paper, was laid over the existing lives of Aboriginal and Māori peoples, rendering the colonies a space for the legal regulation of movement for all who traversed the lands and waters.

In Britain, the purpose of the vagrancy law was to move people on and to return them to their parish of residence, allowing their local area to administer relief under the Poor Law.[4] This removal of people had become quite a business. It led to an urban crisis as people exercised their knowledge of the removal provisions and used them to be ferried back to their locales, as described in accounts of vagrancy in London in the late eighteenth century.[5] 'Strangers' could be unsettling in communities; wandering itself was a sign of mental instability, as well as dangerousness.[6] Historians agree that in the Australasian colonies, the policing and prosecution of vagrants was increasingly a means to maintain social order, with formulations of social control peaking in the nineteenth century.[7] Vagrancy emerged as a habit of life for many of the mobile men and women who were carving out lives across places in the context of convict transportation and its aftermath, or migration and human movement, including between the colonies. Vagrancy was therefore viewed as a social problem of the 'criminal and pauper classes', a phrase later listed in Victoria's police regulations of 1873,[8] and related to law and order in a rapidly forming context with different political and cultural aspects to those in Britain.[9] There was a 'messiness' in laws that sought to create distinctions between types of 'houselessness' that was infused by judgements about people and poverty.[10]

By the early nineteenth century in Sydney and Hobart, convicts who lived and worked around the penal settlements were beginning to exercise some social freedoms, including the possibility of movement between places of work and their homes. Convicts around Sydney, in particular, were part of a growing township with smaller localities, all sites for social interactions between convicts, with Aboriginal people, with the police and those in charge. Yet despite these freedoms, contemporaries viewed these as populations of 'inchoate criminals' who also needed to be contained.[11] It is interesting to reflect on the observation that the community of people living in and among the 'Rocks' area of Sydney was a constantly changing one, with 'new faces, strangers, visitors, itinerant tradesmen, labourers and drifters', but one based in its earliest foundations by people who arrived on convict ships in the eighteenth century and found a place to settle.[12] In Hobart, convicts and Aboriginal people co-existed in an uneasy tension and contest for natural resources in the earliest years, with convicts in different parts of the colony visibly restrained, and a culture of simmering violence ever present.[13] Bushrangers, escaped convicts who disappeared into the bush and survived by committing robberies, presented an early threat in VDL and again in New South Wales over time.[14] There was a strong association between convicts, wandering and escaping, vagrancy charges, and bushranging in the public historical imagination, as sources collated over time in repositories and collections reveal.[15]

Historian Grace Karskens draws upon contemporary writings about the settlement of New South Wales to reflect on the blurry and 'fluid' world of the very early years of the colony, 'a place where it was almost impossible to constrain people, to fix and count them'.[16] In the 1790s, people who became vagrants were described as 'banditti' and were regarded as a threat to order.[17] Runaway convicts sometimes lived with Aboriginal groups in the bush and this intensified the fears about their activities.[18] They were even targeted for roundup from their hideaways around the Hawkesbury river area in the late 1790s to help with harvesting farm crops due to labour shortages.[19] The physical world of the colony, with 'no walls' and dense bush that was easy to escape into, made for what Governor King described as a 'scattered' population.[20] Perhaps these elements explain the perception of Sydney people as a harsh and suspicious 'type' by the 1850s, an observation made by contemporaries.[21]

In Sydney, records of street arrests for Parramatta between 1815 and 1826 show a list of 'absconders', 'runaways' and convicts 'absent' from employment duties, along with three vagrants, two men and one woman, arrested in 1815–17, and one 'common vagrant', a man, arrested in 1826.[22] The policing of convicts changed in the years after 1811, or when Governor Lachlan Macquarie introduced new policing regulations which set out the spatial dimensions of Sydney as districts, each with their own watchhouse for the detention of criminals, along with police assigned to each area.[23] Police had broad power over convicts and non-convicts, especially designed to monitor those seemingly without employment or means of support. In 1825 new Police Magistrate Captain Rossi further professionalized the role of police and their scope. He argued that social change and an increasing number of people coming to Sydney to seek the 'ticket of leave' created a crowded flow of people who threatened the social order by exhibiting traits of the disorderly conduct – idleness, profligacy and loose living – that excited fears about mobility and underlined the risks inherent to a mobile population in the colonies.[24] Rossi was praised by contemporaries and observers like Peter Cunningham, who noted in his *Two Years in New South Wales* Rossi's efforts to remodel police as 'respectable' and efficient in a colony 'composed of such dissolute materials'.[25] Cunningham noticed that the convicts were 'strictly watched'.[26] Meanwhile, policing in VDL under Governor Arthur was performed as a blend of English and Irish policing styles, adapted to suit circumstances.[27]

These fears of the convict class would repeat in subsequent decades and in different colonial locations, including in New Zealand in the 1840s and 50s, echoes of these first few decades of life in Sydney and the new colony of New South Wales. That talk of crimes could be exaggerated in the 'small community' of Sydney did not escape Cunningham, who wrote that conversation often turned on the excitement of a 'bushranger affair, or adroit robbery or burglary'.[28] European women's letters from the period exhibit a tendency to talk up the danger and curiosity of the bushranger in a setting that was potentially confusing about a person's identity and purpose, such as Harriet King who described a man lighting his pipe in the 'men's huts' west of Sydney at Penrith being arrested as a bushranger in 1827.[29] Yet the colonies were full of adventurers and travellers who took risks, including the possibility of getting lost, or coping with snakes, insects, spiders and ticks.[30] Earlier, in 1824, Janet Ranken wrote to her sister-in-law about the young men, strangers in the colony looking around at land to buy, who slept in all kinds of places including outdoors 'in the fields', when visiting more remote parts of the colony beyond Sydney.[31] Over-zealous policing in rural areas resulted in frequent mistaken arrests, including of men working on properties and passing through different places but apprehended on suspicion of bushranging and held in lock-ups on farms, possibly the fate of Harriet King's pipe-smoking man in the huts.[32] The same happened in New Zealand in a later period.[33]

English criminal law was adopted as part of the first Charter of Justice for the colony of New South Wales in 1787, allowing the new colony to establish a Court of Criminal Judicature.[34] By 1828, when the Australian Courts Act came into being, most English statutes in force would apply to matters of crime. However, the Vagrancy Act of 1824 in Britain was seemingly not considered to be directly applicable to the colonial context because its own genesis was in response to the presence of a sizeable group of the 'able-bodied poor' in England; this was a 'class' of people not perceived in early Australia.[35] Legal historians agree, then, that the vagrancy legislation that was crafted for colonial conditions therefore derived from the Vagrancy Act of 1824 in Britain.[36] Colonial governments in Australia and New Zealand could not apply this 1824 law directly to the colonies.[37] This was largely because there was no desire to formulate laws relating to poverty, such as British Poor Laws, and nascent systems of welfare and charity were designed to be responsive to the formative years of settlement.[38] Importantly, the English law of 1824 was a significant influence on the colonies and law making around vagrancy. Its categorization of vagrants adopted the eighteenth-century model of 1740: vagrants were 'idle and disorderly', 'rogues and vagabonds' or 'incorrigible rogues'.[39] Arguably the laws described in this chapter brought the vagrant person inside the law, yet at the same time, conceived of undesirable mobility as being 'outside' the social norms being set down and fashioned in law.[40]

Mobility and empire

Emigration was presented as a solution to the 'evils' of poverty in Britain as early as the 1840s. An illustration in the satirical London magazine *Punch*, published in 1848, contrasted the 'old world' of poor families with the hopes of a new world of plentiful food, sustaining families through work and non-white labour. The scene depicts ragged children with bare feet against the backdrop of smokestacks in the industrializing world 'here', juxtaposed with the harmonious scene of a table groaning with food, set in a vaguely 'tropical' place, 'there'.

Travel writers and diarists documented this curiosity in the colonies they encountered, mostly to deliver news and views of these places to their readers 'at home', which was mostly Britain. Anthony Trollope witnessed destitution on

Figure 2.1 'Here and there; or, emigration, a remedy'. *Punch*, London, 8 July 1848, reproduced courtesy of Alexander Turnbull Library, Wellington, New Zealand REF: PUBL-0043-1848-15. Records/23241802.

the streets of Melbourne when he visited the colonies in the 1870s, writing that '[d]estitute men and women are not entitled by law to be fed and housed at the public expense, as they are in England':

> As far as the law is concerned any man who cannot feed himself may lay down and die. But such is not the result of things as they exist. Poor and destitute there are, though they are very few in number as compared with those among us at home. Work is more plentiful. Wages are higher. Food is cheaper.[41]

Trollope went on to say that the poorest members of society could access benevolent asylums, with the 'comforts of life' provided; he also visited the asylums and gaols of the city, waxing lyrical about the excellent standards of care for the 'needy' and 'afflicted'.[42]

Yet contemporary observations such as this one – that people might 'lay down and die' – was in keeping with the many cases of the vagrants on the streets who were found 'wandering abroad, lying in the open air' in the case of Thomas Guyon in Hobart, Tasmania in 1856, or Catherine Masters 'found asleep by police in an unfinished building' in Launceston, also in Tasmania, in 1860, both of whom received a criminal sentence as vagrants. Such descriptions of the experience of destitution as precipitating vagrancy arrests are extremely common in the historical record. Destitution, when defined as vagrancy, was criminalized, a theme that is developed further in this chapter and in later chapters of this book.[43]

Taking advantage of a developing set of approaches to legal-imperial histories, this chapter brings together the different jurisdictions in this transcolonial world – 'stridently mobile formations' – to demonstrate the explanatory potential of the conceptual framework of mobility to understand vagrancy's past.[44] This chapter focuses on describing the vagrancy laws across the Australasian colonial world as both an imperial legal inheritance, a European invention, and a key instance of colonial law making.[45] Within this frame, it pays attention to local laws enacted to regulate vagrants. Vagrancy laws offer us a means of understanding mobility, partly because vagrant practices involved movement and transience, and also because vagrancy made this mobility highly visible in the public eye. Settler-colonial societies were imbued by a politics of mobility, and the laws of vagrancy express the way ideas about movement were codified over time, also shaping practices of the management of identity. This chapter also asserts the idea that the identities of mobile populations were produced, shaped and transformed through laws and institutions in a dynamic process that, in different places, and over time, acted to regulate and therefore criminalize the vulnerable among these peoples.[46] It examines both the specificity and similarity of each colony's legal inheritance with that of other jurisdictions by considering commonalities and dissonances, paying attention to the significance of shared imperial legal apparatus and practices.[47]

In particular, the chapter's focus is on understanding vagrancy laws across four sites: New South Wales (1835, 1851); Victoria (1852); and New Zealand (1866), with Tasmania's approach to vagrancy slightly different, and covered by the Police Act (1865). Vagrant Acts were regarded by contemporaries as distinct from other criminal laws because they lacked precision about the nature of offence or transgression to be policed. What concerned some observers was the notion that such laws might be used to arrest people on the mere suspicion of criminal activity. This created a sense of unease in societies that were still in formation and where levels of 'disorder' were part of the social world. This chapter discusses this theme in more depth in relation to debates about the introduction of legislation and its passage through parliaments. Vagrancy was imagined in much the same way as it had been in the British context, with the use of categories such as 'rogue' and 'vagabond' proscribing degrees of seriousness embodied in the legislation. These categories formed the overarching concept of 'the vagrant' both in law and in the fashioning of the person of the vagrant that was taken up by newspapers of the period. Newspaper reports shaped thinking in the colonial world, travelling with people across borders and shared from paper to paper, providing common indices of sentiment and understandings of colonial legality, as well as a model for policing using the police gazettes of the period.[48] Communication technologies became central to the creation of a vagrant identity in law and society.

In the colonies, defining the close associations with criminals or 'native' persons through the consorting clauses of these laws was purposeful.[49] Such regulatory practices occurred inside a wider legal context, which the chapter also describes. Legal historians in Australia and New Zealand show the borrowed, distinctive and developing language of laws for the colonies, but the laws of vagrancy have not been investigated in detail or in relation to each other.[50] Laws regulating vagrancy in other places, when examined together, shed light on the ways in which broadly conceived laws designed to control and punish 'personal condition, state of being, and social and economic status' in the context of social and historical changes, shaped particularly by an imperial conception of personhood.[51] The law's relationship to women who had no home was 'long and complex', especially towards the end of the nineteenth century, with the 'rolling momentum of modernity and respectability' in the colonies.[52] This chapter aims to provide an overview of vagrancy in law, attentive to the way localized solutions tell us more about the importance of taking a transcolonial approach to the historical research.

New South Wales

The subject of vagrancy was discussed by colonists in early Sydney. By the 1830s, with many more convicts in circulation, there was a need to enact laws that could help police to monitor and control the movement of people. Magistrates 'were authorized to enter any house at their own discretion' to look for absconders, and employers were obliged to ensure that convict workers had a pass identifying them.[53] Legislation included the 1824 Vagrancy Act, a Malicious Trespassing Act (1827) and the Metropolitan Police Act (1829).[54] By 1833, a Police Act included a 'colourful array of offences'.[55] Yet further legislation was needed to help limit and define the boundaries of colonial space, given the population movement and expansion from Sydney inland.[56] In 1835 a new Bushranging Act made sure that police and citizens would understand the areas of places with towns defined in s. 44, and police to patrol the boundaries. This echoes the older English customs, and the origins of laws of vagrancy, by insisting on the specificity of place and belonging.[57]

The meanings of bushranging had changed over time, as historians note.[58] Waves of bushranging crimes in the 1820s and 1830s led to the creation of the crime of bushranging.[59] Defining the bushranger was in the public interest, with newspapers such as *The Colonist* sharing opinions about the dangers of men who had once been convicts and were now ticket-of-leave men, or absconders, going 'wild in the bush'.[60] A 'second wave' of bushranging in the 1860s promoted changes to policing, mostly because colonists worried that policing was failing, and squatters who occupied the vast tracts of pastoral land wanted to exert more control over their environments.[61] These points are salient to the story of Mary Anne Ward, set out in more detail later in this chapter. Her vagrancy prosecution in New South Wales in the 1860s stands out as an example of the intersections between fears of the bush, bushrangers and crime, and a woman acting both 'out of place' and challenging the norms of gender boundaries.[62]

John Ward's *A Tramp to the Diggings*, published in 1852, presents an account of a society cautious about its inhabitants – all 'rogues' until proven otherwise – and about the dangers of bushrangers. While travelling through the Blue Mountains Ward came upon a small group of up to ten men he was glad to quickly move away from; he too had become suspicious of 'types', noticing 'the countenance of one man … the most roguish and brigand-like in its aspect', which worried him because he was wearing a gold watch and chain and carrying money while travelling the 'wild and peculiar scene all alone'.[63] Emma McPherson was another adventurous European traveller who published her account of experiences in Australia in 1860. After fifteen months of living and moving around with her family – including children – McPherson imagined that 'wild' stories of crime and bushranging were sometimes exaggerated by storytellers. However, McPherson acknowledged that truth could be stranger than fiction, and that the colonies presented 'improbable' narratives:

> As improbable and exaggerated as they might sound at home, it was not difficult to believe them in the silence, solitude and darkness of nightfall in those primeval forests. Besides, I knew well that no fiction could exceed in wildness and improbability, the real histories of some of the early settlers of the colony.[64]

McPherson also noted that the colony's beginnings, and the fact that it still had a large number of 'doubtful characters' living within it, accentuated its peculiar obsession with identity and respectability, a theme that coloured her view of 'class' in Sydney where people tend to demand 'testimonials' of background as evidence of social place.[65] Ward had a similar appraisal of Sydney's people in his writing, noticing a 'Sydney-look' that was a 'mixture of suspicion and curiosity … anxious to discern the real character of an individual'.[66]

Reading the Act to define and prosecute the crime of vagrancy in New South Wales, the intentions of lawmakers quickly surface. 'An Act for the prevention of Vagrancy and for the punishment of idle and disorderly persons rogues and vagabonds and incorrigible rogues in the colony of NSW' (1835) is directed at the population of transported convicts and requires them to notify the police magistrate of any changes in residence. Being on extended probation in this way – itself a form of detention – sent the message that absconding or wandering outside one's designated area was criminal. Wandering was itself explicitly defined, especially in relation to European convicts consorting with Aboriginal 'natives'. Being drunk in public, behaving riotously or associating with known criminals was also a risk, and police powers were clearly extensive. There was little ambiguity about the punishments for people found to be vagrant under this act, including flogging and imprisonment.[67]

Interpretations of the New South Wales Vagrancy Act of 1851 and its precursor of 1835 turned on definitions of persons deemed 'idle and disorderly', 'rogue and vagabond' or 'incorrigible rogue', but also set out the 'offences' of having 'no visible lawful means of support' and other clauses relating to being habitual drunkards, frequenting houses of ill repute, consorting with criminals, consorting with prostitutes, or begging or wandering at large. Police arrests of Aboriginal people using the vagrancy provision were rare – though they did happen, as explained below – mostly because the legislation stipulated that persons who were *not Aboriginal* or children of Aboriginal people, and who could not give a good account of themselves, or who were found wandering or lodging with Aboriginal people, without providing a good reason why, would be charged as vagrants.[68] Although Indigenous peoples were highly vulnerable to regulation and policing, as historians show, in Australia and in New Zealand, the vagrancy laws 'sought variously to limit the debasement of the country's original peoples by those imagined most capable of degrading them'.[69]

Van Diemen's Land, later Tasmania

VDL was part of New South Wales until 1825 and was similarly governed by British criminal laws, with a provision within the 1824 Police Ordinance to regulate vagrancy.[70] The earliest piece of legislation dealing with vagrants through an Act to regulate police to be introduced in VDL was published in the *Hobart Town Gazette* in 1838.[71] This legislation focused on law and order and covered every aspect of life including the maintenance of shop hoardings, waste, animals in the street, as well as the activities of people moving around the towns and countryside. It highlighted the potential for criminal activity by those who were 'idle', 'disorderly', 'wandering abroad', or lodging in barns, buildings or the open air, and extended to people on the open road seeking forms of charity, and women soliciting as prostitutes, as well as people intending to break into buildings with the intent to steal.

Ten years later, the *Hobarton Guardian* reported cases of vagrants who appeared in court, remarking that 'it is quite time that our city was purged of those idle vagabonds', detailing the problem:

> They may be easily recognised by their slinking, dirty, ragged, appearance, and can only support themselves by petty thefts. But there is another class of vagabonds, which may not inaptly be called the 'swell mob' of the genus vagrant. They have no earthly visible honest mode of gaining a livelihood. They manage to sport an outside decent appearance, and prowl about with a swaggering and insolent air. They are to be found mostly at the gaming table, or lounging at the bars of public houses. How they are allowed to escape from being 'policed' requires no great insight to fathom.[72]

Newspapers kept up the pressure in subsequent years with calls for an 'Act for the Suppression of Vagrancy' in 1849, and amendments to existing vagrancy laws in 1858.[73] As I go on to show later in this chapter, discussions about the problem of vagrancy tended to swing between the punitive negative characterization of the vagrant and more charitable views of the impoverished in the 1840s and 1850s, while in the following decades, a greater risk of the overly intrusive nature of vagrancy laws in some colonial settings pushed these debates into different territory.

In VDL, the remarks about the 'swaggering and insolent' were derived from a wider imperial discourse about vagrancy, and also pointed to the desire for an orderly society borne out of convict transportation. There was no specific vagrancy legislation ever introduced in Tasmania, but the Police Act of 1865 referred to the 'suppression of vagrants' (Section 14). There was a pervasive sense of surveillance everywhere in these places. In Tasmania, a revised set of guidance notes for the constabulary issued in 1868 advised that 'Constables are to perform all their duties with the utmost caution and watchfulness, and especially when in pursuit of absconders.'[74]

Port Phillip, later Victoria

Victoria's Legislative Assembly formed in 1851. Managing the rapid population growth and movement around Victoria's goldfields included a focus on vagrancy and destitution. Historians estimate that by the 1850s there were many of the former convicts who arrived in the eastern colonies who were already dead as a result of the impact of the harsh life for labouring men in the colonies, along with poor nutrition, disease and violence; we could add isolation and loneliness to the factors that hastened men to an early death.[75] Laws governing goldfields life included mining acts, laws to regulate licences for gold miners, and laws regulating gunpowder and explosives, along with the regulation of Chinese Immigrants (1855), and the regulation of Chinese residences (1857). Laws relating to Chinese Immigration continued to appear into the 1880s, with deeper concerns about Chinese mobility and the presence of social difference.

The introduction of the vagrancy legislation in 1852 signalled a direct intervention into the lives of people in both the city of Melbourne, and in the rural towns where people were flocking to find work near goldfields. The 'thirty thousand vagabonds' who were circulating around the goldfield in 1851, as the *Argus* newspaper opined, had created alarm about 'idle and disorderly' characters.[76] Immigrants' homes were already attracting attention for their crowded tents near the city.[77] The 'excitement' created by gold rushes was responsible for the lack of 'order' in the colony, and to preserve and reinforce order, laws such as the Vagrancy Act would help to create a sense of space, occupancy and the monitoring of different types of mobility.[78]

The Vagrancy Act of 1852 and its provisions were later incorporated into Police Offences statutes and later amendments throughout the nineteenth century, with reference still made to the 'Vagrancy Act' in policing and prosecution.[79] As with the legislation in New South Wales, the act listed a hundred possible offences and a number of clauses which defined categories of vagrancy under each 'type', such as seven aspects of being 'idle and disorderly'.[80] Interestingly, the vagrancy law was criticized for both its breadth and its vagueness, but also viewed as a usefully flexible law for police to use in practice, even when other laws to regulate space and forms of crime co-existed. This suggests that the vagrancy law had appeal as a law that could offer a shorthand for policing, a theme examined in the next chapter.

Aotearoa/New Zealand

In the early years of the provincial government of New Zealand, ordinances relating to vagrancy were designed to manage the population moving around in the mode of 'settlers' and later, gold seekers. In the South Island, the province of Otago introduced a Vagrant Ordinance in 1861 to 'control the lower elements' of society, which also meant more women were arrested for prostitution.[81] The Ordinance sought to control the movement of those people who were without 'visible lawful means' or who had 'insufficient lawful means of support'. Drunkenness, using indecent language, occupying a house with criminals and women who worked as prostitutes were all 'targets' of the Ordinance, in language that was familiar to anyone who knew the English vagrancy laws.[82] The introduction of specific vagrancy legislation in New Zealand by 1866 came after the influx of people to the colony during the gold rushes to parts of both the North Island and the South Island.

Given its flexibility and potential reach of the vagrancy law, the concept of 'civil liberties' was fiercely debated in the chambers of the New Zealand Parliament. After a new Police Offences Act was introduced in 1884, the Vagrant Act of 1866 was remembered for the 'extraordinary rumpus created in the public mind'.[83] Critics of the new law worried that it was too broad; homelessness and unemployment would be swept up by the law, and provisions to prosecute beggars could, it was suggested, affect miners who moved around the country and lived rough from time to time. The policing of the law also attracted attention. There was concern about the way this new law impinged on local experiences and the authority of local police, especially around the diggings. Others claimed the Bill was an example of 'panic' legislation or that it was too rushed. The debates were extensive over several sittings, but eventually the Bill was passed and the law enacted.[84] Interestingly, the New Zealand Parliament looked to other jurisdictions in the world, including India, seeking comparisons and examples of the impact of vagrancy laws.[85] The colony of Victoria's legislation of 1852 was influential, as with other laws that came from that colony when legislation was created in New Zealand, including lunacy laws.

Historians agree that a new language of social control travelled with European immigrants to the colonies.[86] Hitchcock's interpretation of the earlier laws of vagrancy in England suggests that the categories were 'woolly' and at times, absurd, in the 1700s.[87] Yet the legal categories of person identifiable in the laws persisted over time, also suggesting concepts of personhood and 'othering' practices being made explicit in legislation. As noted earlier, across all the colonial jurisdictions with specific legislation dealing with vagrancy, acts were arranged around the categories of 'idle and disorderly', 'vagabond or rogue' and 'incorrigible rogue'. Police offences statutes covered an array of offences under 'indecency and vagrancy' including prostitution and drunkenness and offered details about specific situations manageable under policing provisions. Two specific aspects of these laws need further explication because they point to the colonial conditions for the invention of the colonial vagrant as a 'person' in terms of the law: the vulnerability of people who could not show any means of employment or support; and a targeted approach to Europeans who consorted with Indigenous peoples.

'No visible means of support'

The first aspect of these colonial laws is the use of the phrase 'no visible means of support' which was used most often in police arrests and in court appearances of persons charged with the crime of vagrancy. There was a common element to this set of categories and descriptors for vagrancy across the colonial jurisdictions, and it related to the deep-seated abhorrence of poverty. Destitution was horrifying to colonial authorities in government. It reminded them that the utopian vision for new societies was being eroded by 'old world' problems like pauperism. Convicts and ex-convicts tended to be recidivist offenders in the early years of the penal colonies. Ultimately, as newspaper reports show, vagrancy laws and police offences legislation swept up the many people who, like Thomas Guyon and Catherine Masters in Tasmania, attracted attention for their sheer poverty entwined with their lack of opportunity in life.

In March 1855 one of these reports was from the *Hobarton Mercury*. It concerned a vagrant named John Spurridge, also listed as 'Spowage', who was charged by DC Fitzsimmons 'having no means of subsistence'. He said he 'had no place to go':

> It appeared that he had only come out of the House of Correction yesterday, and had had no time to get employment, Mr. Abbott discharged him with a caution, recommending him to seek for work.[88]

This was not his first brush with the law. The fact that he was arrested so soon after his release from prison also reminds us of the unforgiving nature of the policing approach to men in his situation. Following his trial in Nottingham, on 21 July 1831, John Spowage had been sentenced to transportation for life and arrived in Hobart from Woolwich colony on the transport *Katherine Stewart Forbes* in 1832. His record – available through the extensive research into the life course of Tasmania's convict populations – shows that he was charged with rape: for 'violently … assaulting and ravishing Mary Anne Lord'. Born in 1812, and aged nineteen when he arrived, he obtained a ticket of leave in 1840, and later received a conditional pardon in July 1845 and was therefore about forty-two when charged with vagrancy after twenty-three years in the colony.[89] In May 1843, he married Mary Ann Griffith at St George's Church in Battery Point, and they had at least three children, Sarah Ann Spoadge [*sic*], born May 1843, George Spoadge [*sic*], born October 1844 and William John Spodge [*sic*], born November 1846.[90] However, his wife Mary Anne died in June 1848 of consumption.[91] To support his family, Spowage had to make the best of his situation. Listed as a labourer and assigned on muster three times to Mr Williamson at Glenorchy, or to Mr John Ferguson at Waterloo Point in the early 1830s, he probably worked as a labourer when he could throughout the 1850s unless he was unable to find work.

There is also evidence that he spent his life in and out of carceral and welfare institutions. More research is needed to find out what became of his children. He was arrested again in June 1855 along with several others for heavy drinking.[92] In September 1865 he was sentenced to three years' imprisonment for stealing a cheese.[93] He was arrested more than once in 1865 for theft, and again in 1872, that time for assaulting a police constable.[94] We also know that he lived in the Cascades Invalid Depot in 1868–70.[95] He died aged eighty-three in the New Town Charitable Institution on 2 November 1895 and was buried in a pauper's grave.[96]

However, just as the vagrancy categories in law were vague, so too was the range of people caught up in its discursive web over time: many different people were the subjects of these laws. Given the flux of colonial life and work, many men in New Zealand 'approximated vagrancy', as Fairburn puts it, and as contemporaries worried when the 1866 legislation was introduced.[97] The appearance of poverty and aimlessness, explored in later chapters of this book that examine the themes of the everyday lives of vagrants, and states of vulnerability, was widespread given the structure of the colonial economies across Australia and New Zealand.

'Consorting' clauses in the colonies

The second aspect of the colonial vagrancy laws that stands out is the use of the 'consorting clause'. There is relatively little scholarship about the meaning and application of consorting clauses in relation to vagrancy laws.[98] Consorting with known criminals was policed, where it could be: this relied on sophisticated knowledge of offenders as much as luck, as shown in stories of policing criminals and their associates later in the period under examination. For offender Daniel Munro, alias Warren, the 'innocence' of being arrested on charges of being 'idle and disorderly' in Wellington New Zealand was quickly dissolved as police indicated his prior offences in the 1890s, including a record of housebreaking, theft, consorting with thieves and keeping company 'with a very notorious criminal' in Masterton, as well as with a 'still worse' criminal in the city. Approached by detectives, 'both bolted' on the night of his arrest.[99]

The background to consorting clauses in Britain suggests that there was a deep unease about the identity of gypsies, people who moved from place to place, had no intention of settling in any one location and who defied notions of community integration by being constantly mobile. As I describe elsewhere, the colonial laws took a specific approach to consorting by focusing on Europeans who associated with Indigenous peoples, rather than including Indigenous peoples in direct policing for acts of vagrancy. Europeans were arrested for being in spaces known to be 'Māori', or for living among and associating with Aboriginal people. This raises the question of whether Indigenous peoples were considered to be vagrants in the eyes of the law.[100] Susanne Davies explains that non-Aboriginal persons associating with Aboriginal people had to explain why, that it was temporary, and show that they were behaving lawfully, otherwise they could be charged as 'idle and disorderly'. Historical research suggests that the lead up to this clause in the 1835 legislation stemmed from fears about the conduct of both Aboriginal and non-Aboriginal peoples – especially convicts – around the early colonial settlement, including worries about sexual interactions, disease and other forms of undesirable mingling. This was a way to exclude Aboriginal people as well as a means of controlling the movement of Europeans.[101]

Both by design and in practice the policing of Indigenous people who were moving from place to place took other direct forms rather than opting to sweep Aboriginal and Māori people into the broad category of 'vagrant'. The laws of vagrancy situated Indigenous peoples as already occupying a world of 'moral failure', as historians suggest, aligning them with the poorest of the poor in Britain, but with a more punitive aspect: the removal of Aboriginal peoples in different colonies, including targeted approaches such as sequestration and separation.[102]

Aboriginal Australians tended to rely on the European towns for food, living around the edges of 'settlements' in the early years of the colony of New South Wales, and again on the outskirts of the city of Melbourne. They were viewed, as historians Lynette Russell explains, as 'beggars and intemperate vagrants' in the 1850s.[103] This 'intimate city' of the growing population created a dependency for Aboriginal peoples who were described in the 1840s as being 'inconvenient' wanderers. The camps were at that time 'unpoliced' and lay 'outside of the emerging city grid … [a place] of drunkenness, gunfire, violence, and of interracial sex'.[104] 'Colonial sentiment' about the lives and status of Aboriginal people therefore shaped ideas about their motility.[105] Some of the issues raised by white contemporaries included a perception of Aboriginal people as inherently 'indolent', while wandering was seen as an activity particular to both Aboriginal and Māori peoples; moreover, the wording of specific consorting clauses in the colonial legislation indicates Aboriginal peoples were not 'vagrants' in the European sense of the word.[106] However, Indigenous people *were* arrested in the colonies on vagrancy charges in the latter decades of the nineteenth century, as Amanda Nettelbeck shows for South Australia and Western Australia, in line with the general increase in policing public order offences.[107]

Of the few recorded vagrancy prosecutions of Aboriginal people in New South Wales, one shows that rural towns observed the infractions of Aboriginal men with a close eye on their perceived threat to local people. Aged around thirty-nine, Charley Ambert was charged with vagrancy in 1878 at the Kiama Police Station and sentenced to six months with hard labour to be served at the Wollongong Gaol.[108] He had been working as a labourer, and had appeared before the courts in 1876, charged with assaulting a man named Tresnan in his home.[109] His defence in the assault case was that he was 'fugged down with grog and hunger' and wandering about inside the man's kitchen in the dark when Tresnan's son discovered him, grabbed him, causing him to fall down and hit his head.[110] Ambert made other court appearances in 1877, and suspicion of him continued to follow his movements.

Eliza White, listed as having no trade, was prosecuted for vagrancy in Cowra in 1878 and sent to Bathurst Gaol for six months. Two other Aboriginal men, charged and prosecuted in 1876 and 1879, were given sentences of six months in prison with hard labour: John Johnson, a horse breaker, whose face was described as 'flat and broad', was sent to Goulburn Gaol, while Thomas Rowe, a stockman, went to Dubbo.[111] These charges all stand out as relatively unusual in the landscape of laws of vagrancy but also suggest local practices of policing Aboriginal people via the vagrancy legislation in Central Western New South Wales.

Although there were very few arrests using the consorting clauses in any colony, specifically in relation to Indigenous people, their very existence shows that the concern about fraternization was another symbol of the regulation of mobility for some people based on the definition of identity and belonging; ethnicity and 'race'. The various colonial legal provisions in Australian legislation were punitive and harsh, as exemplified by cases of two white men arrested as vagrants in an Indigenous camp who were both sentenced to twelve-month imprisonment with hard labour.[112] Over time, Nettelbeck argues, some 'protection' from vagrancy charges afforded by the perception of Aboriginal people as 'outside' the legal concept of vagrancy was whittled away as their 'still presence' on the land represented an obstacle to white progress, disguised as concern about interracial mixing and Indigenous degradation.[113]

In New Zealand, the small number of the vagrancy cases in the data collated from the *Police Gazettes* reveals a similar pattern, with few Māori people charged as vagrants in the nineteenth century. The names of some vagrants, as well as the description by police as 'native to New Zealand', highlights some individual arrests. In January of 1879, Hone Paika, a man aged thirty, with a tattooed face, was arrested in the Hokianga region of the North Island under the vagrancy provisions and sentenced to three months with hard labour. His occupation was 'labourer' and he had a previous conviction in 1878 for larceny, suggesting he may have been known to the police.[114] Harata te Mokotahi was also arrested in the Hokianga region of the North Island in October 1879, suggesting some local policing of Māori. Very little detail was recorded, and Harata was not ascribed any gender, but was described as forty-eight years old and of 'copper complexion' and sentenced to three weeks in prison. A newspaper search suggests Harata was committed to an insane asylum later that month.[115] Aged thirty-one, Raharahi was arrested in Mercer in the Waikato in August of 1877, bearing a tattoo that read 'TAUA KOPEKA' on his right arm; he was sentenced to three months hard labour. His tattoo may have identified his iwi and hapu allegiance to past conflicts between Māori. Sarah Downes, alias Rahena Taone, also had identifying tattoos reading 'WERETENI TOTU' and 'MEHAKA'. Arrested aged in her twenties at Otaki in January 1881 for vagrancy, having worked as a prostitute according to the *New Zealand Police Gazette*, she was later arrested again in March at Masterton, and had spent time in different gaols in between.[116] Rahena (or Sarah) appeared in court as a witness later that year.[117]

These partial glimpses of Māori who were charged with vagrancy offences or who appeared in courtrooms linked to criminal charges remind us of the constant refashioning of the application of laws in practice. In the Australian colony of New South Wales, the story of Worimi woman Mary Ann Bugg – a famous associate and probable wife of a white bushranger – shows how the bending of vagrancy charges could be a process of identifying its utility in relation to Aboriginal people in the middle of the nineteenth century.

Mary Ann Ward (Bugg)

Mary Ann Ward (or Bugg) was tried on 31 March 1866 at the Stroud Police lockup in the Hunter Valley and was described being from Gloucester. Her occupation was given as 'servant'. Born in 1839, Mary Ann was 5 foot 3, her skin was 'dark sallow', she had black hair and brown eyes, a 'slightly cocked' nose, large mouth and chin, and was listed as being a 'half caste Aboriginal'.[118] She was sentenced to six months at East Maitland Gaol. However, unusually, her sentence was remitted less than a month later on 18 April 1866 after a public outcry.[119] Mary Ann was the centre of attention because she was seen as the victim of a political arrest: it was thought that the police were after her husband, the famous bushranger known as 'Thunderbolt', or Frederick Ward. This story about Mary Ann touches on a few elements of the laws of vagrancy, including the prevalent fear of bushranging in the colonies, and the politics of policing in rural areas, but also highlights the question of Indigenous peoples and the uses of the vagrancy laws in relation to their offending.

Mary Ann's early life and relationship with Frederick Ward has been described by a range of historians who have searched for the evidence about her life, including her children, conjecture over her marriages and death through the competing readings of her life in the records.[120] What historians know is that she was born Mary Ann Bugg in May 1834 near Gloucester in the Hunter Valley, the daughter of a convict assigned to the Australian Agricultural Company, and a Worimi woman named Charlotte. She was known to be educated, a fact

Figure 2.2 Bern Emmerichs, 'Mary Ann Bugg' (detail) 2021, reproduced courtesy of Scott Livesey Galleries, Prahran, Melbourne.

that became significant in her vagrancy case later on; she spent time in private education in Sydney until she returned to her family in the mid-1840s.[121] Mary Ann's association with the bushranger known as 'Thunderbolt' began sometime in the 1850s. Ward was a ticket-of-leave man and by the early 1860s was notorious for his escapes from custody on Cockatoo Island, and for his bushranging exploits. Mary Ann was by then accompanying him on his crimes and was arrested while pregnant in 1865, and was known as being a tough accomplice, capable of absconding and guilty of abusing police.[122] This means that her story has been variously appropriated as the story of an 'Aboriginal bushranger', or as a woman outlaw heroine, as portrayed in recent artwork (see Figure 2.2 above), and also evidence of a Worimi woman's history.[123]

William Monckton rode with Thunderbolt and wrote an account of his three years with the man. Ward had a 'softer' side to him, a side he revealed to Monckton, who used his entry into the domestic life of the bushranger in his story of Ward as a family man. Mary Anne appeared to him as 'quite plain'. Her ethnicity was a subject of interest, and Monckton played to that in his description: writing that 'everything about her showed her hybrid origin. Her features, it is true, were fairly well-shaped and regular, but her hair resembled an aboriginal's, and her skin was quite yellow'.[124] Historians tend to agree that it is possible that the vagrancy charge was used against Mary Anne so that her activities with known bushrangers might be contained.[125] Yet none dwell on the charge or its remission in any depth. Kali Bieren's thesis spends time describing the evidence of the arrest and charge, noting that Senior Sergeant Kerrigan told the Police Magistrate that she had told him she had no means of support, and 'no fixed residence'. This meant that Mary Ann was sentenced to six months in prison under the Vagrant Act of 1851, despite Mary Ann defending the charge on the grounds that she was supported by her husband. She was convicted for being 'idle and disorderly, and a companion of reputed thieves, having no visible means of support, or fixed place of residence' and that she could not give a good account of herself.[126] The judgement was debated by locals who campaigned, writing letters to the paper and criticizing the police force. Her case was then debated in the Legislative Assembly and the argument presented focused on her identity as a Worimi woman, with Mr Buchanan, claiming that 'the wilderness was her home, and the wide bush the only residence she possessed'. He went further, posing the idea that the 'original inhabitants' of the colony could not be prosecuted under the Vagrant Act, and that to do so would constitute the 'grossest tyranny and oppression'. Other speakers agreed. Interestingly, they pointed to her being separated from her three children as another 'perversion of justice'.[127]

Magistrate Thomas Nicholls downplayed her origins as the child of a Worimi mother, and pointed to her baptism, her Christian education, her record of employment and her 'settled habits', suggesting that the grounds for arguing against the charge were not accurate.[128] In the judgement handed down on 16 April 1866 by Attorney General Sir James Martin, the arrest and charge of Mary Anne was described as being appropriate under the act. Martin took a different path, paving the way for other uses of the vagrancy law against Aboriginal people who offended.[129] Mary Ann was not living among or 'found wandering in company with' Aboriginal peoples, therefore could not be charged for consorting with them, even though she was 'within their protection'. Most Aboriginal people, Martin said, should not be prosecuted using this law, as they were not all 'civilised'. However, many were like Mary Ann: brought up among

Europeans, people who had 'acquired civilised habits'. The real problem, said Martin, was that the charges brought against the prisoner were flimsy, and not well substantiated, and she was freed. Martin was concerned that such a case, if it was tried in the Supreme Court, would be thrown out.[130]

Afterwards, people weighed in with opinions about the case, about Mary Ann, and about bushranger Thunderbolt, and the politics of policing dangerous characters in the colony. In 1867, Mary Anne was again arrested on a vagrancy charge and sentenced to three months in Maitland Gaol after appearing at Paterson, New South Wales. With 'a few yards of calico, and a few yards of Derry cloth in her possession, for which she could not satisfactorily account', she was deemed a 'vagrant'. A letter to the newspaper by a concerned onlooker – someone who had watched her previous case and conviction be overturned – commented that she was 'as illegally in custody now as when she was arrested and convicted under the Vagrant Act by a bench not many miles distant'.[131]

Conclusions: Responses to mobility

The story of Mary Anne Ward helps to highlight the complicated worlds and experiences of women and men trying to eke out lives on colonial frontiers near the start of the period under investigation. Her story reminds us that vagrancy laws also need to be situated inside the context of a highly mobile colonial world engaged in formation through and in social groupings.[132] The regulation of Aboriginal people in 1860s Victoria and the 'protection' approach emerging in the colony of New South Wales suggested other aspects to population and mobility control. In Victoria in 1869, the Aborigines Protection Act made Aboriginal people subject to European controls. In the same period, New Zealand's land alienation and outright conflict over Māori land also drew attention to the relative freedoms to move around the colony.

Beginning with the regulation of convicts' lives, labour and movement, the policing of mobility in the colonies shows us that 'mobility' itself presented challenges to imperial and colonial authorities, at the same time as it was pivotal to colonial settlement and formation. Vagrants came from all over the world, as shown in the data collated from the colonial *Police Gazettes*, with the majority from parts of Britain.[133] Inherited 'nomadic' tendencies, as historians have speculated, derived from the period of late-eighteenth- and early-nineteenth-century Britain.[134] In Henry Mayhew's extensive account of the London labouring poor, informed by his research into the lifeworlds of convicts bound for transport to Australia in the 1820s and 1830s, offers another view of the 'ragged class' who formed the convict community: these were men and women who grew up in extreme conditions characterized by 'parental neglect or indifference', with casual crime already a way of life.[135]

By the early 1900s, the further restriction of non-white peoples throughout the Australasian colonies had the effect of placing the mobility of some people under question in the public mind. Restrictions on movement were a cornerstone of the governance of populations. These took the form of immigration restriction which affected generations of indentured labourers already living in the northern parts of Australia, as well as Chinese immigrants who populated Victoria, New South Wales and New Zealand, working as market gardeners and labourers, and sometimes as servants. This regulation of peoples across the Australasian colonies was aided by the spread of legal ideas around the British world and was entangled with the work of imperial power.[136] Legal ideas were shared across jurisdictional boundaries, and through the mobility of lawyers, who, like doctors, traversed empire as the development of their professions allowed.[137]

The story of vagrancy laws, with their European genealogy, presents an interesting opportunity to find out more about how transcolonial interventions into human mobility took form and were applied in different settings.[138] The colonies of Australia and New Zealand were not alone in the construction of laws to define the boundaries for movement, especially in relation to the settler-colonial project. Vagrancy laws in the British Empire were used to control 'disorderly Europeans' in many cases, especially around the ports where ships docked and men spilled out to seek adventure and opportunity.[139] The vagrancy prosecution data reflects the diversity of occupational categories among those arrested for vagrancy or for being idle and disorderly where information was recorded.[140]

In India, Canada and South Africa, vagrancy was also defined by concerns about wandering and social formation, with laws imagined in places where Indigenous peoples had been colonized and where immigration was forging social and political relations. There were strong parallels between the monitoring and 'taming' of Indigenous peoples in Australia and other colonies, particularly in India.[141] In urban British Columbia, Canada, vagrancy and prostitution became part of the lexicon of social panic about Aboriginal peoples, with urbanization creating a new understanding of the role played by space in the creation of the identities of the 'vagrant' and the 'prostitute' in the 'streetscapes' of both Vancouver and Melbourne.[142]

Colonial vagrancy laws were created as local responses to the movements of the early population of convicts and people on the move in the colonies, such as miners and itinerant workers. Mobility and what it represented was at the centre of debates about the legislation, including contemporary insight into the curtailment of the liberties of people in the colonies. The view that enforcing the law would lead to strain on policing resources highlights the politics of lawmaking in the colonies, as well as the question of policing practice and the application of laws, as later chapters go on to show. That Tasmania took a distinctive approach reminds that the various colonies enacted legal thinking specific to their contexts and cultures, including the nature of settlement and society and the significance of the convict beginnings of the colony. In New Zealand, the development of separate ordinances followed by one Vagrancy Act also points to the changing role of laws in settler-colonial worlds over time.

Although Miles Fairburn's description of New Zealand as an 'atomised' society has been critiqued by social historians who argue that colonial communities did form and constitute mutuality and reciprocity, his argument about the 'enemies of ideal society' remains compelling in the context of a discussion about vagrancy in the colonies.[143] Legal scholarship has echoed the idea of a legacy of intolerance to people whose lifestyles threatened social cohesion, with the argument that legislation of the 1870s in New Zealand was deliberately 'ferocious' about vagrants and prostitutes.[144] Fairburn points to a masculine world of transience based on itinerant and seasonal work, a condition that he describes as leading to dereliction in some men as an outcome of the 'mentality of caseless striving'.[145] Arguably it was the increasing influx of new migrants who brought with them the 'old-world' concept of 'vagrancy' which continued to be developed in law across the colonial world from the 1860s, as this chapter has outlined. The worlds of vagrants were not only defined by legal restriction but also by their movement in and around towns, cities and in rural areas. The next chapter takes up the role of police and their approaches to vagrants in more detail, including police work and prosecutions using these laws.

3

The policing and prosecution of vagrants

Police were often closely involved in the lives of vagrants. So prevalent was their involvement with minor crimes in early New South Wales that observers like Peter Cunningham commented it was excessive when compared with the 'English bench': police were arresting and charging people for 'insolence, neglect of work, drunkenness, running away, absence without leave so on'.[1] Prosecuted for unauthorized movement, as well as for stopping and 'loitering with intent' in the context of a society bent on settler respectability, urban vagrants were policed using emerging techniques of the police 'beat'. They were subject to police surveillance as shown in the vagrancy arrests tabulated in the various colonial *Police Gazettes*, data that underpins this book and more specifically this chapter. The early years of the colonies of New South Wales and VDL, settled by Europeans in the late eighteenth century, still reflected the English approach to 'moving people on' as endorsed by laws; early modes of policing reflected this and by the 1840s, vagrancy laws tended to highlight people 'who sought to live apart from the rigid discipline demanded by employer or landlord'.[2]

In rural areas, police had to cover different territory to maintain order, relying on local communities and the observations of people in small towns who noticed strangers or people passing through.[3] Tasmanian sources suggest that the population was 'extensively policed' in the 1840s.[4] VDL possessed a 'brutal policing and legal apparatus', with more police per person in the population than New South Wales, and police spread out to check the identities of 'foot travellers' in 1847.[5] Policing was modelled on 'London and Irish forces' as this chapter goes on to describe.[6] There were welfare aspects to their work and in many places, including 1850s New Zealand, police on the streets enjoyed their community status. This can be seen in the account of John Shaw's 'tramp' through the gold diggings of the colonies. Shaw wrote of the policeman in Nelson 'in his blue dress and hard-crowned hat, more frequently engaged in talking over the news of the day':

> At times, however, he has long journeys to perform into the country, to look after distant rogues. On his return, he may be seen entertaining idle people with all the varied incidents of his journey, and laying down the law, as if he were one of the great judges of the district.[7]

Policing was important to each colony, and in local settings, but also in networks of law enforcement across the colonies. Authorities maintained a watchful eye on the 'criminal mobility' that threatened orderly settlements.[8] In the more punitive atmosphere of 1840s Hobart, policing extended to the suppression of harmless events like musical entertainment that was common for people living in and around pubs, such as convicts and ex-convicts.[9]

To explain the role of police, this chapter draws mostly on the *Police Gazette* data and newspaper accounts which recorded court appearances, but also on police regulations and institutional records. Newspapers were an important mode of communication in the period and, across all of the colonies, included lengthy regular court reports. This was perhaps disproportionate to the significance of the crimes being reported, especially vagrancy.[10] Although it could be misleading to rely heavily on these newspaper reports, another way of interpreting the copious reporting of public order offences lies in seeing how police work takes us inside these interactions at the very margins of colonial society, particularly through local expressions and performances of colonial law and its enactment, all of which is evident in policing practices. These practices, documented on paper, reveal the 'paper mobility' of empire that Tony Ballantyne suggests is also central to the flow of information that regulated and shaped ideas about human movement.[11]

Contemporary reports point to the 'public degradation' of vagrants by the police and the courts, and the criminalization of poverty and transience from the 1870s in New Zealand.[12] Susanne Davies writes that in 1880s Victoria, the law gave police 'an unrivalled opportunity to exercise their discretion'.[13] The same can be seen elsewhere in the colonies, as noted by Mark Finnane and Stephen Garton, writing about rates of arrest and police powers across the Australian colonies from the middle of the nineteenth century.[14] The police mostly charged people with 'offences against good order' and petty crimes in the latter part of the nineteenth century, with the charge of vagrancy one example of an array of infringements caught up in the regulation of 'order'.[15] Colonial statistics for police offences are partial: Finnane and Garton state that these are only available in a 'consistent and reliable' format from the 1850s and 1860s, with Tasmania's records only 'regular' from the 1870s.[16] Extant statistics need to be used carefully, as indicated by the statistical analyses by social scientists, and do not always reflect the full picture of policing, as historians show.[17] Overall, my focus here is on the worlds and experiences of vagrants as they encountered the law and police, with data sets allowing me to surface the links to the intersecting records and stories of vagrant lives within a much larger pattern of behaviour and the regulation of vagrants' movements. As microhistories, these stories provide human faces to the data that lies beneath.

Police and policing

Policing was further refined in colonial cities and towns as a set of responses to the colonial environment, including institutions, the perceived threats of hostile Indigenous populations and the tenor of colonial social formation.[18] Criminologists have developed ways to interpret the historical significance of policing for understandings about criminality and personhood, and have also been interested in questions of gender and social difference in the prosecution of crime.[19] Uncovering the sorts of transgressions that provoked colonial surveillance and control reveals more about how the lives of mobile peoples collided with colonial authorities, as well as about the kinds of meanings produced by their appearance in legal settings. A close historical examination of the police work in colonial New South Wales shows that police themselves felt they 'occupied a landscape of suspicion, stopping travellers on the roads to search them and making note of suspicious activity'.[20]

Police were governed by rules and regulations that were formed as colonial policing was being established and explicitly drew on imperial world models. Policing overlapped with styles and cultures of law and order and control including English and Irish constabulary models.[21] These models included militaristic approaches to policing; the sanctioned use of weapons; and the recruitment of able-bodied men.[22] Police culture had developed from the earliest times when constables around the Rocks were bound together by their community of purpose, united in their work to mix among their neighbours, but also to police them, a tension that was not always easy to manage. The mid-century professionalization of the force meant that while in 1819, around half of the constables could not 'write their names', by 1853 this had all changed.[23] What has been described as a 'tense ambivalence' around the position of police in the community was less evident with the guidance of the regulations for the police.[24]

In New South Wales the *Rules and Regulations for the Government and Guidance of the Metropolitan Police Force* set out to create a desired culture of policing in 1853.[25] The guidance described districts to be policed, as well as how police would be appointed. To become a constable, a man had to be aged under forty and to be able to read and write. The expectation was that police would be fit and healthy, would undergo a medical examination, and would be intelligent.[26] This marked a shift from the earlier years of policing the colony which was characterized by the employment of less reliable men: sometimes ex-convicts who were poorly paid, who drank on the job and who were managed by Chief Constables seen as 'petty tyrants' in the eyes of contemporaries.[27] Police had to be able to enact the laws of the colony, engage with justices and perform administrative work, often under pressure, to ensure legal processes were followed. Their duties were broad, intersected with the work of welfare as well as the law, and – as far as the offences of public order were concerned – tended to be repetitive. This repetition was underlined by their ability to make arrests without warrants when identifying 'common prostitutes' or offences involving disorderly and drunk people.[28] Police regulations around identifying loitering tell us more about life in the colonial city.[29] The Sydney Domain or Hyde Park was especially prone to shady characters who frequented the area, lounging and loafing during the day or hanging out in the shadows of the evening, all of which were behaviours known to the Auckland Domain in New Zealand and also to Melbourne's Botanical Gardens in the nineteenth century.[30] In 1868 police requested that the gates to the public domain in Christchurch in New Zealand's South Island be closed 'to keep out prostitutes and disorderly characters', and similar concerns were raised about the city's Hagley Park in 1870.[31] A subsequent version of the *Rules and Regulations* for New South Wales in 1862 reinforced these earlier concerns about public order, refining the relationship between different colonies and practices of policing by including references to the 1852 vagrancy legislation in Victoria, for instance.[32]

Policing the city and countryside was about crime prevention. The *Rules for the Management of the Police Force of New South Wales* published in 1862 asked that police focus on the detection of crime and apprehension of criminals. The focus on the prevention of crime meant that the emphasis was on identifying the intention to commit crimes, allowing police to tune into their suspicions about a range of activities, the people they observed and the places they occupied. The Vagrant Act 1851 was directly referred to in several places, and the duties of police in relation to prostitutes 'wandering the streets' earned a mention. But it was the risk presented by people who looked like they had a nefarious purpose that mattered. People who were carrying a 'picklock, key, crow, jack, bit, or other implement' attracted attention, as did people who were stopping around certain places: 'out-house', 'stable', river, canal, stream, dock, quay, wharf… or just idling in the street or along an avenue, possibly to commit a crime.[33] The places were not the only indicators of intent to commit crime: people intoxicated or incapable of taking care of themselves were also under scrutiny. Other forms of behaviour raised questions about a person's criminal intent including 'wandering abroad', 'begging', 'showing wounds' or exhibiting deformities 'to procure charitable contributions', all of which raise questions about colonial attitudes towards poverty and disability. Finally, anyone who bathed in a public waterway or who put 'filth' and rubbish in public water could also be charged as a criminal.[34] All of these offences interacted with vagrancy.

The Sydney metropolitan police were tasked with covering a vast geographical terrain. The policing districts of metropolitan Sydney were large areas bounded by waterways including Broken Bay, Cowan Creek, Lane Cove River, the Parramatta River, George's River, Botany Bay, and Cape Solander.[35] Local police divisions formed numbered beats and had their own station houses.[36]

The first police in Port Philip, later the colony of Victoria, were the constables who formed a force reporting to the Police Magistrates from 1836, with the development of local district and rural constabulary, city police, native police and a force to oversee the goldfields in the early 1850s. With the formation of the new colony, in 1853 the Victoria Police Force was created with a set of regulations to shape its practices, and the first *Manual of Police Regulations* published in 1856. The Chief Commissioner of Police role was also established.[37] The *Manual of Police Regulations* (1856) was a comprehensive guide for police. In Part One it described police districts, the conditions of entry to the force, promotions, clothing, general duties and more. As in New South Wales, there were expectations that police would be literate, but in Victoria the preference was to admit as new police men who were aged under thirty years, unless they had previously served as police, but even then they were not to be aged over thirty-five.[38] In addition to being able to 'read and write well', they had to provide testimonials of character. They also had to undertake a trial before their appointments were confirmed, and their specific capability for work such as with the mounted police was to be determined after a period of foot service. They had to provide written answers on a test about their work experience, and they also had to swear an oath.[39]

Each of these aspects suggested a seriousness about the police force in Victoria as it faced the challenges of the growing urban population, but also the movement of people arriving during the gold rushes of the 1850s and spreading out from Melbourne to the gold field towns. In Victoria's Regulations (1856), the specific application of legislation was spelled out in greater detail for police. They were instructed how to intervene and arrest people, when to engage with weapons, how to arrest the 'idle and disorderly' without warrants and were provided with definitions of prostitution. Other legislation, such as the Country Police Act, was also cross-referenced with vagrancy.[40]

In 1877 the *Regulations for the Guidance of the Constabulary of Victoria* included more tangible proforma for the practices of arrest, reporting and conveyance of offenders.[41] These regulations were the first since 1856, and related to the Police Regulation Statute of 1873.[42] Tasmania was strongly influenced by English models of policing because colonial government administrator and Premier of Tasmania (1857–60) Francis Smith had first-hand experience of the formation of the London Metropolitan Police under Robert Peel in the 1850s.[43] Policing needed to be reformed in Tasmania: the reputation of the police in the 1840s was imperfect, with claims of police abusing their station in relation to the arrests of women, as examined further later in this chapter. By 1866, decentralized policing meant the mushrooming of an uneven application of the laws by police across several municipalities. In 1898 a Police Regulation Act tidied up what had become a messy system.[44]

Police wore clothing that identified them. Various official regulations listed the clothing items for different police. Police clothing was important to create uniformity and to distinguish rank. In New South Wales, officers provided their own regulation clothes, while members of the general police force were supplied with caps, dress coats, overcoats, trousers, boots and a waterproof cape, as well as some basic pantaloons. Constables were required to furnish a box containing bedding, brushes, combs, razors, underwear and a memorandum book, and were inspected for cleanliness by sergeants. Mounted officers and water police had other requirements and foot police were given arms, with each man to carry a rifle, a bayonet with sheath, a baton, handcuffs, and to carry a pouch, whistle and an identifying number and letter.[45] A photograph album of police wearing uniforms as shown in Figure 3.1 below that were assigned between 1863 and 1918 shows the changing style of official costume, and also illustrates the links between military dress and police uniforms, including insignia and badges denoting rank and status.[46] While the clothing worn by police constables in Victoria was similar to that for New South Wales police, it also had subtle differences, marking policing for each colony out as distinctive in small ways.[47] Being identifiable meant that police work could lack subtlety: offenders scarpered when they saw a detective appear to check out a known burglar on the streets of Wellington, New Zealand, in 1903, probably not for the first or last time in the experience of either.[48]

Figure 3.1 New South Wales Gaol Officials, Darlinghurst Gaol, 1900, NRS-4481-3-[7/16194]=Sh895, reproduced courtesy of State Archives Collection, Sydney, NSW.

Figure 3.2 'Prisoners in uniform, Darlinghurst Gaol', 1900, NRS-4481-3-[7/16194]-Sh897, reproduced courtesy of State Archives Collection, Sydney, NSW.

With the focus on police discretionary power, the language of the police we can find in the different records hints at a degree of familiarity between vagrants and the police, especially in cases of recidivism where individuals were arrested multiple times. Police came to know their communities, mixing with citizens and performing a wide range of duties.[49] Occasionally, we hear their voices in their descriptions of offenders. Charlotte Schmid was a 'showily-dressed young woman' charged with bigamy and tried at the Dunedin Supreme Court in New Zealand in July of 1875.[50] Sergeant-Major Bevan, a popular Irish-born police constable with a distinguished military career in the Crimea, was called to give evidence. Bevan explained that he was aware she had kept a brothel in Maclaggan Street: 'He warned her on one occasion that she would be brought up as a vagrant, and she then promised to leave the town, and return to her husband in Christchurch.'[51] Bevan was no stranger to the mobility of the colonial world, having trained as a police constable in Victoria where he spent time policing the goldfields. Other voices also appear: the colonies were also places where travellers moved around, taking in new places and writing about social habits, groups and milieu.[52] Their narratives offer ways of both seeing and empathizing with those people who lived rough or who were between jobs, and who could not give adequate accounts of their movements.

Identifying and observing vagrants

Around early Sydney, the constables had mingled with the wider community, drinking in public houses and getting to know behaviours that presented within close-knit groups of people. With the greater professionalization of the force including distinctions, rank, types of policing and the rise of theories about crime and criminality, the police became more clinical in their approach to identifying transgressions. In the city of Melbourne police worked the 'beat' in shifts over both night and day. More senior police – the sergeants – had to get to know their assigned locale: local magistrates, entertainment and hotel districts. Constables were to be respected by all people, across all social classes and be respectful to everyone they encountered. Both the Victorian *Manual* (1856) and the *Rules and Regulations* (NSW 1862) are very specific about the hazy time between sunset and sunrise. A police constable could make a judgement about any person 'loitering between sunset and sunrise' in Victoria.[53] In New South Wales, a police constable could 'arrest any person whom he may find between sunset and sunrise lying or loitering in any highway, yard, or other place, and not giving a satisfactory account of himself'.[54]

In the colony of Victoria, the police were encouraged to detail the occupations of people arrested using a helpful appendix of occupational categories. The 'criminal and pauper classes' included 'pauper, beggar, vagrant' as a separate group from 'prostitute and brothelkeeper', with more explanatory entries to aid police in prosecuting cases of prostitution.[55] The policing of people displaying signs of insanity shared some characteristics with the policing of vagrants. Police also played a difficult but much-needed role in managing nineteenth-century lunacy in Victoria, including transporting sick and sometimes violent people suffering from mental illness to support families and protect the public.[56]

The malleability of some vagrants' identities was a feature of the everyday lives of women and men in the colonial world. That involved the ability to move around within the colonies, in some cases, as well as reinvention of the self, in others. People practised 'passing' of all kinds from gender identity to different forms of disguise. The use of different names appears to have been reasonably common in the eighteenth- and nineteenth-century records of convicts and those prosecuted for vagrancy, giving weight to one view that the practice of using an alias had all but died out aside from those of the 'criminal class'.[57] Earlier examples of the use of an alias name suggests that it was a very well-utilized technique for distinguishing between individuals with similar or identical names in the early modern period, had a bearing on 'legitimacy' and places of birth, and was also used by notaries in legal documents.[58] The number of alias names in the different data sets of vagrant prosecutions shows that for people who were seeking to evade the police, perhaps because they had been charged with other crimes, and hoped to slip past authorities. For example, of the sixty-nine offenders in the data with an alias for New South Wales, most used at least one other name. In 1903, the *Australian Photographic Review* announced that in Britain, the technique of photographing fingerprints was revolutionizing police work in cases where identity was hard to fix, in part because of the use of aliases by offenders Prisoners also wore identifiable clothing, as depicted in Figure 3.2 above.[59]

Yet using other names was not always a guarantee of success; these names were noted in the *Police Gazettes,* in court records and newspapers, and could potentially aid the police in their work. One man, John Yates, an offender arrested in Napier New Zealand in the early 1900s, had used at least five names by the age of sixty: Robinson, Campbell, Reay, Thompson and David Brown. With thirty previous convictions, the habit had followed him around, and was recorded with his photograph.[60] Perhaps the 'well educated' Irish Telegraphist, William Crossley, held at Woodville lockup in New Zealand's North Island in 1891, was used to slipping through the net, as he was 'repeatedly convicted' by the age of thirty-four and went by the names 'Harry Clifford alias Clifton alias

Frank Bayley'. This time he was identifiable by his Northern Irish accent, which was noted in the record, and a link was also made to the *New Zealand Police Gazette* entry in 1886 which described the marks on his arms.[61]

More practically, records were not always accurate: names, places and dates were incorrect at the time of entry, misspelt or guessed. A person's known or stated occupation could change readily because work was seasonal, located in specific places or dependent on changing economies.[62] Thinking about how people who lived as vagrants carved out their identities is interesting. People took on a 'vagrant persona' in some instances, becoming 'visible' in a different sense in the community, also suggesting to some scholars that the state of being a vagrant had flexible boundaries.[63] The police used nicknames: the 'swindling parson' or Thomas Roberts arrested in Hay, New South Wales in 1876 was also known as 'Spencer' and 'McDonald'. Servant Jane Maxwell, arrested in Orange, was also known as the 'Red Streak' in 1882.[64] For these reasons, physical descriptions of offenders were vital to police work before photography became the norm in the early twentieth century in some settings. The police 'mugshot' was introduced to the colonies in the late 1850s but not in wide use for a few more decades.[65] Mark Finnane describes the 'standard tools of policing' in use in the Australian colonies by 1912: 'the gazette notice of discharged prisoner details, the photograph, the fingerprint'.[66] In New Zealand, photographs of prisoners were taken in the mid-1880s and often included a focus on the hands of the person to aid identification.[67] *New Zealand Police Gazettes* included photographs of discharged prisoners from 1908.[68]

Photographs collated in the New Zealand Archives as 'Prisoner Photographs' contain mugshots of men charged with vagrancy. The *New Zealand Police Gazette* of 6 October 1909 published a series of photographs of discharged prisoners, including a number of men prosecuted as vagrants. Each man was photographed looking at the camera, and in profile. Other mugshots held in a collection of photographs of prisoners in New Zealand 1902 to 1906 include thirty-eight photographs of vagrants, all male. Among these is John Yates, with his several aliases listed in the notes about his record of offending. By this time Yates was an old man as his photograph shows, and he had been in the colony since 1886, born in 1842 in England. Yates held up his hands for the photographer and his eyes were frowning, his face framed by a beard, but not by hair, as he was balding. He had worked as a blacksmith and labourer and walked with a limp, as one of his legs was shorter than the other, suggesting illness or injury. He was nevertheless sentenced to three months with hard labour. William Ramsay, an American born in 1863, sported a much bushier beard and moustache in his mugshot photograph taken in 1903. He had not been in the colony for very long – a matter of months – and had previous convictions including as a bushranger and thief in New South Wales. In Wellington he had been arrested with housebreaking implements in his possession. He, too, received a sentence of three months in prison with hard labour and would have been more able to withstand the sentence as a younger and fitter man.[69]

Described later in this chapter, Christina Lawson's mugshot also appears in an online collection of police photographs in the New Zealand Police Archive. Like other women photographed in this period, Lawson's face is a reminder of the individual lives behind the vast prosecution data we have, reflecting different stories and experiences. Mugshots appear to us as a treasure trove of archival images, important visual reminders of people and their pasts. Yet the photographs served another purpose at their time of their capture. Writing about the 'tramp' in America, Cresswell examines the documenting of vagrancy in photographs as another aspect of the creation of knowledge about the category of the tramp, a category that was gendered, pathologized and codified.[70]

Overall, police used the vagrancy laws to control and shape public order. 'In the hands of urban police', writes Finnane, 'the vagrancy statues were an instrument for the surveillance of the criminal and dangerous classes', groups which included women working as prostitutes, women and men who lived lives of petty crime, but also the impoverished and destitute. That 'criminals' tended to 'congregate' near hotels and brothels made the job of the police so much more about policing morality as well as wrongdoing, and they were visible in their efforts to clean up the streets of colonial cities.[71] The Chinese people moving around the colony were also more vulnerable to police arrests as shown in studies of the goldfields and mobility.[72]

Vagrant bodies

Vagrancy was already understood as a habit of people who formed a growing 'class' of undesirable people in the British context, with a vein of literary and cultural tropes centring on the notion of the vagrant's body as a 'social toxin'.[73] Not only culture but policing was imported from Britain, with police recruits from England and Ireland coming to New South Wales in the 1850s, evidence of the mobility of thought in the case of practices around identifying vagrancy.[74] Descriptions of vagrants found in the *Police Gazettes* of the period were crafted to aid police in their work, especially when someone evaded a court appearance.

William Finn, aged twenty-six, was 'short and stout', had a dark complexion, was 'clean shaved' and 'generally dressed in dark clothes', and was known to frequent Crown Lane, Woolloomooloo.[75] Men and women arrested for vagrancy bore tattoos, their mouths were missing teeth, their limbs scarred, notably deformed or burned. Some were blind or one-eyed, others were bald, or had large ears.[76] Bodily descriptions added up to 'character' in a few cases when mixed with obscene language or acts of physical resistance. The 'profusely tattooed' Johanna or Lily Barrett, possibly a Māori woman arrested for vagrancy in Auckland in 1899, worked as a prostitute in her late twenties and had at least twelve prior convictions.[77] Bodies also tell us that the lives of vagrants were 'harsh, rough, and marked by poverty'.[78] It was problematic to contemporary observers that police were asked to define those with bodily differences – for instance, 'the maimed, the diseased' – as 'criminal', a theme examined in more depth in the next chapter.[79]

Distinguishing marks and characteristics noted in *Police Gazettes* tended to follow a specific format, with a mention of any photographic record where that existed. An example below includes other detail such as occupation and institutional confinement:

> Rosa Lake, convicted 14/1/1880, female, 21 years old, native to England, convicted of vagrancy, sentenced to 12 months labour, from Addington gaol, 4;9.5", fresh complexion; black hair; dark brown eyes; small nose and mouth; medium chin; long forehead; wicked appearance; also sentenced to 6 months labour for prison offences 6 November 1880, occupation: general servant.[80]

Evidence drawn from the New Zealand sample of women vagrants shows a wide range of physical descriptors used by police in their recorded entries. These included height, facial features (noses were described as medium, straight, flat, aquiline, sharp, small, pug, prominent, and chins described as broad, heavy, receding, heavy and double, pointed; mouths were described as oblique, ordinary, deformed, puckered). Bodies were characterized in terms of build (if stout or slight), markings such as scars or tattoos, complexion (with complexions described as dark, sallow, copper, withered, swarthy, fresh, florid, pale, blotchy, pock-pitted and bloated). Aspects of disfigurement included squints, 'one eye wanting', 'sore eyes', long face, careworn appearance, general descriptions such as 'face and eyes disfigured', and attention was paid to teeth (whether decayed, upper front teeth out or whether teeth were rotten). Other descriptors were also used: 'half-caste', 'expression idiotic', and facial hair (on the chin or lip) was also noted. Injuries such as burns or broken limbs were listed, and any medical or health conditions such as the involuntary twitching of limbs.[81] Accents were also mentioned on occasion.

Among the male vagrants in the New Zealand sample, different terms and patterns appear. Height was only mentioned occasionally, something which might surprise researchers familiar with this type of record-keeping. Men were described as pigeon breasted, or having a sallow complexion, along with florid, fair, fresh, olive, swarthy or black skins. Scars and burn marks were important and frequently noted among men, a large number of whom had burn marks on their bodies. Mouths might be large, and teeth were missing; lips might be 'thick'. Many prisoners had tattooed skin which displayed words, references to family: 'My mother' or had nautical themes. A man's build might be stout, very stout, or slight, or round shouldered. Mental capacity was noted: men might be of 'weak intellect', 'subject to fits', or both 'deaf and dumb', others were 'of idiotic propensities', or possessed a 'vacant stare'. Physical 'defects' were accounted for: there were men with missing toes, or who were 'very deaf', or who had 'lost left testicle' or were missing a joint in one finger. Broken limbs were noticed, along with varicose veins, scarred knuckles, and skin eruptions, or baldness. A stooping gait – which we know now to be a possible sign of a neurological disease – was also recorded in these descriptions.

Age also became a descriptor – both in a basic sense, conveying information, and as a signifier of the criminality of a vagrant offender, young or old. 'Juvenile delinquents', discussed in more detail in Chapter 5 of this book, signified the perils of social dislocation, with families and communities unable to contain young people who might commit crimes. Older people who were either sophisticated in their navigation of a life of petty crime, such as the 'old hands' who appear frequently in court reports and *Police Gazette* notes, presented different challenges to police, often related to the care and treatment of the destitute and the elderly. The 'old hand' was usually a transported convict who had transitioned to being an ex-convict but was involved in criminal activity, and was used in contemporary accounts by convict writers including James Hardy Vaux.[82] In his memoir of policing in the period, William Burrows refers to magistrates knowing some of the men who appeared before them in court by sight as 'old hands' because they had been on chain gangs in the early years of the colonies, suggesting another form of intimacy between the law and offenders.[83] In his encounters with vagrants in prison, John Buckley Castieau noticed men who were 'poor wretches', who were reduced to 'miserable' existences; he felt pity for them, but also disdain for them, a complex response to his work as a goal governor in Melbourne.[84]

Police descriptions of vagrants also intersected with descriptions of people arrested and detained for other reasons. Some accounts remind us of the way mobile lives become visible because of criminal records. One example among many is the story of James Knowles recorded in the *New South Wales Police Gazette and Weekly Record of Crime* in 1863. It demonstrates that identities curated by police and institutions of the law provide portraits of offenders on the move, sometimes by force, but also through escape, or freedoms granted.

> Description of James Knowles, discharged on the 17th instant, from the Penal Establishment, Cockatoo Island; native place London; born 1831, 5 feet 6 ¾ inches high, ruddy and freckled complexion, sandy brown hair, grey eyes, lower front teeth irregular, diagonal scar on centre of upper lip, large wart back of right thumb, A3 flower pot, AW inside lower left arm, third and little finger of left hand contracted from a cut; dressed in a new short blue pea-jacket, lined with red woollen plaid, white shirt and pink or reddish striped Crimean shirt. This offender arrived per "John Calvin," to Tasmania, under the name of Fredk. Bunyan; convicted at Central Criminal Court, London, 5th January 1846, sentenced 10 years. Ran from Mr. Champion, Melville Street, Hobart Town, 13th July 1852; convicted at Police Office, Sydney, 16th February 1853, in the name of Reuben Atkinson, of vagrancy, sentence 2 years' on the roads; again convicted at Albury Quarter Sessions, 17th December 1860, of horse-stealing, in the name of James Knowles, sentence 3 years' on the roads.[85]

This description brings together several themes discussed in this section so far: a former convict, James Knowles, made his way to Tasmania, took different names, was arrested for vagrancy and continued a life of criminal activity in the colonies, and his mobility indicates his life spanned Tasmania, New South Wales and Victoria, suggesting a resourceful and determined mentality. This former convict, turned 'vagrant', sought to escape and evade police, and his miniature life story tells us about the lengths police took to collate descriptions of offenders in their quest for order.

Published police memoirs, where we have extant material, offer other insights into the way police and gaolers viewed vagrants and their bodies. The writings of John Buckley Castieau remind us of the worldviews of police in the nineteenth century in the context of a society with corporal punishments meted out to offenders. In 1874, inside the Victorian prison of Old Melbourne Gaol, a prisoner convicted of vagrancy who was sick with the sexually transmitted disease of gonorrhoea was asked to flog a man who was brought in on a charge of indecency. The flogger-prisoner-vagrant had been 'living with some abandoned women' and his lifestyle mirrored that of another offender who would doss 'in some wretched shelter place in the neighbourhood of the Police Barracks'.[86] Later that same year another prisoner named Billy Weeks who performed work as the gaol 'tailor and barber' was described as having spent most of his life on short vagrancy sentences: 'he is one of the very useful men in Gaol who will work well and willingly', wrote Castieau.[87] These were frightening and violent places: in 1855, Castieau had been 'struck a blow' by a 'notorious vagrant' and he returned the hit; the man was later charged with assault.[88]

Welfare policing

The police in each colony also played a role in policing the poor, which was both about welfare support and suggested that police were obliged to 'punish' persistent poverty and destitution in some cases. Many stories of the police in these instances show that they were attentive to the individuals they found, and used the law in ways that allowed them to offer people some respite from the harsh life on the street. Working with magistrates, as noted elsewhere, they created a 'safety net' for people like Henry Sullivan in Tasmania in May 1863, just as the weather was getting colder and heading into the winter months. The police noticed Henry's conditions, and actively looked for a local solution, even while it may have appeared paternalistic:

> Henry Sullivan, a wretched destitute old man was charged with being idle and disorderly and without any visible means of subsistence. Sub-Inspector Mahoney said that the poor old man seldom had any other shelter at night than that allowed him in the watch-house, but his habits were so dirty that any blankets lent to him had to be destroyed on account of vermin. Mr. Gunn [the magistrate] said that Sullivan would be much better off in gaol, where he would be properly clothed, fed, and kept clean. He therefore sentenced him to two months imprisonment in gaol.[89]

This account shows that police offered blankets to the destitute who lived rough, and that they believed the standards of prison accommodation would help men like Henry.

It was a similar story in the same year, when in October, the police arrested Isabella Cooper for vagrancy because she had 'no visible means of support', having found her in an outhouse in Burnet Street. 'She stated that she had no money, and no where [*sic*] to go to', reported the newspaper of proceedings in the Police Court. 'The Magistrate observed that it would be a charity to provide for her and sentenced her to imprisonment with hard labor for three months.'[90]

Police were both humane and aware of the legal dimensions of their work as set out in the rules and regulations for their work as they enforced the law. The 1853 *Rules and Regulations for Police in New South Wales* referred to 'insane persons' and 'children wandering in the streets'.[91] Dean Wilson argues that police had 'incorporated a "welfare" dimension' to their work from the earliest years of the colony in Victoria.[92] Transporting prisoners and 'lunatics' was one aspect of this work, and it was not always seen as a desirable part of the job by the police.

In an inquiry into women convict prison discipline in VDL in the 1840s, police conduct during their work transferring women prisoners was called into question, revealing that the punishing mood of the colony's policing also created brutes out of police. Providing evidence, a witness was asked about police conduct, and replied it was 'very bad'. They were found guilty and censured for their conduct towards women on warrants: 'for making them drunk, for taking them to disorderly houses in Hobart Town, for leaving them at large and absconding with the warrant'. These police constables had been vagrant men themselves, it was alleged, and had knocked around with unsavoury types of people, 'vagrants, hawkers, or pickpockets'.[93]

A lack of work for men wishing to contribute skills and earn money created groundswell of unspent energy in the community. In 1866, the Inspector General of Police in New South Wales was asked to report on unemployed persons in Sydney. Police and detectives questioned thousands of people and asked them for an account of their names, residence, trade or occupation, whether they were married or had family, their time in the colony and their earnings for the previous six months. The report was provided in October of that year with the proviso that accuracy in the data collected by police was likely to include inaccuracies.[94] Large numbers of the unemployed met in Sydney's Hyde Park to rally about petitioning the government for work in the same month.[95]

Transfer points – from apprehension and arrest to the courtroom

'A morning in the police-court', wrote the John Stanley James as the 'Vagabond', 'is a sad study of Melbourne life'.[96] Observing the proceedings of the police court gave James plenty of fodder to entertain readers in the 1870s, perhaps inspired by Charles Dickens' writings in *The Pickwick Papers*, serialized in the 1830s.[97] He was fascinated by the social and legal institutions that brought him into contact with people from all walks of life, including those he describes as the 'outcasts'.

But he was also interested in the processes of the court and its application of the law, and in the culture of the courthouse. Similarly John Freeman, who also wrote about the police court in Melbourne, observed the work of police in the court, who he described as being 'spry' as well as 'mysterious and knowing', with the sergeant 'pompous'.[98] Movement between the point of arrest, the police court or other courthouse, and gaols points to another form of mobility. These 'procedures of capture and release', as described for nineteenth-century Britain, present an opportunity to analyse the workings of police regulation in practice.[99] In the *Rules and Regulations* (1864) for New South Wales police, constables were reminded of their duties in relation to reporting carefully and clearly so that reports could be sent to the detectives who were responsible for compiling entries for the *Police Gazette*: 'descriptions of offenders should be as clear and minute as obtainable', they were instructed. They were also reminded of their roles in conveying prisoners to the watchhouse.[100]

Police constables were, as historians note, 'diligent' in their detection of crime and 'intensive policing of the roads' in rural areas, paying particular attention to the language used by people they arrested and charged as offenders.[101] Their representation of offences in court was important because of the flow of justice, the oversight of the law by magistrates and those observing lawmaking in the colonies.[102] Although public order offences were low-level offences, they attracted attention in the newspapers, as explained. Sometimes police evidence was not enough to secure vagrancy convictions, as in the case of the three young men arrested in Christchurch in 1900 in relation to the 'consorting' clauses of the law, described in the previous chapter.[103]

There is evidence of movement between places as well as between institutions, with welfare and prison encounters a strong theme. A network of prisons was another result of the move towards a civil society governing its diffuse and growing population of people. These included New South Wales gaols constructed at Berima (1839), Darlinghurst (1841) and out West at Parramatta. There was a gaol at Port Phillip (from date), and prisons at Bathurst, Goulburn and Maitland. A selection of vagrant mugshots held as part of a collection of criminal mugshots from New Zealand between 1902 and 1906 offers evidence of this movement across the colonies, as shown by the notes in each record. George Goddard, arrested in Wellington New Zealand in 1903, had previous convictions in New South Wales, including robbery, and he took at least three aliases. John Cairns was arrested in Dunedin in 1903 aged twenty-two, with seven previous convictions, six of these in Tasmania, including theft, disorderly conduct and indecent language charges, along with vagrancy. American William

Ramsay, whose mugshot was taken at his arrest in Wellington in 1903, had been convicted of housebreaking, being a rogue and vagabond, burglary and vagrancy in Sydney.[104] Prisoners also moved between sites of control and punishment. Woodville Gaol in the North Island was a police lockup until 1896, when it was declared closed by the Governor of the colony under the 1882 Prisons Act.[105] Located at the junction of two mountainous ranges separated by the Manawatu Gorge, Woodville was known as a travellers' rest and a place for hunters to stop. A small collection of cases of vagrants who passed through Woodville in the late 1880s and early 1890s suggests that police gaols in small and remote locations served as distinct points on the vagrant's prosecution journey. These included Englishman John Thompson aged forty-six, who was held in Woodville lockup in transit to Napier Gaol where he was to serve a six-week sentence for vagrancy. McAnally and McLaughlin were two men held at Woodville in February 1889 on their way to Wellington by coach, while the 'ruddy' faced Sophus Christi Twisti, a short man with a slight build, was locked up at Woodville for twenty-one days for vagrancy, being without any visible means of support, in 1890. Described as 'slightly silly and eccentric', Twisti, who had only his swag, a 'dessert knife' and a reputation for begging, was back at Woodville being held on his way to Napier Gaol in 1891.[106]

Evidence from the *Police Gazettes* across all four colonial sites examined here reinforces the sense of the institutional interplay and the role of transfer points for vagrants as well as other offenders. Analysis of the New Zealand data shows that many vagrants did move from town to town, but they did not always move far in geographical terms. They occupied fairly narrow terrain in most cases, with exceptions – those vagrants wanted across the Tasman for repeat offences – being an indication of the possibility for further mobility for some people, mostly men, accused of crimes and seeking new opportunities. Elsewhere I have shown the mobility between institutions including mental hospitals, immigrants' homes, benevolent homes and prisons, arguing that a web of welfare institutions helped to support the colonial approach to mental breakdown in the context of mobility.[107] *Police Gazettes* also show the movement of vagrants between welfare homes, industrial schools, asylums and different prisons. This movement between the colonial institutions of the period was also noted by contemporaries who were critical of the way the vagrancy laws shaped the seemingly endless trail of people who were poor and destitute and were shuffled between these places. As we see in the following chapter, the police also cooperated with magistrates and justices handing down sentences, supporting the convicted to find shelter.[108]

Patrolling gender boundaries

Vagrancy charges affected both women and men in the colonies. The stories of women as vagrants in different chapter of this book demonstrate that the charge of vagrancy was not only used to prosecute men. The different data sets that inform this study do indicate that there were some differences in the way gender was policed.[109] A more granular analysis would show distinctions between gender and urban environments when compared with rural settings, as shown in work by historians interesting in the policing and imprisonment of women.[110] Men who were notorious offenders attracted labels such as 'Kelly the Rake' in the case of New Zealand man John Kelly, who had been in 'every lock-up' in the colony by 1899.[111]

Women also attracted infamy. The 'pug-nosed' Margaret Williams, alias 'Opium Mag', aged thirty-four, was convicted of vagrancy at Waimate in January 1886, and had been in prison for prostitution. By the age of forty-one, she had further convictions for habitual drunkenness.[112] These crimes consistently intersect with vagrancy charges in the many prosecutions of women using the laws of vagrancy. Also in New Zealand, Amy Finlay's story of being policed as a young woman in Ashburton, South Island, in 1891, shows that police were attentive to their role in patrolling gender. Amy was known to be vulnerable because her mother was dead, and her father was 'addicted to drink'. The problem with Amy was her general unruliness: she left home in the night to sleep in the open, under bridges and she spent time with larrikin boys, including 'jockey boys' during race meetings. Police determined that Amy needed to be given the guidance of women who ran a boarding house in Christchurch rather than be sent to the Burnham Reformatory Industrial School.[113] These accounts of police assessing women and their behaviour – the type of conduct that attracted the attention of the police – remind us of the perils of being a woman in public space. Being on the street was dangerous for women, as later chapters also describe, and those women who were brave enough to traverse and subvert expectations of their lives in public spaces often paid the price for their mobility.

Christina Lawson's story

A yellowing 1890 photograph of Christina Lawson as shown in Figure 3.3 below shows her wearing a tall hat adorned with trimmings with confidence, her gaze and posture direct and upright, with her hands held up for the record.[114]

According to the Police Museum note where her image is held, she had been arrested and was sentenced to six months in gaol in February of 1890. Christina Lawson was very well known to the police and in the courts for prostitution in New Zealand from the 1880s to at least 1920. Born in 1858, she was always known by her own name; no aliases appear to have been used or recorded. Lawson showed a pattern of offending that indicates vagrancy had become a way of life for her. She was not especially skilled in evading police detection. It is highly likely that Lawson's movements between Dunedin and Christchurch, and beyond, were somewhat predictable to police. Reading the many accounts of her arrests suggest a life of repeated skirmishes with the law and attempts to get away with small and larger crimes, as well as a heavy reliance on alcohol. She comes across as a bit of a character, reminiscent of the story of Sarah Jones who lived on the streets of Sydney in New South Wales. Lawson's personality was briefly sketched out in court reports periodically reproduced in newspapers.

Christina Lawson was arrested in Dunedin, New Zealand, in September of 1881, for vagrancy.[115] According to the *New Zealand Police Gazette's* record of that specific arrest and charge, she was then twenty-five years old, born in Scotland, and her trade was listed as prostitution. She had come from Dunedin Gaol, a place that was investigated during the early 1880s for abuse and 'breaches of regulations and irregularities'.[116] This, then, was not her first arrest. At five feet one, and without any obvious physical impediments, she must have seemed hardy enough to face a further sentence to time in prison, this time for three months 'with labour'. She had a 'fresh complexion', with 'fair hair, grey eyes' and a 'medium nose, mouth and chin'.[117] Newspaper reports indicate it was not the first time she had been arrested in that year alone: two earlier arrests for drunkenness in February and April.[118] In February she was fined ten shillings and had the option of forty-eight hours in prison; by April, her options had narrowed. By then she was described as a 'habitual drunkard' and was sentenced to two months gaol. It is possible that in that particular week the court took a very dim view of vagrancy, drinking and otherwise disorderly or criminal conduct, as a few other arrests of men for vagrancy also kept the court busy, and sentences of two months were handed out to several defendants.

For many years, Christina Lawson continued to operate on the streets of Dunedin and Christchurch, covering a fair amount of geographical ground in her experiment to live a life of criminal conduct. Lawson appears to have worked as a prostitute from 1880s to 1920s. She had 181 convictions by 1907, mostly for vagrancy and drunkenness. She was still appearing before the courts in 1919. Her story suggests a range of close encounters with the police, courts and prisons in

Figure 3.3 Police photograph, Christina Lawson 1890, Collection of the New Zealand Police Museum Te Whare Taonga o ngā Pirihimana o Aotearoa.

the South Island of New Zealand. She became well known for her recidivism as an offender, a pattern visible in some other instances of vagrancy. Her multiple arrests were not all for vagrancy but tended to align with the broad definition of vagrancy as it was policed on the streets.[119] Lawson was an urban offender, and her 'experience' of being a vagrant is only accessible through reports of her behaviour and character. In telling her story of the life of a vagrant, we can see the way police managed offending alongside the possibility of reform and welfare assistance.

Lawson perhaps fits the profile of those women who arrived in the colony as new immigrants and – perhaps through hard circumstances or lack of other options – were intent on forging careers as criminals, mostly as prostitutes. Repeat offending was common.[120] Some of the commentary around Lawson's arrests fits the interpretation by historians who point out that women's criminal activity was a kind of vicious cycle of offending and the ongoing performance of criminality. In her mugshot taken in 1890, some years after her 1881 arrest described above, Lawson appears composed and sure of herself, suggesting she had agency in her life and chose to live it as she did.

Between 1881 and 1890, Lawson went before the police court or the magistrate's court several times. In 1883, she was arrested for theft, alongside a man named Thomas Lawson, who may have been her husband, or possibly her brother. They were both charged with 'stealing a leathern [*sic*] bag, value 10s, the property of Philip Mitchell'. While she pleaded guilty, Thomas did not. Christina Lawson was given a sentence of three months with hard labour, possibly because she had nineteen previous convictions at that time.[121] Christina and Thomas continued to keep company and turned up in front of the City Police Court in Dunedin again in February 1884. This time Thomas had been fighting in Jetty Street and was fined 5s, with the choice of prison for twenty-four hours. Meanwhile, Lawson's work as a prostitute once more landed her in gaol: not only was she soliciting for clients, but she was also behaving in a 'disorderly manner in the public street'.[122]

By May 1886, again arrested for being drunk and disorderly, Lawson's fortunes were turning sour. This time she was treated with some irritation by police and the court. Arrested by Constable Riddell, who stated she was 'a thorough nuisance', she had 'created a great disturbance' with one witness claiming she had been asked to leave Willis Street in Wellington at least three times. When she did not, she was apprehended and charged. In sentencing her Justice Stratford fined her police expenses and sent her to gaol for seven days.[123]

Christina Lawson's interactions with the police happened so regularly that it is clear she was an identity. Police had also maintained localized and regional records of apprehensions and convictions for prostitution under contagious diseases legislation from 1869.[124] Lawson had probably become an easy target for police arrests, as she claimed in December 1886:

> Accused made a long statement to the effect that the police had a 'set' upon her, but that if the Justices would deal leniently with her on this occasion, she would enter a Home until her husband or friends took charge of her.[125]

In fact, the police stated that they were by now tired of arresting Lawson, who by this time had twenty-six previous convictions recorded; she was sentenced to one month in prison with hard labour. Later in her career, when she had a 'tally' of 121 convictions, the police presented their case to the court, stating 'She is a person very well known to the police, and has been in every gaol in the Dominion'.[126] Lawson's plea for leniency in 1886 must have seemed rich: she was not someone easy to subdue, and this sole mention of her husband (or friends) is the only time such a reference is made in any of the newspaper accounts. During the 1880s and 1890s the police in New Zealand found it difficult to appease the public in their work, a challenge that was remarked upon in the police force's report to parliament in 1895. 'Perhaps the most important duties this department have to deal with', it began, 'is the administration and the laws relating to the drink traffic, gambling, the social evil, and larrikinism'.[127]

Prisons, overcrowded and dank, made conditions for all prisoners harsh, but especially women.[128] As unpalatable as conditions were, some offenders may have sought out constant bouts of gaol confinement for shelter or to receive regular food. Women in prisons in this period were seen as degenerate and dissolute, and prison reform in New Zealand took place over the nineteenth century but in a slow and unspectacular model. 'Hard labour' meant constant work, most likely domestic work for women, while men worked on construction and around the prison grounds. Some prison reform was commencing in 1880s New Zealand but conditions remained harsh. Women and men in the Dunedin Gaol were not separated, as the report of 1883 showed, making for a rough community of prisoners and gaolers.[129] Given these likely outcomes for Lawson, why did she keep offending? By 1912, the *Dominion* noted that 'years of her life have been spent in prisons', and that she had been appearing before the courts for twenty-five years.[130] She seemed to reoffend quickly once she was released, leaving herself vulnerable to police scrutiny. She was part of a loose band of women – Daisy Dale, Clara Dodsworth, Margaret Webster, Honora Setter and Mary McKegney – who were arrested together at various times after drinking and walking the streets.[131] She was a partner in crime and adventure, scaling the walls of the Samaritan Home in 1908 with McKegney.[132]

This part of her story suggests possible solutions other than prison for women who continued to offend. Welfare assistance and institutions were proscribed by the courts to fix the problem presented by Lawson at least twice.[133] In late-nineteenth-century New Zealand, an Act to Provide for the Treatment of Inebriates (1898) helped to foster the establishment of homes for inebriates that would later house people with serious addiction to alcohol and other drugs. The Act followed similar legislation in England and in other colonies including the Cape of Good Hope and Queensland.[134] Women who continued to offend as habitual drunkards in the English context created concerns about the efficacy of short-term sentences and fines, which seemed not to deter women from drinking. Prison sentences did not help, either, as prisons were unable to 'reform' women who were persistent inebriates.[135] In New Zealand, the law meant that judges and magistrates could direct women like Lawson to confinement in homes for inebriates. A further legal tweak in 1906 came in the form of the Habitual Drunkards Act. Under this legislation magistrates could commit a person to an institution for their recovery if they were convicted of inebriety three times in nine months.[136] To ensure this outcome, police could choose to charge a person with drunkenness rather than with vagrancy, taking someone off the streets and not only finding them some form of help, but also lessening incidental policing for alcohol abuse. This happened to Lawson who was convicted in 1907 under the Act and sentenced to the Samaritan Home for two years, as explained in the *Lyttelton Times*.[137]

This experience of the Samaritan Home with Mary McKegney became the subject of a wild night and a colourful report in the 'tabloid' newspaper, *New Zealand Truth*, in 1908. 'A dash for liberty' described the 'grim horror' of the Samaritan Home for its residents as one explanation for the gleeful escape made by two women who were regarded as 'two of the best-behaved women in the institution'. Living in this Home, the account suggested, was a 'prolonged nightmare' for women who had already experienced some social freedom, a 'long run of self-indulgence' and sinned with 'gross delight'; they had to do something to alleviate the boredom. Lawson and McKegney climbed over a wall to get out one night, with Lawson defending her actions by saying she had served months of her two years and was simply following McKegney, who said she wanted to visit her sick mother. While McKegney got out and was returned by police in the morning, Lawson had 'hovered round the building like an unquiet spirit all night', a fact which perhaps influenced the judge to be lenient with her, along with the matron's positive account of her conduct in the Home, when he warned her she was at risk of doubling her sentence. Lawson promised to see out her term 'in peace and quietness'. During proceedings Sergeant Johnston observed that the women had little time to 'get into mischief'.[138]

Yet the mischief did continue later in Lawson's career, and the Samaritan Home proved to be a place where women might bond and continue friendships beyond their sentences. One account of her crimes reveals that Lawson kept a brothel in Christchurch. At this point in her career she had stopped, rather than moving around as a vagrant, and was paying rent. Here, the trail places her in Antigua Street, a few blocks from Hagley Park in the city's heart in 1909. Tipped off by neighbours, the police swooped on the house to find an elderly Julia Cowles, recently released from the Samaritan Home, and Lawson, who was 'consorting' with a man named John Kelly (it seems likely that this is the Kelly mentioned earlier as 'Kelly the Rake'). The court report pronounced she was 'an unlovely-looking middle-aged person of vicious habits', with Constable Harvey testifying she belonged to an 'unfortunate class'.[139] Newspaper accounts, especially the *New Zealand Truth,* of Lawson's exploits over the years became more detailed and poked fun at the court proceedings, especially at the figure of Lawson herself, who presented as comical when she pondered the evidence of the amount of whiskey consumed, denied supplying the alcohol or taking money from men. Kelly 'resented the charge of being an idle and disorderly person' but admitted to 'being on the spree' with prostitutes, but the charge of vagrancy did not stick in his case.[140]

In that case the judge wondered aloud why women in his dock resisted going to the welfare homes and preferred a gaol sentence or a fine. In 1912, when Lawson was sent to an inebriates' institution on an island in the Hauraki Gulf called Pakatoa, she was one of a small group of women and men who were sent to two separate island homes in an experiment in rehabilitation. At other times Lawson refused the shelter of a home, asking instead to pay the fine.[141] Inebriate retreats were also used in other parts of the colonial world including Victoria and New South Wales.[142]

This account of Christina Lawson's exploits offers some detail about her life, yet it is still relatively limited and relies on newspaper accounts and the *Police Gazette.* It also stretches the meanings of vagrancy beyond the use of the label of 'vagrant' in her case, as she was arrested on many different charges, including larceny, drunkenness and idle and disorderly, all offences allied to vagrancy but offering police more specificity for courts and sentencing. In 1869 in New Zealand the Bill to amend the Vagrant Act made prostitution an offence and drew attention to the habits of women who loitered on streets or who congregated in public houses, or who sang obscene songs in public.[143] A vagrancy charge could result in hefty sentences, as the evidence also shows, with one judge advising police to bring her up on a vagrancy charge 'on her next offence' in 1916, presumably because of her many convictions (five charges for drinking in six months).[144] Contemporaries commented on Lawson directly because of her notoriety as a woman arrested frequently for intoxication. A letter to the editor of the *Lyttelton Times* in 1916 asked why it was that the good citizens of Christchurch could allow a woman like Lawson to continue to be 'a standing menace to the good order of the community'.[145] The courts did their best to offer places for safe detention, including through cold winters, and sometimes had to force Lawson to take up options like imprisonment.[146] McGrath, sub-inspector of police in Christchurch noted in 1910 that 'it would be better for all concerned if she were put somewhere to keep her away from the town until after the winter at least', but she was sentenced to seven days in prison.[147] There are accounts of Lawson in the newspapers in the 1920s. She was still offending, being charged, refusing the 'shelter of a home' and attracting attention for her flagrant crimes in the face of the laws of the day.[148]

Unlike Lawson, many other vagrants had even more fleeting representations in the archive. Because she offended and was arrested so often, she came into contact with police over a longer period of time and her type of offending, as well as her seemingly 'incorrigible' criminality, offers us different evidence of a life shaped by mobility. But there were many others like Lawson. In her history of the 'fractured families' in colonial New South Wales, Tanya Evans tells a similar story about Ellen Tighe, who experienced a shiftless mobility as she moves between gaol in Darlinghurst in the 1860s and being charged with another offence – vagrancy, theft, drunkenness, riotous behaviour, using obscene language – and brought by police as a 'well known character' to the police court repeatedly. Her life was spent searching for stability as she faced loss, poverty and separation from her family until she died in 1886.[149] These and other stories round out this picture of what it was like to be a vagrant person encountering police constables in the colonies, whether they were policing the beats of the urban streets in Sydney, Melbourne, Hobart or Dunedin, or the ports and wharves, or responding to reports from rural locations where men slept rough on their way to the next town or farm. The following chapter focuses on the specific determinants of risk for men and women who were living in ways that made them vulnerable to police arrest.

Policing vagrancy contributed to beliefs about acts of mobility. As the debates about new legislation showed in the 1860s, many people were worried about the extent to which ordinary people who were going about their everyday lives might be kept under the surveillance of the state apparatus: the police of the day. These are fears that have taken on greater significance in the age of digital camera, closed-circuit television surveillance and street monitoring of public spaces and private dwellings, as well as shopping establishments, in the twenty-first century. Policing people who were moving around in the colonies was becoming ever more sophisticated through a rising sense of the role played by police in both crime prevention and the creation of public safety, a set of techniques that turned on the identification of difference and on indicators of personhood under definition. This vulnerability is examined further in Chapter 5.

The following chapter reveals the everyday lives of vagrants as they both evaded and encountered not only the law, but also the people around them in a range of circumstances. It was the circulation and activity of the vagrant that can tell us about the way being mobile had different advantages, outcomes or possibilities in the colonies, including for the creation of a range of personal identities. Alongside other accounts of living on the streets, the chapter tells the story of Sarah Jones in Sydney, unflatteringly known in newspaper reports as 'The Cockroach'. Like Lawson, Jones was one of the many women who was 'caught up in a merry-go-round of arrest, incarceration, release and re-arrest over the large part of their lives'.[150]

4

The everyday lives of vagrants

The lives of vagrants reveal much about the everyday mobility that was part of their repertoire. Told to 'move on' by police who they encountered, and through the language of legal judgements in the courtrooms, vagrants were defined by the surveillance which had become routine in colonial-settler society by the middle of the nineteenth century. Newspaper commentary about the vagrant women and men who were found sleeping in the open air, or hiding in buildings or in barns, reinforced their strangeness. Similarly, reports of those vagrants who found opportunities to operate as petty criminals – mostly thieves – tended, on the whole, to focus on the failings of the person instead of expressing concern about support for people in need. In this chapter I examine the agency and creativity of those people living as vagrants by reading sources from different angles to understand vagrancy 'from below', rather than focusing on the implications of these questions for the provision of colonial welfare, a theme for the following chapter.[1] The 'experience' of vagrancy is situated inside a wide social context to paint a picture of the shared and divergent histories of mobility, poverty and welfare across the different places described.

This chapter posits that it may be possible to interpret vagrancy as a 'way of life' in different colonial places through published and unpublished written accounts of vagrant mobility. We are able to see the activities of those people labelled as 'vagrant' by reimagining their lives through the concept of resourcefulness. 'Everyday life' has been theorized by sociologists interested in changing spaces following industrialization and the different population structures that arose with emerging economic conditions of the modern era. Ways of life were affected by physical spaces, the nature of work, and the formation of social groups such as neighbourhoods.[2] To describe the 'everyday lives' of people who lived as vagrants also means finding out about their more precarious lives as they went about the task of seeking shelter, places to sleep, and coping with their bodily illnesses and physical setbacks like injury or disability.

This was a historical period when work in the colonies fluctuated according to seasonal needs and population changes, at the same time as expectations of a self-governing colonial world, preferably one without a visible 'poverty problem', was forming. People had to find ways to survive and thrive outside of existing or nascent systems of welfare and community support. This meant forming social connections and bonds in different places, as well as framing an understanding of 'belonging' and the 'outsider' to existing communities.

Yet from the Aboriginal and Māori points of view, the Europeans were the strangers.[3] The lives of Indigenous Australians had persisted for a long time before the arrival of the British newcomers, the strange invaders who assumed control of their lands. Māori peoples in the 1840s, the time when Europeans 'settled' the places of Aotearoa, were well organized and inventive, as Europeans found. Across multiple fronts and on different shorelines, the British sailors, convicts and immigrants who kept on arriving from the late eighteenth century were printing *their* notions of mobility and settlement onto a place with existing sets of laws, ways of life and stories. Seen this way, the mobility of the Europeans was even more audacious, as were their habits of controlling the movement of others in their midst.

Writing about 'the stranger', sociologist Georg Simmel suggested the 'position of the stranger stands out more sharply if he settles down in the place of his activity', an idea which continues to remind us of the paradox of mobility and 'stopping' for people who were charged as vagrants in the past.[4] The evidence shows that people were moving, all the time, in transient patterns of life that were shaped by their social context, such as the need to work, and the physical world, which was still forming around areas and social groupings. As neighbourhoods and localities sprang up, people took on ideas about settled cultures within them; the whole of the colony could also be said to be a microcosm of a social class of new arrivals who had been there long enough to establish contours and to exhibit a vague hostility to newcomers. In John Ward's perception of Sydney in the 1850s, people took on a 'Sydney-look' that was characterized by 'a mixture of suspicion and curiosity … so anxious to discern the real character of an individual'.[5] As the previous chapter showed, the watching of people in public spaces by police was at the same time drawing the boundaries of gender, ethnicity and class; these were nuanced by the specificity of the social context as well as by local geographies.

The writings of commentators who observed the world of colonial characters and social 'types' present an opportunity to get inside the worldview of the period, so long as we remain alert to the studied practice of journalistic writing of the time. Susanne Davies refers to the way writers Marcus Clarke, John Stanley James and John Freeman each depict these 'outcast' types; she labels the journalists themselves as 'colonial slum journalists'.[6] Graeme Davison and David Dunstan also compared the Australian writing about 'low life' by colonial writers to the generic conventions of the British correspondents of the 1840s, suggesting that colonial writers used London as the 'yardstick' for their portraits of urban place.[7] Looking through the eyes of the James' 'Vagabond' in his essay about the police court in Melbourne, 'The Outcasts of Melbourne' (1876), or through the lens of John Freeman's *Lights and Shadows of Melbourne Life* (1888), for instance, gives the sense that values and identities were already somewhat entrenched in the colonies.[8] Other writings about the colonial world by visitors and travellers such as the novelist Anthony Trollope, or Richard Twopeny, suggest more compassionate readings of houseless people and the destitute that, while also bound by the literary conventions of the age, acted as a check on the social milieu of the urban elite, whose own respectability might be in part derived from good character and charitable action.

Social observation of women and their poverty and mobility in Britain formed the basis of important calls for the social reform of poor laws by the early twentieth century. Embarking on her own 'adventure' in living as a 'tramp', Mary Higgs visited workhouses, wards for 'tramps' and other places where women on the move stopped for shelter. She uncovers, and writes about, the way women could be victims of sexual exploitation, and how women also faced other dangers, a theme examined later in this chapter.[9] In the colonies, women writing about the world of social structures include journalist Catherine Hay Thompson, who, like the 'Vagabond', wanted to experience life in the social institutions of the period to write about them: she spent time in the Kew Metropolitan Asylum in Melbourne.[10]

Despite these opportunities to 'look at' vagrancy (and poverty and illness) by contemporaries, it is more difficult to get closer to the experience of mobility for the person defined as vagrant through the words of contemporary writers and diarists. Discovering the process of mobility – that is to say, how did people *actually live* as vagrants as evidenced by this historical subject of the vagrant – is dependent on being able to read sources carefully and 'against the grain' of interpretation, as so much social and cultural history encourages. Sources include newspaper evidence, photographs, prison and institutional case record notations. Official inquiries into charitable institutions in the colonial period included evidence given by people who were invited to speak about their experiences of charity and poverty; these offer small insights into the lives of the everyday as experienced by contemporaries. The narrative accounts of early settlers in Australia and other sources, including images and fragments of material objects, help us to expand our view of the past of vagrancy.

Observing vagrancy in the colonial world

Writing as the 'Vagabond', journalist John Stanley James conveyed what he saw at the Melbourne police court in the 1870s, calling it a 'sad study' of Melbourne life. The court bustled with people: larrikins, drunks, thieves, youths, working girls, police, volunteers from the Prisoners' Aid Society, the police court missionary and the 'poor creatures' charged with the crime of vagrancy. The 'homeless and the houseless' are contrasted with players who, James observed, were 'on the vag' or who lived as persistent vagrants. Some of those who appeared before the court would 'hear their sentences without a murmur', showing emotions ranging from apathy to fear, and some were clearly penitent. James wrote to capture a record of the social world he found so endlessly fascinating. His essay about the police court comings and goings was as much about the city's street life and cultures of crime as it was a study of people close-up. Places frequented by the criminals who appear before the court also excited James as a writer; the billiard rooms, the concert hall, hotels, gambling dens, as well as slums, all feature in his curious observations of life.

The nature of the lengthy sentences attracted by vagrants – sometimes three months in prison – was a 'blessing' for offenders, according to James. His sense of the desperation of people facing the police court was that their very 'existence' was marginal. He situates them in the places of urban Melbourne:

> Where do the criminal classes of Melbourne live? … I do not suppose any city in the world can show such foul neighbourhoods centred in its very heart. Between Bourke-street and Lonsdale-street, there are a number of lanes, 'terraces', 'squares', and rights-of-way, the present condition of which is a disgrace to the city.[11]

People dwelling here lived in 'hovels': 'low, dilapidated, and dirty'.[12] He was interested in the city's very 'public' neighbourhoods being put on display in these interrogations of behaviours like soliciting for prostitution, being drunk and disorderly, or living rough in proximity to hovels and people who took advantage of those who fallen – sometimes literally – by the wayside. 'Society' he wrote, was of a 'very public kind, the doorsteps, the kerbstones, and the centre of the road forming convenient resting places'.[13] His observations of the city police court were populated by characters such as the 'Yarra Bankers', men living by the Yarra River, along with larrikins. The 'class of outcasts' James focused on here were those who lived outdoors; the vagrants, men and women, 'all of one class':

> They are mostly without family, without friends, without bodily strength, ignorant of any trade, of feeble health, and whose only associates are as themselves. They are vagrants, pure and simple, fear of the law and want of nerve keeping them from being actively criminal, but still ever ready to commit any petty theft … They are generally past middle age, and subsist by begging food, living during the summer in the open air. In the winter, many flock to the Immigrants' Home and Benevolent Asylum; others commit offences to be sent to gaol.[14]

Here, James lets his readers into an interesting lesser-known fact about the vagrants: while many of them had fallen into abusing 'strong drink' or were unable to continue 'plying their trade' as older women prostitutes; others were well-educated men who surprised him with their vast knowledge. His portrait of the vagrants signals an awareness that age played a part in the loss of status, and that health, strength and community bonds were also needed to help people prevent this descent into vagrant lifestyles. He did not see the vagrants as essentially 'criminal' but as capable of becoming criminal if they found themselves desperate enough.

Like James, John Freeman also featured the police courts in his *Lights and Shadows of Melbourne Life*.[15] In the book, Freeman sets up an account of Melbourne's social stratification, fascinated by the vices of the 'dangerous classes': for him, the world of prostitution and drug addiction – with women who worked on the streets closely associated with the Chinese and gambling dens – was the backdrop to his urban tale of social 'types', among them, many mobile people: 'news runners', 'fish hawkers', 'travelling drapers', 'street musicians', as well as 'tinkers', 'beggars' and many others.[16] Freeman draws a distinction between those people who were 'homeless' – who were people on the move between places, and not settled – and the utterly destitute, and he took a keen interest in 'the peripatetics' – starting with 'beggars'.[17] At times, his writing about unfortunate people, such as those 'addicted to drink', is sly and critical; he also suspects some people of deceiving others about their identities. Freeman also writes about 'the elite', especially by observing areas of the city that were thriving with wealth and culture. In his section on the Police Court, Freeman focuses on the way the city court is a breeding ground for crime, with young 'lads' going there to hear proceedings to study legal 'loopholes' and gain information about how to evade prosecution themselves. It was the 'loafers' who called the most 'inconvenience and annoyance' in the gallery, taking up valuable space; and Freeman also indicates that the court always had an audience, with people seeking some form of 'prurient' entertainment by watching others air their 'dirty linen'.[18]

Read together, these journalistic accounts of 'outcasts' tell us about the formation of increasingly finely tuned distinctions between social groups and 'types' of outsiders to settled and civilized society, particularly in urban environments. Although James and Freeman likely intended to share witty views of the people they saw, with satirical elements to indicate their perceptions of social class and the problems faced by lawmakers and police, their often caustic writings reinforced typologies and identities of the period. James was more sympathetic to those he witnessed. These types – 'beggars', the 'houseless', 'travellers' and 'tinkers' – peopled the literary representations of the period around the British world.[19] In reality, some communities of people, including the Romany, faced being ostracized as a result of popular beliefs about their way of life or ethnic origins.[20] Gender and age played a role too; in Australia, as Melissa Bellanta demonstrates, social groups defined by a collective identity such as the 'larrikin' emerged as a threat to community bonds.[21] In rural towns, where most people were known to each other in smaller communities, vagrancy charges were used to move people on or away if their outsider behaviour was upsetting or disturbing.[22] This applied to both women and men, but differences in the policing of women as drunkards or for prostitution could mean that they were more vulnerable to policing in rural areas. The worlds of people on the move were somewhat mysterious to those who observed and worried about them, but they were also ordinary, creative and practical.

Defining everyday mobility

The relevance of everyday life as an object of study has been important to urban historians, sociologists and micro-histories in many different contexts. Historical sociology presents challenges of interpretation: the density of urban life in the present has been read as a site for understanding how strangers mix and mingle, making meaning out of interactions, yet the past throws up challenges of accessibility and viewpoints not easily countered by methods such as the close reading of sources. Vagrants' practices of walking, stopping, resting, seeking shelter, moving on and relocating – creating places for themselves, and also being 'out of place' – are forms of everyday mobility and activity. These were informed by ideas about the deeply entrenched mobility of colonial society. Colin Pooley's work about the mobility of criminals in North-West England, or the everyday mobility of urban London, is suggestive in that it points to the way this concept can be deployed by historians interested in crime and urban life.[23]

The health of the colonial economy depended on a mobile workforce, and forms of mobile labour. The vibrant movement of colonial Sydney, with people moving between ports, wharves, city streets and back again, is indicative of the potential complexity of social interactions between all kinds of people. This was an urban economy full of 'marginal workers' including 'hawkers, fruiterers, match sellers', all 'casually employed'.[24] Hundreds of people including children worked as 'ragpickers' in 1876, scouring the city for old cloth rags.[25] Work could be highly erratic, with jobs allocated day by day, according to chance in part because of shifting demands from pastoralism inland.[26] People seeking work knew that the 'population swelled with the seasons': in winter, rural workers headed to the city, taking their place among the 'vagrants and dossers' as contemporary observers noted; historians can trace occupational seasons via census data.[27] Small 'makeshift' factory work, becoming more common in Sydney in the 1860s and 1870s, was also irregular and often 'casual' work.[28]

Melbourne was similarly uneven in its work opportunities, although the gold rushes of the 1850s and 1860s meant that more wealth flowed through the city and helped to create the growth of towns in the regional areas of Victoria. Low-paid and casual work was, like Sydney, found around the wharves and river, and around the railway yards, and in small factories in the inner west and inner north of the city.[29]

Hobart in the 1840s, like the other colonies, was already suffering through economic recession, with no work for men who were circulating looking for opportunity. This hardship continued until the early 1870s when a 'boom' in the mining of minerals started on the West Coast of Tasmania.[30] In October of 1863, William Burgess was charged in Hobart 'with being an idle and disorderly person, sleeping in the open air, and having no visible lawful means of subsistence'.[31] As a vagrant brought before the court, Burgess – a man who resembled a seaman – had attracted the attention of police because he had been seen 'three successive nights wandering about the wharf'. Once arrested, his opportunity to give the court his status meant that he could get back to work on a ship. In his experience, loitering around the wharf and being able to show his certificate of discharge from the *Calypso*, a ship that had recently been in the port, helped him to evade a longer prison sentence. With the shipping office involved in this case, it also shows that some men benefitted from the protection of their employers:

> The messenger, on his return, stated that the Shipping Master reported that the man could be supplied with a berth in a ship next day, and would be provided with a lodging in the meantime. The Bench ordered the defendant to be imprisoned for one hour, and cautioned him to proceed at once to the Shipping Office on being released.[32]

The shipping industry in and around Hobart and other ports was built on the mobility of seafaring men who moved between places on ships bound for other parts of the colonies for trade, transporting goods and people, and bringing news of other places. These ships docked on occasion and workers sometimes had to find their next berth, as Burgess was able to do. Yet these men 'assumed a potent social visibility as objects of pity and subjects of reform', as Frances Steel argues, possibly because their highly mobile working lives left them vulnerable to a lack of social connections.[33] There were high rates of desertion and absence without leave, making seafarers susceptible to prosecution for these offences of mobility, as well as to vagrancy charges.[34] In the data underpinning this study, sailors are found in each colony's list of vagrancy prosecutions, with men from England, Ireland, Scotland, Jamaica, America, Canada, Cuba, Norway, Finland, Italy, Germany, Sweden and Austria (also Prussia) arrested in many places, many featuring detailed tattoos, such as William Robertson arrested in Wellington in 1881 who wore the 'Scotch thistle and wreath, stars, American banners of war, woman, and anchor on right arm'.[35] Seafaring men were also increasingly supported by the maritime community through Friendly Societies.[36]

Life on the city streets

Life on the streets in the emerging cities of Australia and New Zealand was often smelly, dirty, dangerous and noisy. Urban histories of Melbourne describe the contestation over footpaths, litter and noxious trades, problems of drainage, among other problems experienced by people making their way or finding shelter in the lanes, alleys and alcoves, as well as in public parks.[37] Typhoid infections caused by bacteria, worsened by poor hygiene, killed people in Melbourne throughout the 1860s and 1870s with high rates of infection and mortality in the city's suburbs when compared to British towns.[38] Hobart was scrutinized for its urban and rural living conditions in the 1880s, a series of reports noting the prevalence and threat of diseases including smallpox and typhoid. Public health concerns included the presence of sewage, cesspits and pig sties, all adding to the picture of slums and destitution among children in the colony.[39] Auckland was similarly a place where animals and people lived in close proximity and where sickness and poor behaviours like heavy drinking and fighting tended to affect neighbourly communities and relationships, especially when conflict was obvious and violent.[40]

Both harbour cities that grew up messily around ports and water and the outline of the coast, Sydney and Auckland shared similarities. These were visible through the presence of colonial cultures of exchange and communication with local Indigenous peoples who had been progressively displaced by the presence of military settlements, with the regimen imposed by the institutions of justice and medicine in the early years of the colony. Streets in Melbourne were arranged on a grid, while in Sydney, Auckland and Hobart they were less predictable in their organization. Streets could be narrow, windy and hilly, with people living close to each other and living conditions jostling with leisure and legality every day. It was important for all these places to establish parks and gardens.

Vagrants could be annoying and threatening to other people, either in how they occupied public or shared space, or in their infringement of spaces owned and occupied by others.[41] They may also have been the easy targets of complainants who could tackle the politics of space by blaming vagrants for vandalism or taking up in places where they were not wanted. In June of 1863, John Ferguson, who owned a business in George Street, wrote to the Mayor of Sydney to ask for repairs to his window that was broken by a vagrant named John Hendon, drawing attention to the problem of casual damage by vagrants in the city. Historians point to the prevalence of window smashing by people who were unable to enter cafes or shops, and contemporaries also noted the frequency of this type of property damage.[42] Hendon had thrown a brick bat at the window, and then sought protection, making an application at the police court which was not granted. Ferguson was told by police that taking the matter to court to recover his costs would be a waste of time.[43] In 1877 the Australian Jockey Club complained to the Municipal Council of damage to the fence separating the racecourse from the water reserve caused by a fire lit by vagrants.[44] Vagrants again singled out for their lack of regard for others by William McDonald who suggested they would 'rendezvous' and dump rubbish if he was forced to remove a fence on his property at Lombard Place, west of George Street.[45]

Similar complaints were made about vagrants in nineteenth-century Melbourne. Susanne Davies found evidence of complaints to the police in 1889 made by the owner of the *Age* newspaper, David Syme, who was disturbed by the presence of vagrants in the entrance to his newspaper building. The public library also provided a warm and safe space for Melbourne's 'loafers' in 1887.[46] In each of these Sydney and Melbourne complaints, 'vagrants' were named as a group, blamed for unsociable actions and behaviour, and characterized as an annoyance or worse by the complainant to the council. Borders like fences were important to keep vagrants out and away from 'civilized' spaces, but also to prevent them from occupying empty spaces that they might then colonize as their own. These complaints read as very familiar documents of dispute over social spaces and places; they are opportunistic in their portrayal of vagrants as aggressive and destructive. They also tell us about the people behind the label of vagrant: their individual dealings with shop owners, their group behaviour in seeking warmth and shelter; and their access to clean locations or storage for rubbish – as well as their apparent disregard for other people on the occasions where they were transgressing social norms or laws.

Identities and bodies of vagrants

Given what we know about their habits of life, it is possible that vagrants also crafted their own identities as 'shifters' and relished their chances to escape detection, as described in the previous chapter, and as noticed by the critical Freeman. How they did that was through a combination of associations and stories about their lives, snippets of which appear in court testimony as reported in newspapers. It was harder to hide distinguishing marks such as tattoos or physical features. Physical disability could affect a person's capacity to walk far, or to be secure on the street. 'Being' a vagrant meant adopting some of the characteristics of the 'types' talked about so often in the period. The trope of the sly or evasive criminal, or of the woman who relied on prostitution, could be read as a form of contemporary agency.

Historians speculate that contemporary clothing such as that worn by the labouring men of the period was a kind of 'costume' that created ambiguity in the minds of anyone hoping to 'place' or identify them.[47] Both Freeman and James wrote about the appearances of people who went before the court, noting their 'rags' for clothes, and their body odour.[48] Clothing was likely adopted from earlier phases of colonial life across the different colonies and may have included using animal hide for coats, bags and covering the feet; British-made clothing was not in wide use in the 1800s in VDL except by officials and some free immigrants, for instance, and servants wore jackets made of kangaroo skin.[49] Convicts living in and around Sydney's Rocks district wore typical working peoples' dress in cotton and coarse wool, and later fashioned their own styles of clothing that also set them apart from free settlers.[50]

It is much more difficult to ascertain how people living on the streets or who earned the label of vagrant gained access to health support and care in their lifetimes, aside from tracing the connection between vagrancy arrests and transfers to hospitals or asylums for the insane. The different data sets used in this study show that only a small number of vagrants were transferred to other institutions following their arrests. Being arrested as a vagrant could mean gaining access to basic medical care in a goal hospital, as shown in the records of inquests in the 1840s and 1850s. The report of the chief medical officer in Victoria for 1860 underscores this point: cases of older women and men who were given some medical treatment in gaol, such as a basic diet and rest, resulted in discharges from prison for healthier people who had originally been confined with extreme debility. This '*ad hoc* welfarism' meant that the goal served as a 'hospital' for the sick and infirm who landed there, driving mortality statistics up, a problem that had to be explained in the annual reports of the chief medical officer in the 1860s and 1870s.[51] In Melbourne, Dr John Singleton visited the Melbourne Gaol and was also invited late at night to attend assessments of persons arrested and held in the police lockup and watchhouse. Singleton met people who were suffering from poverty and alcoholism or who had attempted suicide and wrote about his evangelical efforts to rescue them from affliction.[52]

Working from asylum records we can find more evidence of vagrant habits of life: people who were confined inside institutions designated as 'vagrants', taken to the institutions by police, presented as both unwell *and* destitute, probably affected by a lack of nutrition, or an excess of alcohol, combined with the effects of disease. Cases of women and men with dementia, mania, or defined as 'imbeciles' who were arrested as vagrants and taken to the Yarra Bend Asylum in Melbourne or were transferred from prisons to other asylums in the colonies, are a minority of cases, but tell us something about the way social and carceral institutions became a network for managing the colonial vagrancy problem. In the annual reports of asylum inspectors around the colonies the issue of repeated returns of individuals to the public hospitals for the insane from prisons was raised as a difficulty; these 'harmless and incurable' people, often elderly, had nowhere else to go.[53] The confused and confusing history of Emma Thornton, arrested as a vagrant but declared as 'defective', following her confinement at the Yarra Bend in 1906, illustrates the way a person presented to an institution following years of precarious existence: 'says she is 27, her mother 33, that her baby is her little brother'; 'hid knife in [*sic*] her breast'; 'when rescued she had a bunch of coloured rag which she said was very valuable'.[54] If she had worked as a ragpicker, like the hundreds of women and children who operated on the colonial streets, her coloured rag was indeed valuable to her and represented her own survival strategy, along with her knife. Other women may have relied on institutions like asylums and prisons for their safety, including Kate Hinch, who within a week of her discharge from the Auckland Asylum in 1900 'was at the Police Court, as "drunk and disorderly". Patient has spent most of her life in prison', read her notes.[55] Hinch was returned to the asylum by the gaoler at Mount Eden Prison because she was regarded, at the age of sixty-three, as having 'senile decay' and dementia. In Sydney, at Callan Park hospital, by the late nineteenth century, regular committal processes included the homeless, migratory and those with uncertain unemployment, with David Roth suggesting that homeless and vagrancy were important factors in institutional committal.[56]

Dying was also part of the cycle of a vagrant person's existence and yet is rarely the focus of inquiry. Cemetery records discussed by historians sometimes reveal the hidden histories of death for people who lived outside communities of care, as in the case of people living without homes who were part of a religious community.[57] Vagrants who died in unexplained circumstances were subject to medical inquest examinations, as records of mid-century inquests in New South Wales show. The sorry case of Mrs Fell who died as a vagrant, unwanted by the hospital or the asylum but unable to care for herself, was an example of the 'problem' of vagrancy in the 1850s. Mrs Fell struggled to get support despite being infirm and suffering from a 'mental aberration'. She died of exhaustion, and malnourishment, with the jury for her post-mortem examination critical of doctors who failed to admit her to any institution for her protection.[58]

In the records of early inquests for Auckland and surrounding districts compiled from four record books between the 1840s and 1864, there are many drownings, accidents and deaths resulting from extreme intoxication. Several 'unknown men' appear in inquests, found dead on roads and streets, or on boats. Only one man in the collated inquests was a known 'vagrant' and died in prison. In July 1842, John Nunan died after being admitted feeble and in pain. The evidence described in the inquest suggests that he was known to the prison guards, who stated that he was prone to drinking, and that he had been in prison more than once in the past. A fellow prisoner was 'appointed to take care of him' and detailed that '[h]e took one powder, ate some meat, but no bread, and drank some tea. I made him a bed of shavings covered with two blankets, he had three above him and a pillow of his clothes. I attended him til 10pm when I was locked up'.[59] Prison guards said he was 'very feeble' and that he 'could scarcely walk' when admitted.[60]

A few aspects of the everyday lives of vagrants offer greater potential for interpreting mobility. Walking, seeking shelter from weather or for sleep, as well as eating and drinking, can tell us about basic needs. How did the violence of street life also shape the vagrant life? What we know about vagrants and their social connections and bonds within and across communities is also important; the social worlds of the vagrants tend to emerge only as fragments of the stories told about their skirmishes with the law, but evidence of sociality could offer more insight into their tenacity and perseverance as people living 'outside' settled society in the colonial period. Walking and wandering were the mainstay of vagrants, both urban and rural. Reflecting on the physical activity of walking gives us insight into the way vagrants used their bodies to move between places, to occupy spaces and to negotiate their relationships to 'fixed' places.[61] One historical account of ex-convict James Ashcroft maps his movement on foot in search of work.[62] James Cox, whose story is told in more detail in the next chapter, walked long distances between places in New Zealand in search of work.

Shelter and sleep

Contemporaries seemed to be regularly offended by discoveries of people who were 'lodging in the open air'. Yet housing from the earliest days in the colonies was modest, rough, and even temporary, especially in the 1820s in and around Hobart in VDL. Historians suggest that temporary structures resembled the huts used by Aboriginal people, with 'kangaroo hunters, stockmen, sealers, bushrangers and even small farmers' living in basic 'A-frame' shelters made of brush and trees.[63] As the settlement grew and changed, reports of people found 'lying on the ground' or 'lying on some rags near the bridge' became more frequent by the 1860s. Seeking shelter from the weather but also from the outside world and its intrusions on privacy, houseless persons of the nineteenth century had the option of being cared for inside one of the colonial institutions of the period.[64] In Hobart in 1865, Ellen Boylan was charged with vagrancy and 'in lodging in the open air in Goulburn-street, without having any visible means'.[65] Boylan pleaded guilty to the charge, telling the bench that 'she had been at the Invalid Depot, but having come out yesterday for a holiday she had taken drink and stayed out beyond the time'. The newspaper poked fun at her idea of 'taking a holiday', and she was sentenced to three months with hard labour.

Like others, Boylan had arrived as a convict and spent much of her time moving between welfare and carceral institutions. Looking for shelter often meant a cycle of movement between living outdoors and being the recipient of welfare relief such as accommodation in a benevolent home. Boylan's experience of punishment in Tasmania related to her identity as a former convict who had arrived in VDL in 1843 with a seven-year sentence when she was aged forty-one. She arrived with greying hair, and a scar over her left eye, and hailed from Limerick.[66] She was convicted in Hobart Quarter Sessions in 1850 of stealing and sentenced to two years' transportation with hard labour in the Female Factory. She was then convicted of drunkenness three more times in 1855: in June, July and December.[67] In December 1867, she pleaded guilty to disturbing the peace and in February 1868 said she was employed as a servant in a public house called the Plough and Harrow when she was a witness in an assault case. Five men were attacking another man and Boylan was afraid for her life, but bravely tried to intervene before she fled.[68] Later, Boylan found shelter in the Cascades Invalid Depot as a pauper between 1868 and 1870, where she died aged 67 in 1871.[69] Boylan's journey from Ireland to Tasmania was plotted by a life of surviving as an older woman who had few choices aside from domestic work and reliance on institutions when there was no more work, with experiences of the criminal justice system peppering her lifetime and shaping her ability to maintain a stable life in the colonies. Her access to shelter was shaped by these experiences and by her identity as a criminal, pauper and domestic servant.

Open air sleeping was common. Others found creative, if unpopular, ways to get shelter. In October of 1860, Robert Barclay found himself 'an unoccupied house' in Anthill Street, Hobart one Saturday night, but was arrested and charged with 'having no visible means of subsistence'. He told the court that he did have money – and at the police watchhouse he was found with a small sum in his pockets – and that he had offered to pay Mrs Sheehy for 'his lodgings'. Yet his story of seeking a place to stay was undermined by the fact that he was found 'concealed in the chimney of the kitchen' by police, who were alerted by the woman who lived in the house next door. It did not bode well for Barclay, who was sentenced to three months' imprisonment with hard labour.[70] He had arrived in Tasmania on the ship *China* in 1846 on a seven-year sentence, and he lived a life of being 'idle and disorderly', at least as far as the records suggest, until the early twentieth century.[71] In 1866 he was convicted again, this time for malicious wounding, and sentenced to four years in prison at Port Arthur.[72]

Like Barclay hiding in a chimney, seeking shelter in other peoples' houses was a tactic used repeatedly by the middle-aged Maurice Jeffrey. He had been identified in 1899 at the time of his first offence as an American, born in New York in 1861, and he had come from New Zealand's Wakatipu in the Otago region, suggesting he was originally a goldseeker.[73] A commercial traveller, he had first 'caused a nuisance' before he was arrested three more times for being 'idle and disorderly', with each charge attracting a greater sentence.[74] The Tasmanian Launceston *Examiner* presented the evidence against Jeffery, who was 'wandering abroad' in February 1901:

> William Simms, State-school teacher at Invermay, said he had seen the defendant twice. The first time was on January 27 last, when he came to his residence in the morning and went into the drawing-room. When [the] witness came in he was playing the piano, making himself perfectly at home. The defendant asked him for assistance, and he gave him one shilling. On the 13th of the present month the defendant came to the school and again asked for assistance, but this time [the] witness refused him.

Other witnesses agreed that Jeffrey was unwanted in their spaces:

> Robert John Brookes, licensee of the Commercial Hotel, said that during the past ten days Jeffrey had frequently visited his place. Sometimes he paid for a drink and other times he begged one. He would go into the parlour and lie down on the sofa to sleep.

Looking for a place to sleep was entirely rational. Many instances of men and women being found in all kinds of places also show that the police were assiduous in their tracking of unwanted lodgers. People were found 'sleeping under the shelter of an unfinished house'; in stables, 'concealed under the manger'; or asleep 'in an unfinished building', as shown by just a few examples of the many similar reports.[75]

However, Jeffrey's behaviour had become a problem that was getting noticed by the police in more than one place; he had been convicted already as a vagrant at Kelly's Basin on the West Coast of the island of Tasmania. That time he had stated that 'he was a doctor, and was of good family. He had travelled all over the world, and was advised to come to Tasmania for the good of his health'. Heavy drinking was, as the police magistrate determined, 'no doubt the cause of Jeffrey's downfall', stating that he 'was not fit to be at large in his present state, and would be sentenced to six months' imprisonment'.[76] In 1879, James Sullivan was found guilty of sleeping in an outhouse belonging to Robert Thomas and sentenced to a week in prison; he was a man who later repeatedly tested the limits of his welcome at an Old Men's Home in Ashburton, and was severely addicted to drink. In an interesting aside, the court noted that the police said 'nothing was known of the prisoner'. In fact, he was offending outside of his usual locale of Christchurch.[77]

Vagrants seeking places for shelter were seen as a nuisance, as a letter to the Mayor of Sydney from George Kelly and his friends shows in 1883. A vacant condemned building in Engine Street, Ultimo, was creating problems for Kelly and other members of the community, who complained that Engine Street had become dangerous for foot traffic but also for vehicles, and that the building had become a 'harbour for vagrants'. Such an eyesore was not only dangerous, then, but also attracted squatters.[78] People living rough found shelter in abandoned deserted houses, often located in run-down areas in the inner suburbs.[79] Arrested by police for 'sleeping in empty houses', widowed man Edmund McNamara, was taken to the Yarra Bend Lunatic Asylum in the 1891 where it was clear that he showed 'no evidence of insanity', so he was able to get shelter and food; he was allowed to remain for a time as a convalescent patient.[80] The 'aged, the mentally ill, and those with serious ailments' who lived rough were commonly referred to hospitals and charitable institutions or asylums.[81]

For those living on the streets or between periods of secure housing, safe shelter was important for adequate sleep, giving them enough energy for the day ahead which involved more walking between places to stop and shelter. 'Going into the bush to sleep' was, for forty-five-year old Michael Charlton in Launceston in 1906, an act of self-preservation. In between bouts of 'begging from house to house', Charlton was able to hide and rest.[82] For Charlton, the judgement was harsh; with the cooperation of justices, the police had focused on 'scouring the town of the undesirables' who made the place feel unsafe, and he received a three-month sentence.

We can find out where and how people slept and found shelter by examining the reports of people who set out to offer help and assistance to the homeless and unemployed in the urban centres in the colonial cities. Searching the likely locations of the Melbourne unemployed and homeless men late in the 1880s, two Christian missionaries went on foot to the kinds of places where they might find these men. They reported that they spent the night 'going through the lodging-houses, reserve grounds, and the Spencer Street docks, wharves &c', and found 'traces' of men sleeping on the banks of the Yarra River.[83] Physician John Singleton established several night shelters for needy women and men in the 1870s and 1880s in the suburb of Collingwood in Melbourne's inner east. Collingwood was the site of many working families and workers' housing, close to factories and many of the city's charities and religious orders. The men's shelter was named the Blue Bell after a public hotel and was located in Perry Street, and it operated from 1887. The establishment of these shelters was to counter the habits of people who slept rough in 'new buildings, in verandahs, in sheds, or beneath the shrubs in public gardens, on wet nights in empty railway carriages, or to walk about all night', as Singleton wrote.[84]

As shown in Figure 4.1, a photograph depicting a vagrant woman's place to rest and sleep in the Auckland domain in 1915 was described as 'an unknown abode' in a photographic supplement to the *Auckland Weekly News*. The newspaper story (see Figure 4.2) described Elizabeth Allison Woods as an elderly

THE UNKNOWN ABODE FOR SEVERAL MONTHS OF A WOMAN ARRESTED FOR VAGRANCY: A CLUMP OF TOI-TOI IN THE AUCKLAND DOMAIN, WHERE THE UNFORTUNATE WOMAN CONCEALED HERSELF IN THE DAYTIME, VENTURING FORTH AT NIGHT IN SEARCH OF FOOD AND CLOTHES. W. Beattie, Photo.

Figure 4.1 W. Beattie, 'The Unknown Abode', *Auckland Weekly News* (15 October 1915): 50. Reproduced by permission of Auckland Libraries Heritage Collections, AWNS-19141015-50-7.

woman who had lived 'in the scrub' in the Auckland Domain for some time and had also received help from 'some charitable people'. Yet it seemed that the court worried whether 'any of the homes' would take her in. 'She was very weak, owing to her mode of living, and had to be sent to the hospital where she had remained for the last ten days.' Appearing before the court, she was sentenced to a twelve-month period in prison; this sad solution was judged to be the only way to help her to live safely, and to remove her from this public space where her presence possibly offended other people.[85]

Being without a home was a reality for many people who showed up in the newspapers and police records of vagrancy. 'No home' was a newspaper headline

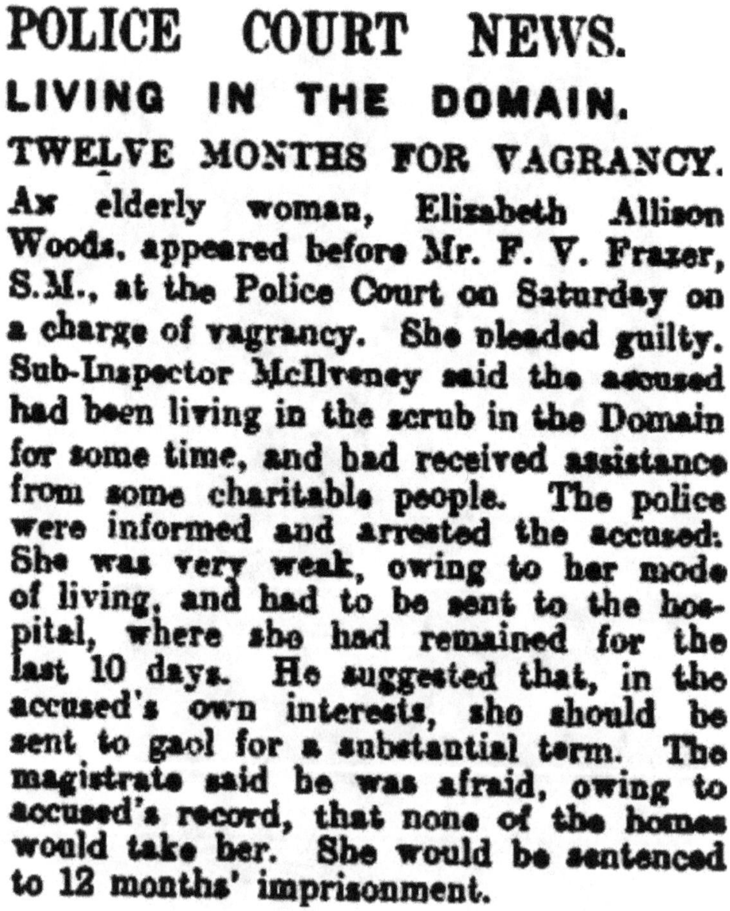

POLICE COURT NEWS.

LIVING IN THE DOMAIN.

TWELVE MONTHS FOR VAGRANCY.

An elderly woman, Elizabeth Allison Woods, appeared before Mr. F. V. Frazer, S.M., at the Police Court on Saturday on a charge of vagrancy. She pleaded guilty. Sub-Inspector McIlveney said the accused had been living in the scrub in the Domain for some time, and had received assistance from some charitable people. The police were informed and arrested the accused. She was very weak, owing to her mode of living, and had to be sent to the hospital, where she had remained for the last 10 days. He suggested that, in the accused's own interests, she should be sent to gaol for a substantial term. The magistrate said he was afraid, owing to accused's record, that none of the homes would take her. She would be sentenced to 12 months' imprisonment.

Figure 4.2 'Police Court News: Living in the Domain', *New Zealand Herald*, 18 October 1914: 5. Reproduced under Creative Commons Licence.

often used when contemporaries were reflecting on the imperfect use of the vagrancy law to manage poverty in the nineteenth century. Boarding houses provided shelter, places to sleep and some sustenance for others on the move. In urban Melbourne, these were distributed around the suburbs of Emerald Hill, St Kilda, Prahran, Richmond and Collingwood.[86] They also most likely offered access to food and drink. Public houses or hotels were centres of communal life for men and some women. Some vagrants might have tried their luck eating food sold or served in public establishments, like 'Hudson', who was charged with theft after he ate food from a bakery and then ran away without paying for it. In a letter to the *West Coast Times* in New Zealand, a correspondent noted that men like Hudson might be 'ravenously hungry', willing to commit a crime because he is 'starving' and has no money.[87] Outside of urban areas, men who subsisted between jobs in rural areas lived on a diet of tea, damper and mutton.[88]

Violence

The streets were dangerous places for people living rough or moving around at night, especially for women. Being addicted to drink and also living as a vagrant made women vulnerable to violence enacted by men. The cases of women raped, murdered or left to die on the streets in colonial cities are shocking in their casual brutality and in what they reveal about attitudes to women who lived rough lives.[89] Catherine Owen, a woman aged about fifty, was raped and murdered by a group of men in 1883, and the report in January 1884 details the crime, and the conviction of four of the offenders.

> A woman named Catherine Owen, about 50 years old, belonging to the vagrant class, has been outraged to death by a number of larrikins at Waterloo, a suburb of Sydney. About eleven o'clock on Christmas night screams were heard at the upper end of the street by two married women, the screams being accompanied by the laughter of a number of young men and boys. The screams continuing, one of the women went out, and asked the larrikins to leave the woman alone. They decamped, but at about half-past twelve Mrs. Logan again heard screams, and went out to the place, when a number of larrikins cleared out, and she found Owen lying naked, her clothes having been torn off with struggling, and her mouth was bleeding. Mrs Logan told her to come 'down to her house', and the woman said she would follow Mrs Logan when she had recovered herself a little. As the woman did not follow, and hearing nothing more, Mrs. Logan concluded she had gone to some other house. The next morning the woman's dead body was found.[90]

Following a reward of £500 for information about the crime offered by the government, several young men aged from 18 to 25 were arrested, and the coronial inquest returned a 'verdict of wilful murder' and four men were committed for trial: Thomas Thornton, William Smith, John Foley and Thomas Conway.

Violence was part of the everyday lives for most people who lived rough, with women more likely to be killed in these public circumstances, as other cases also show. But women who died alone in the streets may also have succumbed to illness and addiction. In February 1876, an inquest was held on the body of Mary Maloney, a thirty-three-year-old woman 'who was found dead in the Eastern Market' in Sydney. A butcher in Leichardt Street gave evidence that Maloney had been a housekeeper, and that she had kept a public house with her former husband, Pierce Maloney. Although she had been married, she was regarded at the time of her death as 'a drunken vagrant, [who] had no place of abode'. The men who gave evidence knew her as being ill, asking for money and looking to get a drink at a hotel. The inquest showed signs that Mary had ingested carbolic acid and had been poisoned, possibly by accident.[91]

Bonds and community

Rural and frontier life was often marked by distance and isolation. Urban communities had different characteristics. The community that formed in early Sydney around the Rocks was created through a shared precariousness.[92] This delicate social balance between security and failure was weighed in the every day by people who lived close by each other as neighbours and found ways to express care and compassion, including for those people who were utterly down and out. Yet in these kinds of new urban communities and places, people still got drink, fell ill, were injured, were in relationships and had babies, or were the victims of crime, and as described above, the streets could also be dangerous and tenuous places to exist.

Communities were formed around dissent as much as around agreement. Historians have shown that more urban women in the colony of Victoria received prison sentences for vagrancy and disorderly conduct offences, postulating that the lives of working-class people in Melbourne were very 'public' and were lived out on the streets in close to neighbours, and were places where sub-cultures of crime likely raised the temperature for conflict between people.[93] The presence of beggars, also noted by contemporary writers, created a visual problem, as well as possibly a threat to peoples' perceived personal safety.[94]

In colonial Auckland people made use of laws to negotiate space, noise, interpersonal relationships and to play out their responses to problems with alcohol, sexual and emotional transgressions, or plain unhappiness about the use of space and resources.[95] Examining traces of a transient population in Auckland between the 1850s and 1875, Dean Wilson found that an urban community was forming around shared understandings of common beliefs about the occupancy of space and the management of tensions around notions of neighbourhood.[96] As people living in close proximity with animals, shared access to water, laneways and areas for children to safely play or move, they also formed ideas about those with insider status and outsider identities, and a culture of gossiping and informal surveillance was noticed by those who observed it as travellers or who were new immigrants.[97]

Sarah Jones

Finding out more about how vagrants managed their everyday lives is difficult because of the partial source materials about any individual person, with sources skewed towards the point of view of observers and critics of vagrant lives. One of the many women who appear in the *New South Wales Police Gazette*, Sarah Jones became notorious for her various encounters with the police. Jones appears several times in the captured data for people prosecuted as vagrants: there are ten entries for her between 1869 and 1877.[98] She continued to offend after that time as shown in court and prison entries in the State Archives of New South Wales.[99] Although the details are relatively consistent each time, subtle changes in the recorded facts about Jones reveal how cautious historians need to be in relation to evidence generated by a limited set of sources. Jones also used a range of aliases, and this fact, along with discrepancies in the record, as well as her own agility as someone who could slip through the net of street surveillance, all mean that our ability to tell a story about her is compromised. And yet we know – in part because of her notoriety – that Sarah managed her everyday existence and continued to survive the challenges presented by colonial urban life on the streets. While this account of her everyday world could also be presented as a narrative about policing, or about the institutional transfer points she navigated, as well as about her criminal activity, here I read her history as evidence of a life built creatively around a series of movements through the spaces she inhabited.

According to the details taken at each of her arrests, Sarah was likely born in Ireland sometime in the 1840s, but she often gave dates in the late 1830s to those who inquired. She had dark hair, and her eyes were recorded as being brown or grey. She did not seem to have attracted any attention for her appearance. This makes her more elusive for the historian than some offenders in the record – especially those whose physical characteristics suggested habits of life or activity. This is even more interesting given the popular nickname for Sarah Jones, which takes on a specific meaning in relation to her fortitude as a woman living as a vagrant over a long period of time.

The common alias noted for Sarah in the *Police Gazette* is an unflattering one: 'the Cockroach'. After its use in the 1870s, this term was popularized in police and court reports in the newspapers, taking hold as shorthand for her in the official notations about her crimes.[100] It highlights her ability to continue to thrive in the grime and grit of the growing city, even though it suggested that the police imagined her to be a nuisance they could not eradicate, as in other cases of repeat offenders including Christina Lawson in New Zealand, whose story appears in the previous chapter. 'The Cockroach' imbued Jones with a sense of her indestructible character: she would live on rubbish and not be deterred, and she would reappear, just when authorities thought she had been removed: 'the "Cockroach" has not yet been squashed', reported the *Australian Star* in August 1888.[101]

Given that the nickname was also noted in court records, it perhaps also served as a record of her identity for people keeping an eye on her movements and charges. Much of the public commentary about her turned on the phrase and used it to depict her, but also the police, as part of an ongoing struggle for control over the street crime she was on trial for committing. The *Evening News* published a little 'ditty' as part of its report on arrests in 1887, with Jones among those arrested: 'they don't know how they come there, and say they're not to blame; they say they don't like Darlinghurst, but they get there just the same'.[102] By the late 1890s one newspaper report claimed Jones 'rejoiced' in the 'delightful' name.[103] There were other aliases used by Jones, showing that she was able to evade detection at times, hoping to put police off the scent. The names Theresa Brophy and Theresa Jackson, as well as Mary Jackson, are listed in the official records for Biloela Gaol, an old convict prison on an island near Balmain in New South Wales.[104]

Sydney's streets, mapped out by police as districts to manage populations, were also spaces for work, travel and leisure. There were laneways and alleys giving access to doorways and privacy, especially away from the main streets or corners where groups gathered. Working as a prostitute likely meant soliciting for paying customers around the streets of the red-light district. Sarah's own movements through the city are not easy to track, and frustratingly are not always mentioned in the newspaper reports of her arrests. She was likely most often found around the central city area including Macquarie Street. Sydney was a place where it was relatively easy to obtain alcohol and to frequent public houses. Sarah Jones was often viewed through the prism of the common charge of being an 'inebriate', along with many other women and men who chose to enjoy these habits of life in the city. The most popular drink was beer: it was easily brewed and was the most available source of alcohol in the colony.

The Police Court, as the 'Vagabond' described for Melbourne, was a place of coming and going, performance and despair, and readily promoted the dangers of vice in urban life. For those presenting in Sydney's Central Police Court on the corner of Druitt and George Streets from the 1830s the experience was similar. By 1889 the Police Court moved from the site of the central markets to Liverpool Street, giving the police more opportunity to use holding cells and interact with courthouses.[105] Sarah Jones also spent stretches of time at Darlinghurst Gaol. This prison was part of Sydney life: the institution itself was a founding one, and its physical presence – with the gaol built by convicts in the 1820s – served to remind people that the city was part of an ordered society, one governed by laws and with responsibilities towards lawful citizenship. Yet it was also a frightening place: execution by hanging took place at Darlinghurst Gaol until 1889, with public hangings conducted to crowds until 1852.[106] Between the 1870s and late 1890s, Sarah Jones was sent to Darlinghurst at least twenty times, with ten of these clearly for vagrancy charges as the prosecution data shows.[107] 'Be it ever so humble there's no place like gaol for a "tough specimen"', read the newspaper report titled 'Home, Sweet Home'.[108]

Conclusions: The meanings of vagrancy in everyday life

These indications of the life lived by Sarah Jones, assembled as a short narrative, are fleeting. There are echoes of the story of Christina Lawson here, too, showing common elements in the worlds of women who opted or were forced by circumstances to exist in these marginal ways, but who nonetheless carved out spaces and 'careers' as offenders over time. The women and men whose everyday existence featured in the records of crime and punishment remind us of the exigencies of living rough: the need for shelter, sleep, food, protection from violence, and human contact and friendship. The sheer practicality of life on the street for vagrants meant that luxuries like human community may have been difficult to create, but the evidence also shows the strength of human bonds and emerging communities of care and welfare in the stories here, even though the slices of life available are momentary glimpses of a busy dynamic colonial context that range across places and with local characteristics.

It is paradoxical that colonial society was both ambivalent about mobility and yet founded on the grand project of immigration and settlement. Demographic transitions during the nineteenth century created the conditions for massive upheaval and transition, and disruption to the lives of many people around the world from Europe and Britain to North America, Australia and New Zealand. The idea that everyone had access to opportunity was a fiction that propelled immigration. Yet mobile identities were shaped by both socio-economic circumstance and shared understandings and collective expectations. Using stories of the people in need in the colonies, and also the writing of one-time vagrant James Cox in New Zealand, the following chapter examines the question of socially vulnerable people.[109] It expands on this set of reflections about different identities, looking at the way that 'difference', including vagrancy, was bound up with gender, sexuality, age, socio-economic class, ethnicity, as well a set of intersecting ideas about persons who presented a threat or challenge to settled order and colonial progress in the context of economic depression and a growing class of the very poor. Although stories about vagrants tended to be disparaging, there were citizens and charitable organizations working to ameliorate the conditions for the poor, and they also produced ideas about social groups deemed more vulnerable to policing and poverty in colonial society.

5

Worlds of vulnerability

This book has examined the lives of many people like Sarah Jones who were labelled as vagrants because they came into contact with the law throughout the 1870s and 1880s. Laws subtly evolved over time, and the police used legislation in different ways across the time period studied here. Historians point out that estimating actual numbers of 'vagrants' who were arrested by police is difficult: their motility means that it is hard to capture the sheer size of the group of mobile vagrants, since prosecution data can only represent the number of people who collided with both police and the courts, and who therefore earned the label of 'vagrant'. Likewise, Stephen Garton's examination of people 'out of luck' in Australia's past points to the difficulty in estimating the extent of historical poverty.[1] Garton points to social survey data in the British context such as statistics collected to reflect the populations of London or York around the turn of the nineteenth century, noting similar data does not exist for the colonial period in Australia.[2] In Britain, a Royal Commission into the Poor Law in 1909 continued concern over pauperism and characterized responses to vagrancy and poverty into the early twentieth century.[3] Both vagrancy and poverty remained significant social and cultural concerns across the British world, also featuring in political responses to social problems which included illness, ageing and welfare support for people in need.

In Britain, prosecutions for vagrancy rose steadily, until almost 40,000 people were prosecuted each year under the Vagrancy Act by 1913.[4] In the Australian colonies, over 86,000 people were convicted of offences against good order, which included vagrancy, by the end of 1910. Earlier data, counted at intervals, shows more than 30,000 convictions in 1875, and more than 57,000 in 1885.[5] In New Zealand, vagrancy prosecutions increased in the years after 1850, which as Fairburn argues was one consequence of immigration; vagrancy rose from being the thirteenth most common crime in 1850 to the third most common crime by the 1880s, and in 1879, the number of vagrancy prosecutions peaked at 29 per cent of every 10,000 people in the country.[6]

In this chapter, different experiences of vagrancy, including the factors that made people vulnerable to policing or regulation – such as poverty and unemployment – show another side to the history of vagrant lives in the colonies. Official inquiries and social statistics offer glimpses of the colonial world mediated by the emerging governmentality of social welfare. In Chapter 1, at the outset of this study, I noted the changing concept of vagrancy and the formation of a 'modern vagrant' type who troubled contemporary policy makers.[7] The history of the rise of this idea of the new modern vagrant is examined as part of this chapter, showing the way the vagrancy concept was adapted and used at specific historical moments to signify social concerns or economic shifts regarding mobility as well as stability of employment and social attitudes towards poverty.

This chapter offers another model for understanding the meaning of vagrancy, one that links the evidence back to histories of social welfare and institutional care. Histories of vagrancy 'from below' speak to the structural nature of class, poverty and social formation in the colonial era. Law was a structure that sought to control and classify people in its enactment and performance of justice. People could evade or interact with legal structures as the previous chapter explored. They brought their own agency to being vagrants, and to being mobile in a world of regulation. Using the theme of vulnerability in histories of vagrancy and the regulation of mobility helps to create a stronger historical relationship between law and the social institutions of the period, such as asylums, benevolent homes, immigrants' homes, hospitals, charities and other places.[8] Describing different aspects of the profile of those more vulnerable to police surveillance and regulation offers a reminder of the socio-economic factors at play in creating definitions of unauthorized mobility that are also relevant in our present moment, reminding us of the tension between the specificity of the vagrancy laws and categorization of 'the vagrant', and the enduring, more elastic meanings of category of the outsider. These ideas are examined in more depth in the final chapter of this book.

More specifically, this chapter looks closely at the formation of a social 'underclass' of people unable to conform or succeed to settler expectations who became the equivalent of the paupers in the old world but without a 'poor law'. The impact of the 1890s economic depression – an era that led to economic devastation for the very poor – reinforced the need for a new concept of vulnerable persons in the law as historically defined through the regulation of vagrancy, with contemporaries noting the risk in continuing to arrest the poor for 'no real offence'.[9] Therefore, this chapter examines available research findings to show

how a history of vulnerability to policing and imprisonment can be plotted and framed as a study of social cohorts within a larger population, allowing us to test and reveal the historical meaning of 'vulnerability' itself. It is important here to remain attentive to the potential of an intersectional analysis, showing how age, ethnicity, disability and gender, meant that people became more visible to police enforcing the laws that tackled unwanted mobility such as vagrancy.

Vulnerability also allows for some new thinking about the way that specific populations were positioned socially and culturally within the politics of mobility. Using vulnerability as a frame tells us more about mobility as a common threat to social stability. As Tony Ballantyne notes for New Zealand, mobility was ever present in the colonies by the latter part of the nineteenth century, but had begun to be contained; the 'helter-skelter' days of the 1850s and 1860s 'where men chased rumours and parties criss-crossed the landscape' were replaced by regular train and coach services, mail deliveries, and cultures of towns and cities.[10] Alan Atkinson has shown how the Australian colonies were similarly mobile places, also focusing on communication such as postal services, rail and human movement for adventure and opportunity.[11] In these more 'settled' communities, mobility not only made some members of colonial society 'visible' to the lawmakers, but also rendered them invisible at the same time: being elderly, having a form of physical or mental disability, or failing to conform to norms of gender or ethnicity could mean that people were sentenced to a life of being mobile and slipping through the social cracks of order and opportunity. They were then compelled to remain 'unmoored' and risk taking in their lives, constantly moving for survival.

One man who experienced a lack of mooring in the later stages of his life was James Cox, whose story has been retold by historian Miles Fairburn. Cox's account of being a 'vagrant' and living as a mobile worker establishes the concept of being a vulnerable person in the colonies from the point of view of the vagrant himself. Although he was not arrested for the crime of vagrancy, like the other individuals whose stories flow through this book, his perspective is important to establishing the meanings of vulnerability and historical 'precarity' and is examined later in this chapter.[12]

Vulnerable social groups

By the end of the nineteenth century, plenty of contemporary observers found that vagrancy laws had criminalized being poor for a long period of time. Writing in the New Zealand paper in 1900, *The Nelson Examiner*, one editor described the way that legislation 'evolved' with regard to the 'curious crime' of vagrancy:

> [T]o apply indiscriminately to the lurking tramp … to the dying woman found on the doorstep, or the foundling infant left on the kerbstone. … In order that they might be housed, fed, restored or even buried … they must be charged, convicted, and thereafter passed on to the charitable or other institutions, or even to the common gaol.[13]

Historians have shown that local gaols and asylums in the colonies routinely became places to send the very poor, sometimes the very old, and certainly those found to be vagrant.[14] Sometimes those people sought out such institutional 'care' or put themselves into situations where they were more vulnerable to police apprehension. This cyclical experience points to what historians writing about Britain have suggestively described as a 'makeshift economy' of survival strategies, with crime being one strategy to manage living in poverty.[15] Pointing to seasonal work, seasonal use of charity and specific times when crime peaked, historians also uncover one of the reasons communities may have feared the uncertain and periodic threat posed by the vagrant. For instance, 'swagmen, tramps and vagrants' were groups of men whose episodic mobility in rural parts of the colonies was viewed with mistrust.[16]

'Vulnerability' as defined by social histories of welfare, institutions and illness in the late nineteenth century effectively tends to group together the people who found themselves destitute and criminal, with welfare agencies attuned to these risks in particular. Sickness, disability, youth, old age, but also being a migrant, or losing a spouse or family protector through death or desertion, could result in extreme poverty, evidenced by so many of the micro-stories of vagrancy found in contemporary newspaper reports. 'Infirmity' had become a category in colonial census data collection by the early 1870s, and encompassed different forms of impairment including blindness, deafness and mental illness.[17] Increasingly, children, unskilled workers and rural people were viewed as more vulnerable to destitution, especially as the colonial societies described in this study began to create more robust and purposeful types of relief and support.[18] Writing about representations of 'the tramp', historians have identified social types and tropes in the literature of the nineteenth century relevant to discussions about understandings of vulnerability and beliefs about vagrancy. For example, the 'sentimental motifs' associated with impoverished children were also attached to 'homeless men and helpless waifs' who found themselves 'friendless' and alone like orphaned children.[19]

Specific ethnic groups also faced challenges in colonial society. Chinese miners from Canton to the Otago goldfields had been invited by the Chamber of Commerce in 1865. While general Chinese mobility in New Zealand was 'unregulated' in the 1860s and 1870s, leading to concerns about the Chinese presence, historians show that these mobile workers were networked together by familial and professional associations and played a role in connecting parts of New Zealand (and the Australian colonies) to world economies.[20] Other ethnic groups potentially provided points of communal identification, such as the Jewish community in Melbourne. Yet poverty could result in social breakdown and isolation for even close-knit communities. Three successive reports of inquiries into charitable institutions in Victoria revealed widespread destitution and rates of pauperism, including alarming stories of poor people being buried unidentified in unmarked graves.[21] Research suggests that Jewish people were also buried unidentified despite claims made by contemporaries for a cohesive and united cultural group.[22]

As the previous chapters of this book show, the vulnerable people in the colonies included those who had no home to go to, the destitute, the sick, disabled and diseased, children, the elderly, and women who worked as prostitutes and 'juvenile delinquents', as well as Aboriginal people and Māori people. Several groups are described more fully below to help explain the concept of vulnerability in historical context: the aged, mobile families, juveniles, people with physical or mental disability, and mobile workers or men seeking work during economic downturn. Put another way, what the prosecution data tells us about these groups, especially in relation to the intersections between categories, also sheds light on the hidden risks of being poor and mobile in the colonial world.

Old age

When combined with age, gender also played a role in making a person vulnerable to poverty and vagrancy. This was especially true for older women. Historians show that the majority of women prosecuted as vagrants in Victoria were 'from the ranks of the poverty-stricken'.[23] Older women were especially vulnerable to minor public order charges given the shrinking opportunities for work and the lack of access to aged pensions until after 1900. Victoria Nagy argues that access to charity was restricted and limited by 'stringent conditions'.[24]

The case of an 'Old Hand', Ann McCoady (also recorded as McAvady) reported from the Hobart police court in 1890 again reminds us of the lives of repeat offenders whose lives were caught in the cycle of policing and gaol time for petty offences, including vagrancy.[25] In McCoady's court appearance, police seemed to reinforce the need to confine her for a lengthy period:

> Ann McCoady was charged with being an idle and disorderly character, with no visible means of support. She pleaded not guilty, but after hearing the evidence of Constable Samuel Smith and Sergeant Blakeney, the Magistrate sentenced her to six months' imprisonment remarking that defendant had been 13 times convicted for a like offence, and no less than eight times for larceny.[26]

Ann McAvady, born in Dublin Ireland, had arrived on the *J. W. Dare* (*John William Dare*) in 1853 as Ann Kenny. She was then aged twenty and married Thomas McAvady also known as Mcaveady in Hobart Town on 5 April 1853, aged twenty-one. Thomas, from County Mayo, Ireland, arrived as a convict on the *London* in 1851, aged twenty-four. He died in 1864 of 'traumatic tetanus' and was buried as a pauper, and left Ann a widow.[27] She was admitted as a pauper to the Invalid Depot in New Town on several occasions, variously named Ann, Mary Ann or Mary McAvady.[28]

Ann's offending continued beyond her sentence in 1890: she was again imprisoned for drunkenness, aged sixty-three on 16 August 1892.[29] Although her age is inconsistent, she appears to be the Ann McAvady who died in the Charitable Institution in Hobart on 27 August 1894, aged seventy-six.[30] Ann's story tells us that women who were left behind as widows did not always fare well as sole agents. They could be left impoverished if their marriages were also patterned by poverty, and homelessness followed. Many vagrant women were alone and without support. Margaret Tennant has shown that New Zealand faced growing numbers of the elderly who were homeless in the 1880s. Older men, in particular, were unable to compete for work, and men dominated in the group of homeless aged over sixty-five years; New Zealand statistical data shows a steady increase in the population of men aged sixty-five and over in homes for the aged.[31] It became important to see these older people as a separate group and to distinguish their needs from those of the many younger people in the colonies also seeking refuge, including young families.[32] The aged were becoming infirm and incapacitated.[33]

Mobile families

Children and families were also caught up in the policing of mobility. Stories of family groups on the move indicate that vagrancy was not only a 'crime' of individuals who looked out of place or suspicious but was also applied to adults with young dependents who were seeking work and shelter. Elsewhere, Maree O'Connor and I show the plight of families on the move, arguing that by examining stories of vagrant families, we can find out more about the way approaches to vagrancy were gendered.[34] For example, poverty could shape parents' responses to care, making families more mobile in search of work and shelter; or separating children from fathers or mothers. Families in each of the colonial sites examined in this book were affected by fluctuating colonial economies, problems of housing and employment, as well as sickness and death. In her study of vagrancy in Victoria Susanne Davies reports that in the 1890s economic depression in urban Melbourne, families were forced out of housing and lost possessions, became destitute, and were suddenly homeless with dependents:

> The depression brought unprecedented misery for unskilled labourers and their dependents. With few resources to fall back on, these men and women quickly descended into extreme poverty. … [In 1892, the *Age* newspaper reported that] 'privation, want and semi-starvation' stalked the unemployed and their families. It claimed that hundreds of homes had been stripped bare, as men and women had gradually sold all of their possessions to buy food. Unable to pay rent, others were forced onto the streets.[35]

Despite the view that vagrancy was a problem of men seeking work, these economic conditions created more arrests of women as vagrants in Victoria, as Davies shows. She explains the vagrancy prosecution rates through both a demographic analysis of the changing urban population, with unemployed men leaving the city in large numbers in search of seasonal work elsewhere, and also the impact on families, the lack of work for women, and an increasing desperation among women who were deserted by men and living in poverty.[36]

Yet homeless families had concerned colonial authorities in earlier decades because they drew attention to a lack of work for male breadwinners, and the prevalence of vagrant men in the colonies.[37] If families 'dispersed and divided' because of economic pressures, they also created new family structures and many more men who presented as slightly wild in their quest for work.[38]

A story in the Tasmanian newspaper the *Cornwall Chronicle* much earlier, in March 1860, also showed that the dominant view was that 'traditional' families were settled, not on the move, like the family of James and Margaret McDonald:

> James McDonald, and his wife Margaret, were charged with being idle and disorderly characters, sleeping in the open air, and having no visible means of subsistence. The defendant's [*sic*] who were simple looking creatures and were accompanied by two children of the respective ages of about six and four yours,

> were found on Sunday night in bed on Cox's Hill, near Mr Harvey's, having encamped there for want of a better lodging. McDonald said he was a blacksmith, that he and his family had walked up from Oatlands as he was promised work in town, but arriving on Sunday night without money to pay for lodging, and the children being knocked up with the journey, he was compelled to take shelter somewhere until the morning. He said if discharged he could obtain work, and His Worship liberated him and his wife, and advised them to save money to support their family on future journeys.[39]

James and Margaret McDonald were doing their best for their family; they had not abandoned their children, and they were following the promise of work. Despite the unorthodox nature of this family's life, there was no signal that this was a 'criminal family' which was the other 'ugly' problem of the mobile family. Yet as in the case of similar arrests of family groups, it was the fact that this was a family 'out of place' or resorting to behaviours that made children appear vulnerable that was concerning to police. In 1882 another family was subject to the same type of surveillance when they were on the move between the New Zealand town of Lyttelton and Christchurch, but their experience was one of surviving 'homeless, sleeping in outhouses, or in any place … they could find shelter'.[40]

Whenever identity was in dispute or curious, questions were raised about the nature of family relationships, as in the case of Johanna Clarke and William Clarke who were arrested together on 27 May 1868 in Yass, New South Wales. Johanna was a forty-seven-year-old servant from Cork and William was twelve, and they claimed he was born in NSW. It was unclear whether he was her son, and further research does not shed any light on their relationship.[41] Family groups that fell apart because of poverty also produced young people who were at risk of lives of poverty and crime, as the cases of the very young who were vulnerable to police arrests also show.

Juvenile delinquency

Young men and women were highly vulnerable to arrest as juvenile delinquents. Newspapers barely paid attention to vagrant families in the reporting of vagrancy, mostly because it was individuals who were the focus of policing and prosecution. Yet this historical period was marked by a very mobile migrant. Elsewhere, I argue that 'historians have shown that "transiency" came to define most communities of nineteenth-century North America and Western Europe.

Not all of this movement was by individuals: small groups and families were often "in motion".[42] Historians also provide evidence that families became fragmented and scattered because of poverty.[43] The result was that children became homeless, were sometimes orphaned, and often had to rely on lives of petty crime.

The 1870s witnessed a rise in the numbers of 'street urchins' in the colonies, with local social surveys showing the impact of family breakdown and destitution in Auckland in 1872.[44] Children were taken to industrial schools and orphanages, destitute, or as criminals. They were detained under the Vagrant Act in the 1860s and 1870s, but, after the 1880s, separate colonial laws governed the regulation of homeless children including the Industrial Schools Act in New Zealand (1882). Amendments in 1895 meant that children who were found begging, or who were without means of subsistence, or who were found wandering or sleeping in the open, could be held in custody for their own protection. In Victoria, children who were perceived as being 'neglected, or in moral jeopardy' could be sent directly to industrial schools or placed in foster homes from the late 1880s.[45]

Therefore, despite the lack of explicit laws to govern paupers as in Britain, there were attempts to protect vulnerable people through legislation. The examples of New Zealand and Victoria remind us of its purpose. The Destitute Persons Act (1846) and the Deserted Wives and Children Act (1840), respectively, made it possible for women to pursue maintenance from their husbands who deserted them.[46] Legislation governing the growing population of people who were deemed to be 'insane' and who needed mental health care, such as the Victorian Lunacy Statute (1867) and the New Zealand Lunacy Act (1868), meant that families could seek out assistance when mental illness created family tension or affected the family economy. By the mid to late 1880s in both colonies, systems of welfare protection came in the form of social institutions such as asylums, hospitals, benevolent homes and charitable institutions.

Women and men also lost their children to processes of protection, with children made subject to forced mobility between social institutions and the courts. Their familiar and distressing stories of family dispersal remind us of the long history of child protection that was tied to understandings of family mobility and precarity. In Launceston, Tasmania in 1866, the case of William Stokes went before the Police Magistrate:

> William Stokes, a boy about 15 years of age, charged with being idle and disorderly, and without visible means of subsistence, or place of abode, was discharged, as Mr Bryant, of the Market House Tavern, interfered on his behalf, and gave him food and shelter.[47]

When community friends and protectors did not step in to help, children and teenagers were sent to industrial schools or prisons, as the story of Catherine McGafferty, 'a bright looking little orphan' in 1881 Launceston, Tasmania, shows. McGafferty was pregnant, and while she did have someone to intervene on her behalf, she was sent to prison as a vagrant:

> The case was a peculiarly painful one, and the Police Magistrate in passing sentence remarked that he was actuated by feelings of pity, and that her incarceration would be a charity rather than a punishment.[48]

Young girls and women were subjected to a particular form of moral scrutiny and gendered surveillance, as demonstrated by feminist historians.[49] In 1896, an article titled 'Nobody's daughters' published in the *Christchurch Star* drew attention to the plight of adolescent women who were arrested as vagrants. Unlike vagrant men and older vagrant women, who could be taken to a home, or boys who should be disciplined, vagrant girls were depicted as the focus of much 'worry of the police and the distraction of the bench'.[50]

Physical disability

The colonies were places where inheritances from the 'old world' of Europe shaped thinking about poverty, destitution and physical disability. It was a sense of disgust at the sheer abjection in the combination of poverty and disability that European observers conveyed in their writing about visits to colonial India, for instance, with 'thronging … transient masses of disabled beggars' who presented a challenge because of their mobility.[51]

As noted in the previous chapter, the social institutions of the period included asylums for the insane. People confined in hospitals for the insane came from all walks of life and experiences, including disability and vagrancy. Studies of the populations of these institutions indicate that in the 1840s, early in the life of the Australian colonies, such institutions tended to house 'men, usually vagrants or itinerant workers', and that the institutions themselves played a role in the identification of the 'most dangerous' people in society.[52]

In 1863, a letter to the *Argus* newspaper in Melbourne made 'An Appeal for "Vagrants"' in the colony, suggesting that in the midst of plenty, 'there are some unfortunate classes unprovided for':

> The maimed, the diseased, and the unfortunate widows and destitute children are insufficiently cared for. It is scarcely right that an unfortunate cripple should

> be treated as a vagabond, and sent to prison under the Vagrant Act, merely to provide sustenance.[53]

Those 'unprovided for' were often people with physical disability or what was defined as 'mental deficiency'. Some of these were sent to institutions such as the asylums for the insane, where their experiences ranged from neglect to abuse.[54]

James Sullivan, a man prosecuted for vagrancy in Christchurch, New Zealand, continued to attract the attention of police throughout the 1870s, fined frequently for being drunk and disorderly. By September 1880 he was very ill: seen by two doctors, admitted to Ashburton Old Men's Home and to a hospital, the charges of vagrancy were remanded twice. On his fourth appearance before court on 17 September 1880, the vagrancy charge was withdrawn. Although his 'insubordinate' behaviour was seen as disruptive – leading to his expulsion from the Old Men's Home – he was also physically disabled: 'the doctors said that the man was a cripple and not fit to do any work' in October 1880.[55] Sullivan appears in the database of New Zealand vagrancy prosecutions which also shows he had previous convictions. In March 1879, he was arrested in Timaru. Said to be a 'hawker' from Ireland, Sullivan was described as aged forty-nine, with a pale complexion, and his left side paralysed. Another prosecution entry for 1881, when he was arrested in Christchurch, lists him as a 'shepherd' from London, but his physical description is identical – eye colour, hair colour, pale complexion and his left side paralysed. Despite his physical challenges, Sullivan moved around the colony's South Island and his paralysis did not prevent his sentences with hard labour on these occasions.[56] This microhistory of James Sullivan is interesting because it shows, once again, the interplay between social institutions, the police and the courts, and highlights the considered use of the vagrancy charge as well as interactions over whether prison was the right place for this man. This was likely to have been dependent on a particular justice sitting in judgement, as well as the medical evidence provided by the doctors.

Sullivan was just one of many people who carried a physical disability. There were others who were paralyzed, such as Catherine Carroll. Elizabeth Maher was an epileptic dressmaker. Samuel Jones was subject to fits. Bridget Keys was nearly blind. John Riley was a mute. Bridget Duck was deaf. Isaac Berry, arrested in Walcha on 28 December 1874, had lost his left arm and his right hand was crippled. Ah Sing, who was arrested on 5 November 1879 was a blind cook from China.[57] Each of these vagrants, arrested in New South Wales in the 1860s and 1870s, faced significant challenges in terms of daily survival, including inside social or carceral institutions like prisons or asylums, as historians demonstrate.[58]

In 1877, a man named John Williams was charged with a vagrancy offence. His case appears in the data for this study: he was tried at Rangiora in New Zealand's South Island on 17 July and sentenced to one month in prison aged sixty-five; he was known to be a labourer, and from Scotland. He had an alias: 'McFarlane'.[59] He was arrested again in the Otago area after his initial charge and sent back to prison for a further three months with hard labour, and this time his case attracted some public attention; it was reported in the *North Otago Times* in August that year:

> No *real* offence. No; only the imagined one of poverty and old age. In these advanced and enlightened times one would scarcely have thought that the inhabitants of prosperous Otago, with its numerous churches and charities, could have experienced the pang of reading in the annals of its law courts such a record [Emphasis in the original].[60]

The editorial goes on to examine the role played by the police in arrests like this one, and to point to the need for the protection of the 'poor and friendless'. There were other newspaper reports around the colonies pointing to the same social problem and expressing similar concerns about the use of the vagrancy law when it came to the very old. New Zealanders were highly aware of the role played by their charitable institutions, including the homes for old men and old women; yet these were not enough, or not always suitable. Time and again, as stated earlier, it was reported that justices had no choice but to send a person to gaol for shelter and respite; a point that reminds us of the range of mobility 'transfer points' in the career of the vagrant.[61]

Being out of work and mobile made some people desperate. In his personal writings about 'being out of work', Thomas Dobeson, who also spent time among the unemployed of Sydney in the 1880s and early 1890s, ruefully observed the statistics for suicide in 1889, noting that among the deaths were people without very much money, such as one man who left as his assets 'a hand saw & a horses' bridle' or the 'Chinaman [who] left 2/6 behind him'. Yet some departed the world with more to leave behind, suggesting suicide was also the reaction to different life challenges; another man left 'two horses, a saddle, a swag & five pounds ten shillings in cash'.[62] The 'failing men' in the economic depression of the 1890s in New Zealand were facing a loss of status, too; some men had been without work for many years and felt their usefulness to families and communities had come to an end.[63]

Mobile workers

The swagmen of colonial Australia and New Zealand were, according to contemporary writer John A. Lee, 'men occasionally willing to do a day's work for a night's lodging and a couple of meals'. These men were distinct from 'sundowners', who would 'walk from station to station during the day', sleep under a haystack, or somewhere outdoors, and 'make their appearance at that hour before the "whares" or huts provided for them, and demand from the owners supper and shelter'.[64] Sundowners worried colonial authorities so much in Victoria in the 1890s that data about their movements was presented in the Legislative Assembly and reported in the *Argus* newspaper.[65] There was genuine concern about the population losses from Victoria to the west, as well as about the desertion of women and families. In addition, for the men who lived off the land, there was a sense of threat as they appeared to lurk and wait for their moment to work; accounts of theft, violence and dramatic responses to being turned away by a station owner or a kitchen could result in episode like that described by witnesses. Writing about New Zealand, Lee suggests this 'vagrant fraternity' could become discontented. Some larger stations employed a cook to look after these roving workers; it was the appearance of many at once as 'uninvited guests' that might cost a household more in time and provisions.[66]

Lee was realistic about the temptations of drink and crime these men faced, and he was sympathetic, to a point; yet for him, 'sundowners' appeared to be less sympathetic characters, often appearing as 'ungrateful' and 'irresponsible' men in these accounts of the period. What is significant here is the fact the pastoral industry relied on some mobile labour: the properties were acquitted with huts and shelters for the men, and it was in the interests of stations to treat them well so they would return for the seasonal work in shearing or mustering, or other forms of work around the properties, cultivating a type of worker and employer loyalty that could be sustained throughout periods of economic downturn, such as times witnessed in the 1890s across the colonial world.[67]

The meaningful association between changing fortunes among the labouring poor and vagrancy has been established in Britain. Following the Napoleonic War, a wider economic recession began, and the earliest prosecutions of vagrants as offenders in the wake of new laws including the Poor Law of 1822 formed a pattern of managing the itinerant workforce by the early to mid-nineteenth century, shaped in part by growing industrialization and urbanization. In Australia and New Zealand, two economic depressions, first in the 1840s and then in the 1890s, signalled a crisis for a mobile labouring population. Jessica Gerrard's interpretation of the meanings of homelessness over time points to the shifting meanings of 'productivity' as it was historically construed, but also to the persistence of the association with being economically productive and a full citizen.[68] This occupational mobility was felt across the Pacific, with gold rushes creating 'an interconnected corridor of migration' for workers and miners.[69] In the North American context, 'tramps' were heavily policed, with the 'suppression' of tramps in the 1890s providing another link to the spread of ideas about dangerous and 'unproductive' mobility.[70] Just as police had counted out of work men in the Australian colonies, so too were American tramps subject to a census, this time by a sociologists interested to study the population and its characteristics; in the 1870s, the legislation around tramps and the pejorative language used to describe tramps has echoes of the Australian and New Zealand approach to vagrancy.[71]

The colonial labour market depended on mobile workers to meet the fluctuating demands of the colony and its population. The previous chapter's description of the nature of work in Sydney set out the way work was precarious and could turn quickly if conditions around wharves and city industries were compromised by changing events or supplies of raw materials. In New Zealand, many occupations were commonly understood to be 'transient', with both skilled and unskilled work affected by the economic depression late in the nineteenth century. New occupational classifications were also bound up with clashes over working conditions and rights as industrial debates came to define the start of the twentieth century for workers.[72] It mattered who was mobile among the workers; for instance, restrictions were introduced late in the nineteenth century to control non-white labour. In many industries, Aboriginal and Māori mobility was superseded by European mobility. Mobility was gendered, as argued throughout this book, and specific type of social identity through labour such as prostitution was forged through its meanings.

Dobeson also describes not waiting around in Sydney for work in the late 1880s if there was a way to find activity restorative, pointing to another form of mobility for men who were seeking work:

> Been away for five days fishing. They say it is a poor heart that never rejoices. A party of us took some food, a blanket & tents & took a ticket for Gosford, distant 52 miles. We arrived there after going through some grand country. … It was cold and wet when we got to Gosford. We found an old empty house in the darkness, lit a fire & had some supper.[73]

Dobeson and nine other men – all unemployed – enjoyed beers, a trip into the 'one-horse' town of Gosford, and then walked 12 miles with their swags on their backs through very rough terrain and poor roads to look for work north of Sydney. Another man, Irishman William Farrell, wrote about his search for work in the 1880s as he made his way to Victoria, documenting his honest account of drinking too much when he could not work to support his large family.[74] In the 1880s in New Zealand, John A. Lee witnessed similar feats, writing about the men who walked and walked and then 'died along the tracks'.[75]

Mobile peoples like these groups were a force for change, even though unemployed men were 'unpopular objects of charity'.[76] The unemployed gathered in public places, protesting the lack of work. Dobeson rightly notes the incredible work it took to create railway lines, tunnels and roads north of Sydney, up through the Central Coast of New South Wales. Where was the work now, long after that convict labour had developed access to the territory inland from the Sydney settlement? The instability of work on offer across the colonies in the nineteenth century created sub-populations of mobile men, and as noted earlier, destitution among women and families, especially prominent in the colonies from the middle of the century. One of these individual men seeking work was James Cox.

In New Zealand, Miles Fairburn asserts, there was a problem distinguishing the large number of the 'colony's roving men' from vagrants, due to their outward appearance, the irregularity of colonial employment and what he saw as a lack of social cohesion on the colonial frontier.

> In housing, diet, dress, speech it was largely impossible to pick out the 'loafer' from other foot-loose men or even from the more settled. For example, swaggers either slept in the open, or in the single-room 'swagger's hut' … or in unoccupied shacks; but 'sleeping rough' was just as much the practice of shepherds, drovers, gumdiggers, pioneer landholders.[77]

Ambiguities based on dress, habits of life and popular 'types' clouded the picture for contemporaries, confusing the public and leading to arrests of 'respectable persons'.[78] Tennant also notes the way the unemployed were linked with degeneracy or 'intransigence' in the public mind.[79] This was a perception that persisted for some time. In 1909, 'Another labourer' wrote somewhat hyperbolically to the *Evening Post* newspaper in New Zealand to point out that young men seeking work would easily be confused with vagrants and charged as such: 'if they go, and tramp, and sleep in shanties, or sheep-pens, nowadays, they are liable to come up before the magistrate on a vagrancy charge'.[80] A few years earlier, labourer James Cox, writes historian Miles Fairburn, described his own prospects as that of a 'vagrant with little hope of ever getting out of the wretched life' in his diary during a lean year.[81] The everyday experiences of Cox over a period of months give us more insight into what 'being vulnerable' meant for working men.

James Cox

New Zealand labouring man James Cox (1846–1925) kept a diary between late 1888 and early 1925. Cox had emigrated to New Zealand in his thirties after youthful adventures like walking in Europe and working as a clerical assistant for the Great Western Railway Company. He arrived in the South Island of New Zealand, living in Christchurch until the need for work drove him northwards to Wellington in 1888. Fairburn estimates that Cox wrote around 800,000 words, some of which is minute detail about his movements and working life.[82] During the years 1892 and 1893 he recorded his life as a 'vagrant' on the move between places in New Zealand's two islands. He told the story of his extreme discomfort and loneliness, as well as his physical pain and recovery.[83]

The existing historical presentation of Cox's narrative places it into the context of the worlds of men who were seeking work and contributing to the industries of flax, timber, sheep farming and agriculture. Cox's ability to work was often shaped by external forces over which he had no control. He therefore represents a group of men, some of whom had far less capability than he did to withstand the stressful conditions of being out of work and constantly looking out for employment to sustain them.[84] By re-reading Cox's ideas about 'being vagrant', we can add to our interpretation of stories about mobility in this period as experienced by labouring men who were part of swell of 'workless men' among the 'tramps and swaggers on the roads'.[85] In 1892, as historians remind us, the whole labour market of the lower North Island of New Zealand was 'acutely depressed'. Wages and employment had dropped from 1879.[86] Like so many other men – as asylum records also show – Cox was plagued by feelings of instability. He was without social networks, writes Fairburn, and this meant he was less able to cope with 'life on the road'. Fairburn claims that Cox was not 'well adapted' to his 'migrations'. Yet Cox was articulate, shared his thoughts in writing: we do not always have the evidence for other migratory labouring men to know what they felt about their mobility. What we can say is that Cox offers us some insight into the likely cultures of vagrant men in the period, allowing us to build a richer story of vagrancy as an experience of vulnerable people.

Vagrancy was often precipitated by episodes of poor mental health, and Cox's experience tells us that when relationships between people broke down, and poor health was also a factor, men could find themselves alone and terribly self-reliant. When Cox left his position at a sawmill – odd jobs and cooking – he was not getting along with his employer Ted Jones.[87] In March 1892, Cox had only a small sum saved when he walked away from Jones and went to Palmerston North, a town in the North Island. He seemed anxious, restless to stay moving on 22 March: 'I am tired already of nothing to do but do not know which way to look for work, I must not stay here much longer.' His compulsion to keep moving continues and a few days later he writes that he needs to go on the next journey to Marton to find work. To get there, he took a train, and he walked, and he stayed in boarding houses, a common practice among men seeking work. The boarding houses of the late nineteenth century appeared along railways lines in places where men might be moving for temporary work.

Cox's feat in walking long distances in poor shoes (he cut out the heels, for instance, to reduce the pain in his feet) and with cut and battered feet also reminds us of the physical nature of being vagrant and mobile.[88] Cox had to carry a swag, and he was unhappy about having to lug it around, complaining about disliking it in 1892.[89] Fairburn reproduced Cox's treks in three separate maps showing his Autumn trek in 1892; his trek of Spring that same year; and his Summer and Autumn trek of 1893, each one plotted by places, distances and dates.[90] These maps reveal the extent of what Fairburn calls Cox's 'migrations' which mirror those of many other men, some of whom he meets along the way. The company he keeps from time to time brings his spirits up and clearly shows the value of sociality for the solitary working man's well-being. But at other times he falls into very black moods, such as his period of depression in April of 1893. He could be anxious and fussy about his situation or his work.

Sometimes, as Fairburn notes on several occasions in his narration, swaggers were not welcome at stations and were actively discouraged, a blow to Cox and his company as they sought both work and temporary stays for food and drink, as well as a bed for the night. Much of what Cox records about his journeys reinforces the insights offered by other writers including Lee. There were men who hid all day and then appeared at day's end; there were others who were addicted to drink and could do no work; there were acts of generosity and kindness along the way. When he became a cook's assistant at Waimarama in 1893 he worked hard, ate well and also managed to reflect on his lot, hoping to write letters and get time to himself, but instead found he was at the beck and call of the workers, also writing letters for other men who could not write because they were illiterate.[91] Fairburn tends to be impatient and sometimes critical of Cox, even suggesting he 'frittered' away his earnings when he spent time recovering in boarding houses after his long stint of work. No doubt he was sometimes unpleasant company himself, but he was striving for both work and social connection. He was physically – and mentally – worn out. In his period of depression in 1893, Cox covered up to 32 kilometres a day, over what Fairburn describes as 'some very rough country'.[92] He was not alone: these men who walked and remained mobile were perhaps staving off the inevitable stasis of stopping and succumbing to their fates.

Men like Cox could develop injuries at work that left them weak, unable to undertake forms of physical labour, or at worst, left them permanently disabled. As Lee put it, 'men worked until they could no longer be of use; they walked until they could walk no longer'. One man who perished in an old mens' home in Oamaru in 1911 aged ninety after years of walking was Robert (Barney) Winters, according to a photograph in the *Otago Witness*.[93] Also known as 'Barney Whiterats', Robert Winters was believed to be an entertainer who was born in London in 1821. In New Zealand, he became known as figure of curiosity in North Otago following his stint as a seaman who abandoned ship in the late 1840s and became an itinerant worker who performed for children with a show using white rats.[94] There were men all around the Australian colonies with similar identities and lifestyles; they were known as the 'nomad workers', and they were often depicted in official photographs by the late nineteenth century.[95]

Finally, Cox, in his old age, battled illness and surgery for cancer. He had managed to eke out a life in his later years by trekking, working and seeking shelter. He became acutely aware – both as an observer and as someone with lived experience – of the poverty of being an unskilled labourer who faced long periods of time without work, and who had to mix with all types of people to get by. He was literate and had started his life as the child of relatively successful small farmers in England. If we applied a psychological interpretation to his experiences, we might suggest that he was broken by the early death of his father, that migration to New Zealand exacerbated his sense of isolation and loss, and that his life took a turn for loneliness and desperation as a result.[96] He, like so many others, was tossed around of the vicissitudes of mobility and of being mobile, forced to be on the road for lengthy and punishing periods of time. His days ended in a home for elderly men in Caterton, where he was comfortable and surrounded by a community and friends, where he died in 1925.[97] This was not the way so many others who had been arrested for vagrancy found their lives by the time they died in the colonies in the same period.

Escaping the old world?

Historians explain that the colonies experienced a collapse of the labour market in the 1890s. The 'Here, and There' cartoon published in *Punch* in 1848, with its sly look at the promotion of emigration (see Figure 2.1), extolled the possibility of escaping 'old world' destitution. When looking back from the early 1900s, it signalled a harsh reality. By the early twentieth century the meanings of vagrancy across the British world had become a topic for discussion as reported around the empire's newspapers. In March 1906, the *Hobart Mercury* published a long story titled 'Vagrancy, British and Colonial' which worried about a rising 'poverty and distress' caused by unemployment. Wary of 'indiscriminate charity', the editorial passed judgement on 'useless, reckless and dishonest persons' who left women and children abandoned, or who were too lazy to find a job and make an honest living. Instead of viewing the swelling ranks of unemployed as a structural problem, the piece defined the greater problem of 'habitual vagrancy', a situation affecting the United States as well as Britain. 'Most of those who wander about the country, ostensibly looking for work', noted the author, 'are the very persons who do not want to find it'.[98] One writer whose pseudonym was 'Wanderer', or Elim Henry D'Avigdor, wrote about the 'professional unemployed' in New Zealand, and about ticket-of-leave convicts from Australia who arrived in New Zealand looking for work. His view was that the professional unemployed manufactured their discontent and grumbled loudly about being out of work but were less inclined to look for work or to perform it.[99]

In fact, in 1904, the Salvation Army made a similar call to establish labour colonies by sending 'reformable' vagrants to the actual Australasian colonies to reduce the number of dependent vagrants, an emigration proposal that was widely condemned.[100] The aim of the *Hobart Mercury* editorial was to criticize the approach to charity and welfare in the English context; it cited the growing number of vagrants converging in London at Hyde Park Corner, and it highlighted the controversial idea of reforming the unemployed in labour colonies. Its tone sits in contrast to many other moderate reports and reflections in the colonial press identified as part of this chapter, including the more enlightened discussion of the 'unfortunate pauper' in *The Star* in 1901.[101]

The period between 1840 and 1910 drew the colonies of Australia and New Zealand colonies into a world economy based on raw materials supplied to manufacturers and workers in industrializing Britain. Factories and production had also started to drive employment in colonial cities, but the places where wool, dairy, meat, timber and sugar were processed and exported around from colonies to Britain were prioritized for white European workers from the late 1890s and increasingly following 1901 and the Immigration Act in newly Federated Australia. For men, being physically fit and able dominated working prospects, and for women, reproduction was favoured as contribution to the health of the colonial world and emerging nations of Australasia.

New Zealand politician and social reformer William Pember Reeves paid attention to the problem of the working man who was out of work in his influential book *State Experiments in Australia and New Zealand* (1902). He pointed to the similarities in the approach taken in the colonies of both New South Wales and New Zealand in the 1890s, where the concept of the 'Bureau of Labour' took hold as a place where men could register for work. Reeves noted the problem of the vagrants in cities who arrived from elsewhere – their mobility this time a way to move them on from one place to another – and the identities of the 'lazy, the utterly useless, and the social outcast' who tended to 'herd together'.[102] Again, he drew a distinction between the 'wandering swagmen … [who were] chronic vagabonds who tramp along' without really wanting work, and those 'genuine' swagmen who would 'take anything'.[103]

The new 'modern vagrant' type emerged at a time of modernizing labour practices. This type appeared to signal a difference between the 'old-style beggar', people who were truly destitute, and those who were itinerant workers in a world where being itinerant and seeking work was a sign of 'unemployability'. An editorial in New Zealand's *The Star* titled 'How he may be treated in future' directly tackled the change in the concept of vagrancy. The 'new modern vagrant' was found by observers in England and Wales to be male and living 'an unsocial existence'. He was 'content' with 'miserable surroundings', and resisted reform:

> The majority of the class are in the able-bodied period of life – seldom below sixteen or above sixty-five years. They are not an ill-fed class – their bodies as a rule are well nourished; they are much better clad than they used to be, and their boots generally are sound.[104]

These men were judged able to work but were more militant in their claims for better conditions and also wanted more control over their working lives. They also had access to forms of leisure, unlike many men who preceded them. The pamphlet issued by the Salvation Army's William Booth in 1904 was reprinted by his son, Bramwell in 1909, who described the growing numbers of vagrants as 'less amenable to police control' and as 'more aggressive in their methods of preying on the community'.[105]

Conclusions

Historians have used vagrancy as a window onto historical processes including economic processes, labour and human migration, urbanization, and responses to poverty such as welfare and legislation. Among the processes Paul Ocobock identifies, the 'formation of subcultures among the poor' is important to this book and the stories within it.[106] Patterns of vulnerability were based on social difference and the politics of mobility and identity. Describing well-known narratives of welfare in the nineteenth century, historian Shurlee Swain has showed that 'vignettes' of poverty had powerful tropes such as pity, lack, and disgust for the objects of need and charity, including children, the very vulnerable: we can therefore see 'vulnerability' itself as a category that attracts powerful signifiers.[107] These have become deeply entrenched in the social and cultural order over time. From Henry Mayhew's 'roving' and 'restless' poor of Britain in the 1820s and 1830s, with their vagrant identities articulated in a social survey with a wide readership, to later travellers' writings about the colonial world and its characters, we can discern influential and entrenched ideas about undesirable mobility that signalled the inherent tendency to dependence on state and charitable organizations: a definitive vulnerable class.[108]

Experiences of vagrancy, as the story of James Cox suggests, could leave deep scars on individual people. Fairburn suggests that Cox suffered dreadfully during his 'days of darkness': these were periods of 'extreme adverse contingency … when he was more or less continuously on the move for approximately a month at a time.'[109] Fairburn also argued that 'the visibility of social derelicts in the colony' was symptomatic of a more widely felt loneliness.[110]

Vulnerability also offers us powerful explanatory potential as we select themes and focus on specific topics through socio-legal histories to shed light on enduring human problems. It foregrounds, as Fineman argues, 'social experience as well as institutional arrangements under law' to frame a social justice interpretation of history, asking historians to 'pay attention to the persistence of … constant human needs over time.'[111]

Although people fell into mobile lives or were forced to stay on the move to seek work or shelter, which made them far more vulnerable to police arrest and sentencing by the courts, wandering may also have had appeal for its own sake. Being mobile could also be an expression of freedom and adventure, of refusal to stay still, as the final chapter of this book demonstrates.

6

Adventure, wandering or predation? Regulating mobility

The story of James Cox and his experiences tramping across New Zealand shows that, contrary to persistent beliefs about 'loafers', not all tramps 'hated work' or avoided it; in fact, many men and women searched for gainful employment and purpose throughout their lives in the colonies.[1] This often-hopeful and highly peripatetic quest involved physical and mental effort. Yet the mobility of these people became symbolic of their lack of fixedness and settlement: permission to be mobile was attenuated in the colonies. Histories of wandering peoples, including labourers, capture the essence of mobility as both forced and a consequence of social, economic and cultural disruption. These histories sit alongside stories of adventure in the period, offering alternative narratives of cultural change and colonial 'types', as well as mythologies of the bush, rural life and leisure.[2]

In writing a history of 'vagrancy from below', this book has told the stories of just a small few of the many thousands of vagrant lives in the record. These stories are suggestive of all kinds of experiences of mobility for marginalized peoples across the colonies in Australia and New Zealand. They also have a relationship with similar narrative accounts of 'tramps' and vagrants in other places around the world, revealing a pattern in the production of meanings about vagrancy in a range of colonial settings, from American jurisdictions to African, but also in other historical and geographical settings including Asia.[3] The quest for freedom to live without constraints, including pursuing a life on the streets, is one theme expressed among the cases of people arrested as vagrants. In other examples, vagrants became wanderers, and were forced into mobility through poverty and a lack of social connections. Some vagrants were feared because of their propensity for 'predatory' crime, such as opportunistic thefts, physical assault or lurking with intent to prey on unsuspecting people in public. Habitual reliance on alcohol – a form of survival for so many vagrants – also compromised safe streets for the 'respectable' societies being crafted in the colonies during the nineteenth century. Rural mobility for seasonal work characterized the lives of many more people, especially men, and the vagrancy charge was applied in some places to continue 'protecting' tenuous frontier communities from a perceived lack of order.[4]

This final chapter shares some additional evidence of the insider account of being vagrant or witnessing vagrancy to provide an extension to the themes of the previous chapter. It examines adventure, wandering and predation as interpretative themes for the history of vagrancy as mobility, and concludes by reflecting on the conceptual contribution of this book as a whole.

Adventure: Types and narratives

Examining both the romanticized and critical contemporary views of the 'tramp', historians and literary scholars notice tropes in the cultural construction of vagrant identities. These literary representations functioned to create powerful meanings of vagrancy in everyday life. Negative descriptive typologies of the vagrant mattered in their historical context because they 'affected the lived experience of mobile people'.[5] Representations of different versions of destitution and poverty, or work, unemployment and social class, found their way into social reports and informed official classifications, just as they seeped into colonial and imperial discourse about welfare and charity over time.[6] Yet there is a politics of writing a history of 'vagrancy from below': finding out more about vagrants means moving beyond the 'illusory caricatures' in fiction and popular depictions, including art.[7] Another problem noted by historians is the ambiguity of identity in the past; the way that both in representation and in life, different peoples' experiences are comingled and difficult to distinguish, creating the sense of unease about the vagrant person; in the period of the nineteenth century both in Britain and in the colonies, there was 'a large mobile population in which itinerant labourers were mingled with the destitute and with the old-style beggars' who become one group of 'vagabonds' in the public mind.[8]

What we might call the registers of mobility in the past are many and varied, located in published and unpublished written accounts of vagrancy. Vagrants' practices – walking, stopping, resting, sheltering and relocating from one part of the colony to another – were experiences informed by ideas about the ever-present and deeply entrenched mobility of colonial society. Adding to the complexity of unwanted mobility, colonial citizens sometimes experienced intimate encounters with unwanted mobility in the person of the vagrant. Narrative accounts by travellers across colonial Victoria and New Zealand provide a different view, and show curiosity mixed with fear in depictions of colonial mobility, views which persisted from the 1850s into the 1870s and beyond. *Glimpses of Life in Victoria*, published anonymously in 1872 but thought to be the work of colonist and squatter John Hunter Kerr, included a chapter entitled 'Travellers'. Kerr described the many people who wandered looking for work or who lived rough and dwelt in the bush. Some of these men were defined by the law as 'idle vagabonds'. Others were more respectable, but the problem for contemporaries, as historians note, lay in distinguishing between men who were shirking work and those genuinely impoverished.[9]

The reality of this life was stark: many men and women commenced their travels in Britain and ended up in the colonies utterly spent. In his autobiography *Days of Crime and Years and Suffering*, convict writer Owen Suffolk described his 'life as a vagabond'. He referred to being 'foodless' then 'houseless' and 'bedless' on the streets of London, destitute. There in these early days of vagrancy he learned that 'the state was kinder to the criminal than to the poor', a belief that shaped his life as a criminal.[10] Suffolk, whose writing has been described as inventive, drew on his experience even if he also embellished it. He noted that from his 'vagrant haunts and associations' he had learned about 'the rights of a vagabond' as well as social views of poverty.[11]

Margaret Crowther writes that the fear of the vagrant 'gradually diminished' in the nineteenth century in Britain, in part because of more effective policing. This had the effect of transforming the figure of the vagrant into a 'petty criminal'.[12] She suggested that in 'frontier societies' the image of the romantic tramp becomes appealing.[13] Writing about the American idea of the tramp, Alistair Robinson points to the 'versatility of British conceptions of vagrancy' as he takes a closer look at frontier society, suggesting the appeal of the tramp lay in its expression of liminal characters who represented possibility and transgression in an era of highly mobile populations including immigrants, but also displaced Indigenous American peoples.[14]

In Australia and New Zealand, the ideal of the 'swagman' shows that in part, one conception of the vagrant was romanticized. Travel writers tended to select popular 'characters' to depict for readers interested in the adventure of an imagined vicarious colonial journey. John Hunter Kerr was worried about the sight of 'stout lazy fellows lying two or three together, stretched at full length under the slight shade of a tree' before they turned into 'sundowners' and sought shelter at a local swagman's hut or station.[15] Some narratives skirted closely to memoir while others were more fanciful. In 1853, William Howitt's tale of travelling in Victoria recounts an encounter with a 'strange crazed shepherd', who he depicts as a 'visionary'. The story has a mystical aspect, suggesting that men who lived as eccentric wanderers may have had access to a depth of understanding that most men did not. When Howitt and his party find this man, he is walking in search of a station for work, carrying a bundle over his shoulder. He is dressed in typical 'swagger' clothing. Even though he seems 'harmless', he is a stranger, and in this narrative, he comes to represent the fears that circulated about lone, wandering men. He explained he had been a shepherd for property owners at Mount Macedon but that he had lost the ability to supervise because of rheumatic gout, and the station owners had told him to seek help from a benevolent home. Howitt and his companions were disbelieving, suggesting that this man 'a poor, crippled, crazy man' would not have been left to seek help like this:

> But this is a common phase of shepherd lunacy; the idea that something had to be done a long way off, by which they are induced to wander from place to place till they frequently sink and perish in the bush. It was evident, from the state of his wardrobe, that he has been long wandering about. … His memory was obviously almost gone, probably from the effect of the ailment on his brain.[16]

This man had, by Howitt's estimation, lost touch with his age, his background and his purpose. This type of man – a solo, lost shepherd with insanity – was a colonial character who appeared in the asylum records in the 1860s. Men who had been working on the land or seeking gold sometimes found themselves quite alone and went 'mad'.[17] Howitt goes on to explain this man was well educated, speaking of literature and ideas; Howitt and his party offered food, company and warm blankets by a fire. In the morning, Howitt was astonished when this man continued on his way with his swag, even though he was wracked with pain and moaning in the night. 'It really gives one a miserable idea of shepherding, and of the little care taken of the old, or insane shepherds, to see them thus wandering about', he wrote.[18] One of his observations was that the man was childlike, had become simple, and was needy, a vulnerable person, just as others concluded about the very old who became insensible as vagrants living on the streets.

John A. Lee's writing about New Zealand in the 1880s described in the previous chapter reminds us that the swaggers were real men.[19] Lee grew up on a property where a cottage was used by these men and he played games of 'being a swagger' as a child. He knew the men by name and he knew their stories. He knew what they ate, and what they took away with them as provisions for the road.[20] 'The thousands of men on the roads sought work. A job was the golden fleece. From Otago, Southland, Canterbury, Hawke's Bay, Wairarapa … the story was the same'.[21] The *New Zealand Graphic* printed a reputed account of one man's life as a swagger in 1893, possibly written by a journalist, but layered with 'the spirit of independence' associated with the swagman's identity at that time. The piece argued that men seeking work in the colonies belonged to a class of people who tried to be innovative and responsive to the changing labour market; they did not see themselves as farmers, but as workers: 'many of the vagrant class are old hands; men who have travelled by sea and land, whose intelligent conversation and knowledge' would surpass that of the 'fifty-acre cockatoo' selecting land.[22]

In her work about travel writing in New Zealand, Lydia Wevers pointed to the characterization of the 'mobile, volatile population' of the colonies.[23] She identified 'rovers and ramblers' who produced 'texts of motion', finding mostly adventure in the 'footloose male travellers' who wrote about their movement around New Zealand.[24] In general, Wevers found writers produced 'reiterated stereotypes and cliches', especially when describing the natural world. By contrast, Ken Gelder and Rachael Weaver find similar 'types' of characters, but in Australian fiction, and they tie their analysis of these fictional types to the production of meaning about the colonial economy. It follows that the production of social identities served a purpose for contemporaries interested to define an emerging social and cultural milieu or structure.[25] They point to the social categorizations made by writers such as Anthony Trollope, John Freeman, Richard Twopeny and Marcus Clark.[26] The writers were themselves mobile, and could move freely, unlike many others in the colonial world including those people they captured in their descriptions of life and society.

Some colonial writing by women shows other sides to the nature of the vagrant encounter, such as forms of personal intimacy, as I have commented elsewhere.[27] Pioneer woman in the South Island of New Zealand, Sarah Amelia Courage wrote about her 'encounter with a vagrant' in a mini-drama about a 'rogue' and quick-witted character who transgresses the boundaries between the outside world and her domestic space.[28] Courage lets down her guard because she feels sympathy for the man who arrives weary, and she lets him have a cup of tea in the kitchen. Despite expressing her fear of him – far of the stranger in her midst – the next morning, she realizes the man appears confident and relaxed, and she sends him away, only to find her domestic servant leaves with him. This story, probably embroidered by Courage, points to the flavour of contemporary storytelling in the colonies: 'the effect of the stranger at the door: his oddness, liminality, guile, and effect on others'.[29] Similarly, Kerr noted the threat of the 'ruffian' figures, men who thieved food from the cook, and tended to see the swaggers as a 'thankless set' in colonial Victoria.[30]

Wandering: Places and spaces

James Cox's movement has been interpreted as 'blind wandering' and 'meandering' in terms that show how forms of mobility that did not fit the settler norm or pattern continue to be positioned historically as problematic.[31] Fairburn uses pejorative language to describe his movement: for instance, Cox 'trudged'. Although it is not straightforward to represent vagrants' stories as either narratives of resistance or liberty, or of repression, it is possible to see patterns of prosecution and recidivism as expressions of vagrants' using the laws of the day to 'subsist' on urban streets over decades, as some evidence describes. The notion of 'wandering' seems to turn on the fine line between liberation from social expectations and moral degradation, often expressed in contradictory representations of 'the tramp'; yet, as historians have put it, 'most men were on the road because they had few other choices'.[32] Observers of the colonial world included travel writers who singled out the wanderers they saw because their identities were ambiguous and drew attention to the central paradox of colonial expansion and freedom.[33]

'Wandering' presented many colonial jurisdictions with difficulty in relation to local populations, including in India and in some African colonies, and in relation to Aboriginal peoples in Australia. The wandering insane, for instance, created concerns about how to contain mental illness at a time when the large institutions for those people designated as insane were designed to house troublesome populations, alongside prisons. In India, where separate institutions existed for the 'natives' and the 'Europeans', this loose wandering did not fit the British colonial mode of governance and control; local authorities established bureaucracies of monitoring mobility including laws about different forms of behaviour such as vagrancy.[34]

Historians of empire have been at the forefront of writing about the complicated networks of people, things and ideas that produced new ideas about mobility.[35] Colonial sites had been formed through the movement of peoples: the conquest of Indigenous peoples in the name of exploration and expansion; convict transportation; and waves of migration to further establish colonies as imperial outposts. In keeping with settler-colonial histories which emphasize the implementation of imperial rule 'on the ground', Cresswell's interpretation of the potential of the 'mobility turn' for historians highlights the production of mobility within local power relations. Cresswell suggests that the 'mobility' of people at scale from the sixteenth century led to significant interventions by local authorities such as tighter controls on movement and 'new forms of surveillance' of people on the move; this could include the use of social institutions, such as those used to house vulnerable people.[36] More precisely, Cresswell explains, mobility can have a 'furtive and transgressive character to it, crossing boundaries, breaking definitions … [and] threaten the quest for fixity'.[37]

The movement of vagrants in the colonial world is a good example of this transgressive mobility. Put more precisely, the settler-colonial world was already formed by mobile settler populations whose very ability to move around freely was based on curtailing the movement of Indigenous peoples, as well as those whose movement presented a threat. In the colonial world, 'some mobilities [were] dependent on the immobilities of others', and mobility could have 'visible effects' in relations of power.[38] Here, all the 'lifeblood of modernity' characterized by the flows of migration and arrivals, overland expeditions and journeys, and networks for rail and communications, the freedom of movement was tempered by the fear of what it meant.[39] In turn, it was the emergence of modernity – defined by Durba Ghosh and Dane Kennedy through the 'markers' of 'social order' – that was also driving an urgency around settler mentalities of movement.[40] Edward Said argued that vagrants, along with others like 'homeless wanderers and nomads', are the result of imperial power grabs at different moments in history: both at the high point of imperialism and in the age of decolonizing empire.[41]

Transcolonial history draws attention to the complex relations of empire, with imperial models for the laws of vagrancy establishing the framework for legislation. Ghosh and Kennedy write that transcolonial histories help to address the 'multiple networks of exchange that arose from the imperial experience, networks that connected colonies to one another as well as to Britain and stretched across geographical and political boundaries'.[42] This book has shown the importance of connecting legal history with the problems and rewards of national, transnational and global historical scholarship, also arguing that we should pay closer attention to the mutually productive relationships between law and colonialism.[43] In thinking about imperial and colonial histories, another contribution of this book lies in the connections it makes between places, as well as revealing untold histories about vagrancy in specific local sites. There are no detailed histories of vagrancy in Tasmania and New South Wales, and no other study that brings the four colonies discussed here into one interpretive frame.

Looking at the way certain forms of regulatory texts such as legislation and guiding principles and rules for police in the use of vagrancy laws shows the common and shared legal inheritances across place, as well as their specific local challenges. Without many existing micro-historical studies of policing in smaller locations aside from rural towns like Yass or Orange in New South Wales, or in growing urban places like Melbourne and its inner suburbs, the temptation is to elide descriptions of policing vagrancy across places: a trap for any study of more than one site. Similarly, looking at inner city communities in formation, such as Auckland or Melbourne, tends to bring different places into one conceptual world of the streetscapes and laneways, the problems of living close together, of children looking for ways to earn money or adults scrapping over infractions.

It is here that we could consider the value of the mobility paradigm's concept of 'moorings' to shed light on the problem of the outsider identity. As suburbs, cities and towns created their cohesive communities, they looked to keep out transients and itinerants. The very settled nature of the community meant that newcomers could be considered disruptive or even dangerous. A newcomer or outsider might be a person who arrived to seek work, but who was unknown to the people in that place, or who asked for a meal on his tramp through the countryside. And if a whole family appeared, looking for shelter and food, the imagined threat presented was possibly based on scarce resources for the people who were already there. They themselves may have struggled to feed families. In this way, moorings – or being relatively 'settled' in neighbourhoods and localities – could produce the intruder, or the identity of the vagrant whose movement threatened the status quo.

This book opened with the description of the Jim Crace novel *Harvest*, in which such 'moorings' quickly become more unstable, also revealing the way the mobility of 'others' can disrupt settled populations. Such interlopers tended to look like outsiders rather than appearing to blend in. Although methodologies drawing attention to histories of the body have been practised by historians in many contexts, the vagrant's body as it was understood through the behaviour, habits, experiences and interactions of people in the past has rarely been the focus of inquiry.

Predation: Crime, law and order

Whether or not prosecuting vagrancy hinted at fears about wandering, the unfettered and unproductive world of adventure, or mostly of criminal predation, it was movement that underpinned the framework to understand vagrancy as a crime. As Lauren Benton argues, the mobility of laws and legal practitioners around empire produced a kind of 'layered' effect as far as understanding law's operation was concerned. It gave rise to a 'fluid legal politics surrounding subjecthood and authority', Benton suggests, an idea that can productively be applied to the creation of vagrancy legislation in the Australasian colonies.[44] Vagrancy stayed on the statute books for some time. By the late twentieth century, such laws were seen as outlandish and entirely foreign.[45]

Yet homeless people in our own time have also been subject to the triumvirate of criminalization of being on the streets, physical removal from locations and social marginalization in public discourse. By looking at prosecutions using vagrancy laws in the past we can uncover a consistent pessimism about behaviour. There is also a long history of slippage between representations of the 'mobile poor' and vagrants, dating back to the early modern era in Britain.[46] The development of categories of vagrancy in law in the 1600s informed the guides for police, who in turn developed concepts of poverty, vagrancy, desertion, strangers and travellers in an evolving and complex lexicon that reveals an increasingly mobile society.[47]

As argued throughout this book, the concern about convicts and ex-convicts as they made their lives in early New South Wales and VDL was the beginning of a larger pattern of regulating people across the colonies. In the 1850s and 1860s, gold mining drew thousands of people from many parts of the world to the goldfields, including Chinese sojourners. The 'excitement' and disorder of social change and population growth, as well as the feverish search for gold, created the conditions for family separations and poverty.[48] Lunacy legislation, which, like vagrancy laws had earlier imperial models and laws in the 1840s, developed across the colonies from the 1860s as a response to the need for larger custodial and curative institutions.

The policing of young people and 'delinquency' in the colonies is another common element across the different places and legal jurisdictions described here. Gender also played a role in the shaping of the vagrant identity. Cresswell points to the question of the woman as 'tramp', and along with other scholars, notes the transgressive nature of the concept of a woman vagrant, despite her actual presence in the prosecution data as shown in this study.[49] Philippa Levine has argued that 'prostitution, crime and mobility formed a heady trio'.[50] Mobility and criminality were already inextricably linked in the minds of the European colonists when it came to the convicts transported for crimes ranging from petty to serious, and women convicts had already been tarnished with the association between their sexualities and bodies and criminal behaviour.

It is likely that women who were labelled as vagrants were possibly far more threatening than men seen as vagrants because they 'represented the breakdown of the traditional household and loosening of sexual mores. These women were seen as unredeemable and left to ride the rails on their own terms'.[51] In another way, social class also offered some women the potential for different forms of mobility. Writing about the histories of prostitution around the British Empire, Levine suggests that poorer women's mobility in colonial spaces was less 'fixed' by family responsibilities, familial roles and sites of family property than that of women of the middle and upper class.[52] Meanwhile, unemployed men attracted attention because they were outwardly mobile and present in political protests in the colonies.

These accounts of vagrant lives also illustrate the deeper meanings of the prosecution data by showing the intersections between gender, class, ethnicity, disability and age in the group of people arrested for vagrancy over time. The story of James Cox acts as a reminder of the lived reality for men and women who lived precariously and became vulnerable to economic change. Although he was never arrested and charged with vagrancy, many others like him were. He writes about his experiences of social discord and a lack of harmony, possibly because he clashed with employers, or because he showed an angular personality that was not a good fit for the social milieu he occupied. His account of living rough through the depression of the 1890s when he identified as a 'vagrant' gives us an insider's perspective of the lives of people who were marginalized and living as outsiders to communities and society at large.

In writing about the histories of vagrants from these diverse points of view, this book has also tried to foreground the current potency and potential of mobility studies in a rapidly changing world, giving this study a sociological inflection and orienting readers interested in a multidisciplinary approach to the meanings of vagrancy in historical perspective.

Mobility in the colonial world – and we can say, across the British world – was regulated in three ways.[53] First, mobility was regulated through the *legal apparatus* that deemed some acts of mobility illegal and criminal, punishing the mobile for transgressing into spaces and places where they were forbidden to go. Second, mobility was regulated through *modes of surveillance*, including via textual and photographic modes. Forming the basis of this study, the *Police Gazettes* and social institutions captured detail about people who were on the move. Third, in the observations of contemporaries who wrote about colonial society and its people and created its *narrative 'types'* in accounts of people who were making their way, mobility was regulated as categories of 'outsiders' were forged for identification. At the same time, these narrative types could constitute valid identities for people seeking to use them, both as projections onto others and as lived personas. This history has aimed to uncover these worlds of vagrants through a selection of 'life stories', with mobility a part of the analytical approach to read these patchy, reconstructed accounts of being a vagrant.[54] These outsiders took on 'vagrant personas' for themselves in different moments and as far as we are able to discern through a range of sources.

This approach is useful because it suggests that there is no exactitude about the history of vagrancy, but rather, a series of interpretive moves historians might make to get closer to understanding vagrancy in the past. Writing about the vagrancy law in Britain in 1824, Alistair Robinson suggests that the 'vagrant state' was 'porous'.[55] He arrives at this understanding through the common understanding of the breadth of the vagrancy law, which was often described as 'flexible', both in Britain and in the colonies. Robinson says that this 'amorphous' meaning of vagrancy flowed onto the measurement of the incidence of vagrancy as a crime as seen in statistics, which is again repeated in the colonial data used in this study. What interests me here is what he describes as the 'unaccountability of itinerants'.[56] Reading this idea of porosity to create a theoretical model to interpret vagrancy is suggestive in the sense that it makes the vagrant identity an 'empty' category, able to be filled by shifting descriptors; and in the context of this study, it also applies to changing meanings of unwanted mobility in the colonies.

The theoretical possibilities of the mobility paradigm provide us with a deeper and more helpful model to understand the history of vagrancy in its fullest sense, building on the idea of the 'politics of mobility' outlined by mobilities scholar Tim Cresswell. In his argument about the politics of mobility, Cresswell highlights the elements of power, representation and the embodiment of mobility, all of which clearly emerge in a study of vagrancy.[57] Relying on theories of criminality, for instance, or ideas about 'otherness', offers some potential. Yet by further inscribing the multiple possibilities presented by mobility as an interpretive framework, we can see the way that a vagrant's identity was also formed in relation to movement, lack of movement, the politics of space and place, and inside the problematic of colonial mobility itself. The idea of the 'mobility turn' has been attached to social science research and less often taken up by historians, with some notable exceptions, such as the work by Tony Ballantyne focused on imperial and colonial worlds.[58] Yet historical terrain is ripe for the analysis of mobility as a productive category in relation to human movement and its regulation.

By examining the prosecution data for vagrancy across the colonies, this book has also aimed to shed light on the political meanings of vagrancy prosecutions and social controls over some peoples' movement in the period to 1910. During this time, changing understandings of how society should operate and meld together, as well as shifts in policing and legislation, created evolving meanings of mobility in the colonial world. Earlier discussions in this book outlined other forms of the legal regulation of mobility that should be read in tandem with this discussion of vagrancy: the policing, confinement and sequestration of Indigenous peoples, including through legislation in Victoria in the mid-1860s, land alienation for Māori in New Zealand and Aboriginal 'protection', among other forms of regulation, are all pertinent here. Immigration restriction was another outcome of the hyper-vigilant attitude towards mobility in the nineteenth century.[59] Controls over indentured labour in parts of the Oceanian world also suggest a political plane for the experience of mobility.[60]

Throughout this book, the evidence of vagrancy shows that the many stories of vagrants have been coded in the 'words and statistics of others: police, sociologists, employers, and journalists'.[61] By sharing these stories of the worlds of the vagrant, we might come closer to knowing the human experience of vagrancy. While we remain attentive to the historical specificity of the formation of the category of 'the vagrant', we also learn much by understanding its continual resonance in our present. By using mobility as an interpretative concept, we gain a sense of the politics shaping the vagrant experience over time.

7

Epilogue

The precarious present

Reflecting on these histories of vagrants, it is useful to imagine the past inflected in our present. Writing in this reflective and self-reflexive mode can offer the historian access to the physical and emotional content of the past.[1] In my current neighbourhood, I've noticed several people who live and sleep 'rough': houseless, but not without friends and community. One woman who lives outdoors finds shelter in doorways, lanes and on the porches or verandahs of businesses overnight. She wears a distinctive dark uniform of clothing and a hat, and she presents as someone keenly watching life on the streets she inhabits. Older men tend to collect together. A younger woman sits just inside an alcove at the entrance of the supermarket – often a locus for communication with other women and men – sometimes with a small fund of coins and notes accumulating on a mat near her feet. One day she had a small white kitten with her, and at other times she has had a boyfriend for company too.

I was deeply sad to see a notice scrawled on the wall, written on more than one surface in chalk and in pen nearby, announcing the death of one of the men who was mourned by his friends on the street.

There are very few places for people to sleep or find shelter. My daughter showed me images of 'anti-homeless architecture' also known as 'hostile architecture' – seats with hard metal divisions, a series of vertical poles arranged in alcoves – to prevent people from resting or sleeping in public space. It is estimated that people in Australia who live rough walk around 4 kilometres a day, or 28 kilometres a week: they are highly mobile people which contributes to the social unease about their identities and 'place' in society.

Over the past few years, individuals and collectives of people who live on the streets and seek charitable assistance in Australia has grown, with 'homelessness' recognized as a significant social problem. During the 2020–1 period of the pandemic, some cities in Australia offered hotel accommodation to the houseless, signalling protection and safety, but also demonstrating political expediency in the face of social unease about rates of COVID infection.

In 2022, a conservative politician in Australia called for the vagrancy legislation to be reintroduced in Queensland to criminalize people living outdoors. As it is, vagrancy laws conceived in the nineteenth century persisted well into the twentieth century, long past the time of their validity as an approach to human problems of belonging and economic stress. Vagrancy laws were only repealed in some jurisdictions in the 2000s and labels of 'homeless' have replaced the vagrancy concept. These laws have attracted attention during periods of progressive law reform.

Now, the number of people living rough is also patterned by an increase in the public visibility of mental illness following the closures of large mental hospitals from the 1980s. This relationship between mental illness and vagrancy also has a long history and was one entry point to this topic for me as a researcher.

Although we cannot ascribe the same historical meanings to 'vagrancy' in the past and 'homelessness' in our present, there are echoes of the past treatment of vagrants in our present. Tim Cresswell suggests we could consider the 'role of the medieval vagrant in the constitution of contemporary mobilities'.[2] This might seem a stretch of the historical imagination, yet I can see the parallels in experience, discourses of mobile people, and historical repetition in terms of economic change and similar pressures on our welfare systems, and definite similarities in constructions of poverty and the 'deserving' and 'respectable' or 'undeserving poor'. Cresswell argues that we need to understand mobility as having a past, as something deeply stitched into our historical experience. One audience member at a seminar where I spoke about this research in October 2022 mentioned the idea of a 'long vagrancy', meaning a elastic period of time during which meanings of vagrancy have been continually produced, overlaid and also experienced: in our twenty-first-century moment we witness so much human suffering and mobility intertwined with the problems of economic stress and housing unaffordability.[3]

The common thread between vagrancy and homelessness, suggests Cresswell, is 'place': the way places are inhabited, understood and controlled produces the meanings of those people who live without houses or shelter.[4]

This book is written to bring humanity to the lives and stories of 'vagrants' who appear in the historical record. These people were the subjects of much social commentary in their own times. They have also been written about by historians interested in social, cultural and urban life, and by scholars interested in law and order. Because my own experience as a historian has been entwined with my interest in the way the present echoes the past, I am conscious of trying to lay bare the lives of historical characters who have no opportunity to write back or to comment on my interpretation of their world. To counter this problem, I represent their lives as narratives woven into a larger history of the way nineteenth-century citizens made sense of the curious mobility of people who were labelled as 'vagrants'. These accounts of vagrant lives are sometimes speculative and involve acts of historical imagination.

My hope is that this book takes us into the stories of the past as these continue to resonate with us in our own time, and that it reminds us of the precarious present.

Annotated guide to data and digital sources

In addition to the Bibliography provided at the end of this book, this guide is designed to explain three areas of research central to this book. First, I describe the vagrancy prosecution data sets used in this study, including explaining their creation and accessibility to readers. My preference here is to enable researchers to seek sources of data and to become active users of these, rather than extracting some of the data in partial representational tables or graphs. Another reason this guide is useful to interested researchers is that the data collected over time differs in a range of aspects including selection, sampling and format, leaving both gaps and uncertainties in terms of using definitive data in this study, and opportunities for researchers interested in quantification to use the data sets in their own work. Second, I set out the different digital and online collections made available to public users by relevant research repositories and libraries. Third, this guide offers some further advice regarding the use of interactive online research collections made available to users by researchers through programmes and projects, such as collaborative research in the field of policing, crime and justice histories.

Vagrancy prosecution data sets *c.* 1860 to 1910

Extant historical *Police Gazettes* for the colonies studied here are held in archives and libraries in microfilm or microfiche format, with some digital collections also available online. There were thousands of discharged prisoners who were prosecuted for vagrancy listed in the different editions of the colonial *Police Gazettes.* At the beginning of Chapter 5, an estimate of the overall numbers of vagrancy prosecutions by the early twentieth century at the start of provides a reminder of the extent of the 'vagrancy problem' in the minds of colonial authorities. In the past, it has been difficult for historians of crime and policing to draw on accurate sources of data relating to criminal prosecutions. Yet it is possible to use the discharged prisoner lists to provide a suggestive account of vagrancy prosecutions, and to marry this with other data.

The benefit of digitization projects means that historians have more possibilities in terms of linking records, finding individuals, tracing court and gaol records, and searching digitized newspaper reports for references to vagrants. Yet problems remain: the amount of potential material now available online is both patchy in its coverage and immense; plotting any meaningful way through the digital records also needs to be done with care and attention to the ultimate aim of the research.

Vagrancy prosecution data for each of the colonies between 1860 and 1910 was gathered for this project in different stages and is therefore not easily compared or represented. The common principle used in data collection for each colony, with data gathered at different times, was the focus on vagrants who were convicted, sentenced and who spent time in detention.

The initial research work took place in New Zealand. All discharged prisoners convicted of vagrancy in every third year for a full year from 1877 to 1900 comprise one separate set of data for this study. This data was collected by me as a series of photographs, with fields of data then noted from these photographs and entered into a Microsoft Access database which was then extracted into Excel. This data set is a sample of 1,187 vagrant prosecutions over the period, with a few individuals appearing more than once. The data was analysed by a research assistant and includes rich qualitative material such as comments on the physical appearances of vagrants. This data is not yet deposited in a public online repository but will form the basis of a digital project to provide greater access to users in future.

Additional data sets include all discharged prisoners convicted of vagrancy as listed in the *Police Gazettes* in New South Wales, Victoria and Tasmania from *c.* 1860 to *c.* 1920. These were provided by Hamish Maxwell-Stewart as separate Microsoft Excel sheets for each jurisdiction and correspond to his extensive research into convict lives across the colonies. Each data set reflects differences between the colonies in terms of legislation, policing and the extant archives. The vagrancy prosecution data for Tasmania is collated for 1865 to 1923. There was no specific vagrancy legislation in Tasmania, so the relevant prosecution data is based on charges ranging from 'idle and disorderly' to 'vagrancy' as established in the police offences law. The vagrancy prosecution data for Victoria is collated from 1864 to 1906 and includes detailed qualitative comments entered by researchers. The vagrancy prosecution data for New South Wales is collated from 1866 to 1924 and includes fewer descriptive comments about individual offenders. The New South Wales data overall shows a much lower proportion of offenders prosecuted for non-indictable offences than the Tasmanian and Victorian data.[1]

The Australian Data Archive (ADA) hosts these data sets in the 'dataverse' as shown below. In this 'dataverse', research articles and findings are linked to data sets where these exist and offer more possibilities in terms of understanding the data and its potential uses.

The Australian Data Archive
https://dataverse.ada.edu.au/dataverse.xhtml?alias=ada&q=police%20gazette

A research assistant for this project provided more detailed work on the NSW *Police Gazettes* for two decades (1860 and 1870) by using TROVE (an Australian online repository). That data is set out in Excel spreadsheets and corresponds with the data set provided in the 'dataverse', with the advantage that more details about prosecutions were entered which offer amplification of the research materials across demographic categories; this data set also includes descriptive comments about offenders. For Tasmania, a different research assistant provided data for all vagrancy prosecutions based on statistical returns. As with the data collected in New Zealand, these data sets are not yet deposited in a public online repository but will form the basis of a project to provide greater access to users in future. These interventions have been useful as this book has focused on the question of different colonial sites and policing practices.

In keeping with this ethos of make available data open to users, throughout this book, the different sources of information about vagrancy prosecution are used to highlight possible future thematic pathways that could be drawn out from the separate sets of data by researchers who are able to access publicly available data sets. For instance, the concentrations of urban and rural vagrancy prosecutions in the context of colonial populations; the birthplaces of people prosecuted as vagrants; gender, age and occupational information; the charges and sentences in relation to jurisdiction and time period; and descriptive data contained within charges and captured in the *Police Gazettes* and other sources. Data will be modelled within the Time-Layered Cultural Map of Australia (TLCMap) for future uses to visual prosecution patterns, or elements of vagrants' mobility. See: https://tlcmap.org/

For example, comparing two specific jurisdictions, Tasmania and Victoria, yields interesting results because they had similar rates of prosecution. Some aspects of the prosecution data stand out: the data shows that former convicts in Tasmania received longer prison sentences, and that convict absconders were more likely than others in the population to be charged as vagrants. Women were more likely to be prosecuted as vagrants than men, but more men were prosecuted overall. In both places, being Irish was a risk, with more Irish-born charged as vagrants and included in the records.[2]

Additional early statistical data can be located in the Australian Bureau of Statistics historical collections online, including the lengthy section on 'social condition' first published as part of a statistical overview of the Australian colonies in 1904. In New Zealand, similar sources of statistical information can also be located online.

Australian Bureau of Statistics, *A Statistical Account of Australia and New Zealand, 1902-03*, at https://www.abs.gov.au/AUSSTATS/abs@.nsf/DetailsPage/1398.01902-03?OpenDocument, URL accessed 4 August 2023.

New Zealand History/Nga korero a ipurangi o Aotearoa
https://nzhistory.govt.nz/politics/working-with-statistics

Future scholarship could include data visualization methods to show the large number of people prosecuted as vagrants using a colour palette. Using this kind of visual methodology as a representational practice would reveal the array categories such as age, gender, birthplace and occupation in alternative ways and enable the production of new knowledge.

Research repository websites

Official libraries, archives and repositories in Australia and New Zealand have made specific data sets available to researchers. Ranging from immigration and convict records to online exhibitions about themes such as 'criminal characters', these data sets are useful to the study of vagrancy and mobility. The selection of sites listed here is based on my research for this book. In particular, some of those listed – especially the digitized newspapers in Australia and New Zealand – have been a valuable source of information about vagrant lives, movement and criminal prosecutions, aligning with the prosecution data and adding depth to the cases of recidivist offenders such as Christina Lawson and Sarah Jones. Former convicts appear in some of the lists, allowing us to find out more about convicts who were charged with the crime of vagrancy in the Australian colonies. Researchers have collaborated with libraries and archives to produce and share data including visual representations such as vagrant mugshots in online exhibits. Some of the researchers involved in this work have produced several academic publications about the prosecution of vagrancy. The 'Vagrants and Murderesses' site held by the Public Record Office of Victoria, together with digitized sources held in TROVE or PapersPast (all digitized newspapers in New

Zealand), each offer points of connection and the amplification for individual cases and collective storytelling.

Assisted Immigration Records
State Archives Collection, Museums of History New South Wales
https://mhnsw.au/indexes/immigration-and-shipping/assisted-immigrants-index/
Convict Records
https://convictrecords.com.au/
Criminal Characters
https://criminalcharacters.com/resources/prisons-and-punishment/map-of-australian-prisons/
Museums of History New South Wales
https://mhnsw.au/stories/
Online register of criminal prosecutions at the Public Record Office of Victoria: https://prov.vic.gov.au/explore-collection/explore-topic/justice-crime-and-law/register-male-and-female-prisoners-1855-1947
PapersPast
https://paperspast.natlib.govt.nz/newspapers
TROVE
https://trove.nla.gov.au/
Unemployed in Sydney, 1866
https://mhnsw.au/indexes/unemployment/unemployed-in-sydney/
Vagrants and Murderesses
https://vagrantsandmurderesses.com/

Research projects with interactive data capability

New Zealand's Lost Cases Project and the Australian Prosecution Project provide more fleeting glimpses of vagrancy as a crime as they both focus on different parts of the criminal justice system, with the Prosecution Project focused on courts hearing criminal trials, but also incorporating *Police Gazettes*. I have included the latter here as a good example of the model of an accessible research site with data available to users even though it will not yield much on vagrancy as a topic. In this book, the Lost Cases Project did prove to be a helpful source of information for a few cases as cited in the text. The travel writing project is an exciting interactive site with potential to represent far more colonial writing in a visual map than the examples used in this book. Digitized texts in that collection will reveal far more about mobility and vagrancy – especially narratives about vagrancy in the colonies – than I have been able to discuss here.

New Zealand's Lost Cases Project
https://www.wgtn.ac.nz/law/nzlostcases/default.aspx
Nineteenth-Century Travel Writing
https://www.austlit.edu.au/austlit/page/24009237
The Prosecution Project
https://prosecutionproject.griffith.edu.au/

Finally, and as a brief example, blogs and articles in *The Conversation* also show the potential for linking data and research to wider audiences and users. Alana Piper and Victoria Nagy have written about 'Disorderly Women, Broken Windows and Social Outcasts' for their blog published by the Australian Women's History Network, 18 October 2017: http://www.auswhn.org.au/blog/victorian-female-prisoners/

Notes

Chapter 1

1 Jim Crace, *Harvest* (London: Picador, 2013). Reviewers of the novel comment that it is set in an indeterminate time and place; see Clare Sestanovich, 'Logs vs. Dead Donkeys: The Tweet That Helped Me Make Sense of Jim Crace', *The Atlantic*, 10 September 2013.

2 I thank Dr Kate Bowan, Australian National University, for suggesting this phrase as applied to my study.

3 Margaret Keegan, *Press*, 19 August 1902: 2; Christina Lawson, numerous instances, see *Lyttelton Times*, 2 October 1905: 3.

4 *New Zealand Herald*, 8 June 1900: 7.

5 As noted about New Zealand by Miles Fairburn, 'Vagrants, "Folk Devils" and Nineteenth-Century New Zealand as a Bondless Society', *Historical Studies*, 21, no. 85 (October 1985): 50.

6 Mark Finnane, *Punishment in Australian Society* (Melbourne: Oxford University Press, 1997), 78.

7 David Hitchcock, 'Editorial: Poverty and Mobility in England, 1600–1850', *Rural History* 24, no. 1 (2013): 3.

8 This surveillance is described by Kirsty Reid in *Gender and Empire: Convicts, Settlers and the State in Early Colonial Australia* (Manchester: Manchester University Press, 2007), 97–8. Convict and ticket-of-leave households in Van Diemen's Land were kept under the watchful eye of authorities from 1816 onwards. In early Sydney convicts were watched by constables from 1811. They wore distinctive dress as described by Paula J. Byrne in *Criminal Law and Colonial Subject: New South Wales 1810–1830* (Cambridge and Melbourne: Cambridge University Press, 1993), 156–7. See also Andrew McLeod, 'On the Origins of Consorting Laws', *Melbourne University Law Review* 37, no. 103 (2013): 114.

9 Amanda Nettelbeck has written about the creation of the 'Aboriginal vagrant' in three colonies/states of Australia in the wake of Aboriginal 'protection': see 'Creating the Aboriginal Vagrant: Protective Governance and Indigenous Mobility in Colonial Australia', *Pacific Historical Review* 87, no. 1 (2018): 79–100.

10 Stephen Garton, *Out of Luck: Poor Australians and Social Welfare* (Sydney: Allen & Unwin, 1990), 36.

11 New Zealand poet R. A. K. Mason, b. 1905, wrote a poem called 'On the swag' that was published in 1934. It conjured the 'romantic' experience of a swagman as a Christ-like figure fed by households on his journey. New Zealand historian Miles Fairburn notes that more romanticized conceptions of vagrancy were formed after the mid-1930s in his account 'Vagrants, "Folk Devils" and Nineteenth-Century New Zealand as a Bondless Society', 495. Julie Kimber notes the mythologizing of the 'Australian identity' of the bushman which shares a North American strand of romanticization of these characters; see Kimber, '"A nuisance to the community": Policing the Vagrant Woman', *Journal of Australian Studies* 34, no. 3 (September 2010): 288. See also Jessica Gerrard, 'The Interconnected Histories of Labour and Homelessness', *Labour History* 112 (May 2017): 155–6.

12 These include A. L. Beier and Paul Ocobock eds., *Cast Out: Vagrancy and Homelessness in Global and Historical Perspective* (Ohio: Ohio University Press, 2009); David Hitchcock, *Vagrancy in English Culture and Society, 1650–1750* (London: Bloomsbury Academic, 2016).

13 See, for instance, Zelinsky's theory of mobility and demographic transition (1971) in Colin G. Pooley and Jean Turnbull, *Migration and Mobility in Britain since the Eighteenth Century* (London: UCL Press, 1998), 8.

14 Philippa Levine, *Prostitution, Race and Politics: Policing Venereal Disease in the British Empire* (London and New York: Routledge, 2003), 187.

15 Ocobock, 'Introduction: Vagrancy and Homelessness in Global and Historical Perspective', in *Cast Out*, 21; 19.

16 Hitchcock, *Vagrancy in English Culture and Society*, 1–20.

17 Tony Ballantyne, 'Mobility, Empire, Colonisation', *History Australia* 11, no. 2 (2014): 12.

18 On using criminal records to find out about mobility, see Pooley and Turnbull, *Migration and Mobility in Britain*, 14–15.

19 Sally Engle Merry and Donald Brenneis, *Law and Empire in the Pacific: Fiji and Hawai'I* (Santa Fe: SAR Press, 2004), 6–10; Lauren Benton, *A Search for Sovereignty: Law and Geography in European Empires, 1400–1900* (New York: Cambridge University Press, 2010), 137; Moloughney and Stenhouse, 1999; Angela Hawk, 'Going "Mad" in Gold Country: Migrant Populations and the Problem of Containment in Pacific Mining Boom Regions', *Pacific Historical Review* 80, no. 1 (2011): 64–96.

20 Historical accounts of insanity and confinement in Australia and New Zealand include Catharine Coleborne, *Insanity, Identity and Empire: Colonial institutional confinement in Australia and New Zealand, 1870–1910* (Manchester UK: Manchester University Press, 2015).

21 Tim Cresswell, *Place: An Introduction* (Oxford: Wiley-Blackwell, 2015), 175.

22 Coleborne, *Insanity, Identity and Empire*, 100–3.

23 See Catharine Coleborne and Maree O'Connor, 'Vagrancy, Mobility and Colonialism', in *Handbook of Historical Geography*, ed. Mona Domosh, Michael Heffernan and Charles W. J. Withers (London: SAGE, 2020), 374–89.
24 My own study of asylums as social institutions in this period, *Insanity, Identity and Empire* investigates the meanings of identity in the Australian and New Zealand setting.
25 See Amanda Nettelbeck, 'Creating the Aboriginal "Vagrant": Protective Governance and Indigenous Mobility in Colonial Australia', *Pacific Historical Review* 87, no. 1 (2017): 79–100. See also Catharine Coleborne, 'Consorting with Others: Vagrancy Laws and Unauthorized Mobility across Colonial Borders in New Zealand from 1877 to 1900', in *Empire and Mobility in the Long Nineteenth Century*, ed. Peter Merriman and David Lambert (Manchester, UK: Manchester UP, 2020).
26 Bruce Kercher, *Outsiders: Tales from the Supreme Court of NSW, 1824–1836* (Melbourne: Australian Scholarly Publishing, 2006), 8–9. Kercher's framing of outsiders in law (see pp. 171–9) is specific but follows the social history conceptualization of the 'outsider' also found in work by Eric Hobsbawm, *Bandits* (London: Pantheon, [1969] 1981).
27 On humanities research and the mobilities paradigm, see Peter Merriman and Lynne Pearce eds., *Mobility and the Humanities* (London and New York: Routledge, 2018); see also a Special Section of *Transfers: Interdisciplinary Journal of Mobility Studies* focused on 'Settler-Colonial Mobilities', 5, no. 3 (December 2015).
28 John Urry, *Mobilities* (Malden: Polity, 2007), 32–6.
29 Tim Cresswell, 'Towards a Politics of Mobility', *Environment and Planning D: Society and Space* 28 (2010): 17; Tim Cresswell, 'The Production of Mobilities', *New Formations: A Journal of Culture/Theory/Politics* 43 (2001): 11–25.
30 Ballantyne, 'Mobility, Empire, Colonisation', 37.
31 See *Law/Text/Culture*, 'Making Law Visible: Past and Present Histories and Postcolonial Theory', ed. Nan Seuffert and Catharine Coleborne, 7 (2003).
32 Graeme Davison, J. W. McCarty and Ailsa McLeary eds., *Australians 1888* (Sydney: Fairfax, Syme and Weldon, 1987), 230–5; 249.
33 Elsewhere I show a trans-colonial historical approach to underline this regionality and shared history of legal practices in the case of mental health; see Coleborne, *Madness in the Family: Insanity and Institutions in the Australasian Colonial World 1860s–1914* (Basingstoke and New York: Palgrave Macmillan, 2010), 15–42.
34 Alan Atkinson, *The Europeans in Australia: A History*, Volume 2 (Melbourne and Oxford: Oxford University Press, 2004), 247.
35 Andrew J. May, 'Good Fences: Affective Sociability, Neighbourly Relations, and Australian Municipalism', in *Urban Emotions and the Making of the City: Interdisciplinary Perspectives*, ed. Katie Barclay and Jade Riddle (London and New York: Routledge, 2021), 114.

36 On the slums of Sydney and Melbourne see Garton, *Out of Luck*, 36–42.

37 Cresswell, *Place*, 175.

38 The introduction of the Old Age Pension in Australia and New Zealand is discussed by historians including Margaret Tennant, 'Elderly Indigents and Old Men's Homes 1880–1920', *New Zealand Journal of History* 17, no. 1 (1983): 3; John Murphy, *A Decent Provision: Australian Welfare Policy, 1870 to 1949* (Farnham, Surrey: Ashgate, 2011), 61–4.

39 Fairburn, 'Vagrants, "Folk Devils" and Nineteenth-Century New Zealand as a Bondless Society'.

40 Susanne Elizabeth Davies, Vagrancy and the Victorians: The Social Construction of the Vagrant in Melbourne, 1880–1907, Unpublished PhD Thesis in History, University of Melbourne, 1990.

41 Fairburn, 'Vagrants', 50.

42 Charlotte Macdonald, 'Crime and Punishment in New Zealand, 1840–1913: A Gendered History', *New Zealand Journal of History* 23, no. 1 (1989): 13.

43 Kay Daniels, *So Much Hard Work: Women and Prostitution in Australian History* (Sydney: Fontana/Collins, 1984); Judith A. Allen, *Sex and Secrets: Crimes Involving Australian Women since 1880* (Oxford, Melbourne, Auckland and New York: Oxford University Press, 1990).

44 Christina Twomey, *Deserted and Destitute: Motherhood, Wife Desertion and Colonial Welfare* (Melbourne: Australian Scholarly Publishing, 2002).

45 Julie Kimber, 'Poor Laws: A Historiography of Vagrancy in Australia', *History Compass* 11, no. 8 (2013): 540.

46 Alan Piper and Victoria Nagy, 'Versatile Offending: Criminal Careers of Female Prisoners in Australia 1860–1920', *Journal of Interdisciplinary History* 48, no. 2 (2017): 187–210; 'Imprisonment of Female Urban and Rural Offenders in Victoria, 1860–1920', *International Journal for Crime, Justice and Social Democracy* 8, no. 1 (2019): 100–115.

47 Victoria Nagy, 'Women, Old Age and Imprisonment in Victoria, Australia 1860–1920', *Women and Criminal Justice* 30, no. 3 (2020): 151–71.

48 Garton, *Out of Luck;* Margaret Tennant, *Paupers and Providers: Charitable Aid in New Zealand* (Wellington: Allen & Unwin/Historical Branch, 1989).

49 Kimber focuses on the story of Annie Larkins in 'A Nuisance to the Community', 281–7; see also the approach taken by Janet McCalman in *Vandemonians: The Repressed History of Colonial Victoria* (Melbourne: Miegunuyah Press: 2021). N. J. Crowson also uses the technique of creating 'life stories' to flesh out the experiences of vagrants in late-nineteenth-century England; see 'Tramps' Tales: Discovering the Life Stories of Late Victorian and Edwardian Vagrants', *English Historical Review* 125, no. 577 (2020): 1489–526. Some of the 'identities' are sketched in social histories including Garton, *Out of Luck*, 39.

50 A. L. Beier, *Masterless Men: The Vagrancy Problem in England 1560–1640* (London and New York: Methuen, 1985), 51. See also Cresswell, *Place*, 175, writing about the transformation of social hierarchies and 'traditional patterns of rights and duties'.

51 Beier, *Masterless Men,* 68.

52 Beier, *Masterless Men*, 65; Crowson, 'Tramps' Tales', 1522.

53 Coleborne, *Insanity, Identity and Empire*, 36.

54 Susanne Davies, '"Ragged, Dirty … Infamous and Obscene": The "Vagrant" in Late-Nineteenth-Century Melbourne', in *A Nation of Rogues: Crime, Law and Punishment in Colonial Australia,* ed. David Phillips and Susanne Davies (Melbourne: University of Melbourne Press, 1994), 156.

55 Martha Albertson Fineman, 'The Vulnerable Subject: Anchoring Equality in the Human Condition', *Yale Journal of Law and Feminism* 20, no. 1 (2008): 8–9.

56 Precarity is discussed by recent social scientists in the following works: See, for example, Clara Han, 'Precarity, precariousness, and vulnerability'. *Annual Review of Anthropology* 47 (2018): 331–43; and Julie McLeod, 'Vulnerability and the neo-liberal youth citizen: a view from Australia'. *Comparative Education* 48, no. 1 (2012): 11–26.

57 In other disciplines, different mobile methods can disturb the social science research model, such as walking interviews, participant-observation and co-design of research data. However, historical research mostly already involves being mobile. The difference here could be said to be about the awareness of the archive as a site of production of knowledge, as I show elsewhere: see Catharine Coleborne, 'Institutional Case Files', in *Sources and Methods in Histories of Colonialism: Approaching the Imperial Archive*, ed. Kirsty Reid and Fiona Paisley (London and New York: Routledge, 2017). See also Victoria Haskins, 'Decolonizing the Archives: A Transnational Perspective', in *Sources and Methods in the Histories of Colonialism,* 61.

58 Urry, *Mobilities,* 42; Tim Cresswell refers to 'spaces' of the regulation of mobility including prisons; see 'Towards a Politics of Mobility', 27.

59 Urry, *Mobilities*, 39; see also David Lambert and Peter Merriman eds., *Empire and Mobility in the Long Nineteenth Century* (Manchester: Manchester University Press, 2020), 11.

60 Crowson writes about the methodological challenges presented by vagrants' mobility; see 'Tramps' Tales', 1489.

61 Crowson, 'Tramps' Tales', 1507.

62 This process started with my work 'Crime, the Legal Archive, and Postcolonial Histories', in *Crime and Empire 1840–1940: Criminal Justice in Local and Global Context,* ed. Graeme Dunstall and Barry Godfrey (Devon, UK: Willan Publishing, 2005).

63 Alecia Simmonds, 'Legal Records', in *Sources for the History of Emotions: A Guide* ed. Katie Barclay, Sharon Crozier-De Rosa and Peter N. Stearns (London and New

York: Routledge, 2020), 79. On using legal records, see Byrne, *Criminal Law and Colonial Subject*, 11.

64 For a good example of the powerful work of legal narratives, see Debra Powell's doctoral research about infanticide in New Zealand: Debra Powell, A History of Infanticide and Child-Homicide in New Zealand, 1870–1910, Unpublished PhD Thesis in History, University of Waikato, 2013.

65 See my commentary about the uses of the *Police Gazettes* in Catharine Coleborne, 'Law's Mobility: Vagrancy and Imperial Legality in the Trans-Tasman Colonial World', in *New Zealand's Empire*, ed. Katie Pickles and Catharine Coleborne (Manchester, UK: Manchester University Press, 2015), 95; and Coleborne, 'Consorting with Others', 144.

66 M. A. Crowther, 'The Tramp', in *Myths of the English*, ed. Roy Porter (Cambridge: Polity Press, 1992), 98.

67 Crowther, 'The Tramp', 98.

68 Alistair Robinson, *Vagrancy and the Victorians Age, Representing the Wandering Poor in Nineteenth-Century Literature and Culture* (Cambridge: Cambridge University Press, 2022), 12; Crowson, 'Tramps' Tales', 1489.

69 The data sets used in this study are explained in the Annotated guide to data and digital sources at the end of this volume. See also K. Inwood, H. Maxwell-Stewart, D. Oxley and J. Stankovich, 'Growing Incomes, Growing People in Nineteenth-Century Tasmania', *Australian Economic History Review* 55, no. 2 (2015): 187–211; H. Maxwell-Stewart, K. Inwood and J. Stankovich, 'The Prison and the Colonial Family', *History of the Family* 20, no. 2 (2015): 231–48.

70 A survey of the *Otago Police Gazette and Record of Crime* for 1863–5; 1864–7; and 1867–9 held in the State Library of New South Wales indicated shared policing roles for police in different colonial jurisdictions; SLNSW Q343/0.

71 Hitchcock, 'Editorial: Poverty and Mobility in England, 1600–1850', 1.

72 Tim Cresswell's *The Tramp in America* (London: Reaktion Books, 2001) examines the body and image of 'the tramp' including through photographic evidence.

73 Kimber also makes this point about the importance of humanizing the past; see Kimber, 'A nuisance to the community', 286.

74 The practice of telling individual stories plotted against large data is becoming an established way to create new narratives of fields of social history. See Hitchcock, *Vagrancy in English Culture and Society*, 1–20.

75 Lambert and Merriman eds., *Empire and Mobility in the Long Nineteenth Century*, 11.

76 Ballantyne, 'Mobility, Empire, Colonisation', 33.

77 See https://criminalcharacters.com/, URL accessed 9 February 2023. See also an online register of criminal prosecutions at the Public Record Office of Victoria: https://prov.vic.gov.au/explore-collection/explore-topic/justice-crime-and-law/register-male-and-female-prisoners-1855–1947.

78 On bushrangers, see: Byrne, *Criminal Law and Colonial Subject*, Chapter 5: 129–51; Bruce Kercher, *An Unruly Child: A History of Law in Australia* (St Leonards: Allen & Unwin, 1995), 104–5.

79 Hitchcock, 'Editorial: Poverty and Mobility in England, 1600–1850', 2.

80 Miles Fairburn, *Nearly Out of Heart and Hope: The Puzzle of a Colonial Labourer's Diary* (Auckland: Auckland University Press, 1995).

81 Aparna Nair, '"They Shall See His Face": Blindness in British India, 1850–1950', *Medical History* 61, no. 2 (2017): 184–5.

82 Nair, '"They Shall See His face"': 192; see also 'Melbourne Beggar'. *Illustrated Melbourne News*, 18 June 1872: 128.

83 This idea is developed in more detail in Chapters 5 and 6 of this book. See 'How he may be treated in future', *Star*, 26 April 1906: 2.

84 As Crowson notes in the English context, not all vagrants were 'outsiders'; some were those who chose to live as vagrants inside communities' see Crowson, 'Tramps' Tales', 1490.

Chapter 2

1 On the convict transport, see https://convictrecords.com.au/ships/mangles URL accessed 24 July 2023.

2 'Central Police Court', *Sydney Morning Herald*, 12 January 1878: 6.

3 Jan Kociumbas, 'All That Glitters', in *The Oxford History of Australia, Volume 2, 1770–1860: Possessions* (Melbourne: Oxford University Press, 1992), 314.

4 See, for instance, David Hitchcock, *Vagrancy in English Culture and Society, 1650–1750* (London: Bloomsbury Academic, 2016); Beate Althammer, 'Roaming Men, Sedentary Women? The Gendering of Vagrancy Offenses in Nineteenth-Century Europe', *Journal of Social History* 51, no. 4 (2018): 736–59.

5 Tim Hitchcock, 'The London Vagrancy Crisis of the 1780s', *Rural History* 24, no. 1 (2013): 55–6.

6 Audrey Eccles, '"Furiously Mad": Vagrancy Law and a Sub-Group of the Disorderly Poor', *Rural History* 24, no. 1 (2013): 25–40.

7 Julie Kimber, '"A nuisance to the community": Policing the Vagrant Woman', *Journal of Australian Studies* 34, no. 3 (2010): 277; Janet McCalman, *Vandemonians, The Repressed History of Colonial Victoria* (Carlton: Miegunyah Press, 2021), 19; Mark Finnane, 'Law and Regulation', in *The Cambridge History of Australia*, volume 1, ed. Alison Bashford and Stuart McIntyre (Melbourne, New York and Cambridge: Cambridge University Press, 2013), 399–405.

8 See the *Regulations for the Guidance of the Constabulary* (Victoria, 1873).

9 Elsewhere I have written about other colonial contexts and the legal regulation of mobility and vagrants, also explaining the links between concerns about mobility and

populations of concern including Indigenous people, women performing work as prostitutes and immigrants; see Catharine Coleborne and Maree O'Connor, 'Vagrancy, Mobility and Colonialism', in *Handbook of Historical Geography*, ed. Mona Domosh, Michael Heffernan and Charles W. J. Withers (London: SAGE, 2020), 374–89.

10 Jessica Gerrard, 'The Interconnected Histories of Labour and Homelessness', *Labour History*, no. 112 (May 2017): 173.

11 The phrase is used several times in relation to the underlying rationale for vagrancy laws in Andrew McLeod, 'On the Origins of Consorting laws', *Melbourne University Law Review* 37, no. 103 (2013): 103–42.

12 Grace Karskens, *The Rocks: Life in Early Sydney* (Melbourne: Melbourne University Press, 1997), 52.

13 James Boyce, *Van Diemen's Land* (Melbourne: Black Inc., 2008), 63–141.

14 Bruce Kercher, *An Unruly Child: A History of Law in Australia* (St Leonards: Allen & Unwin, 1995), 104.

15 For instance, the National Library of Australia holds biographical cuttings relating to individuals like Frank McCallum, also known as Captain Melville, a bushranger who was an ex-convict from VDL who operated in Port Phillip/Victoria in the 1850s. He was arrested on vagrancy charges early in his career in 1849. See Biographical cuttings on Frank McCallum, former vagrant in the early 1800s, containing one or more cuttings from newspapers or journals, NLA Collection.

16 Grace Karskens, '"This Spirit of Emigration": The Nature and Meanings of Escape in Early New South Wales', *Journal of Australian Colonial History*, 7 (2005): 9.

17 Bruce Swanton, *The Police of Sydney: 1788–1862* (Canberra: Australian Institute of Criminology and NSW Police Historical Society, 1984), 9.

18 Swanton, *The Police of Sydney*, 16.

19 Swanton, *The Police of Sydney*, 19.

20 Karskens, 'This spirit of emigration', 9.

21 John Shaw, *A Tramp on the Diggings* (London: Richard Bentley, 1852), 230.

22 Paula J. Byrne, *Criminal Law and Colonial Subject: New South Wales, 1810–1830* (Melbourne: Cambridge University Press, 1993), 173–6.

23 Byrne, *Criminal Law and Colonial Subject,* 156.

24 Byrne, *Criminal Law and Colonial Subject,* 157.

25 Peter Cunningham, *Two Years in New South Wales* (London: Henry Colburn, 1827), 64.

26 Cunningham, *Two Years in New South Wales*, 63.

27 Stefan Petrow, 'Policing in a Penal Colony: Governor Arthur's Police System in Van Diemen's Land, 1826–1836', *Law and History Review* 18, no. 2 (2000): 351–95.

28 Cunningham, *Two Years in New South Wales,* 65.

29 Harriet King, Letter to her husband in 1827, from *Dear Fanny: Women's Letters to and from New South Wales, 1788–1857,* ed. Helen Heney (Canberra: Australian National University Press, 1985), 105.

30 Shaw, *A Tramp on the Diggings*, 241–2; 268–9.

31 Janet Ranken letter, 1824, from *Dear Fanny*, 77.

32 Alexander Harris, *Settlers and Convicts: Recollections of Sixteen years' Labour in the Australian Backwoods, by an Emigrant Mechanic*, 1847; chapter 8, 'Arrest of Free Emigrants on Suspicion of Being Bushrangers' (Melbourne: Melbourne University Press, 1994), 75–84.

33 Miles Fairburn, *The Ideal Society and Its Enemies: The Foundations of Modern New Zealand Society, 1850–1900* (Auckland: Auckland University Press, 1989), 249.

34 McLeod, 'On the Origins of Consorting Laws', 177.

35 McLeod, 'On the Origins', 118.

36 Gerard Curry, 'A Bundle of Vague Diverse Offences: The Vagrancy Laws with Special Reference to the New Zealand Experience', *Anglo-American Law Review* 1 (1972): 523–36; Julie Kimber, 'Poor Laws: A Historiography of Vagrancy in Australia', *History Compass* 11 (2013): 537–50.

37 Peter Spiller, Jeremy Finn and Richard Boast, *A New Zealand Legal History* (Wellington: Brookers, 1995), 85.

38 Julie Kimber sets out an explanation of the way welfare and charity approaches approximated poor relief in the colonies; see 'Poor Laws', 539. McCalman argues that the English Poor Law criminalized poverty by the 1830s; see *Vandemonians*, 19.

39 Alistair Robinson, *Vagrancy in the Victorian Age, Representing the Wandering Poor in Nineteenth-Century Literature and Culture* (Cambridge: Cambridge University Press, 2022), 12. See also Eccles, 'Furiously Mad', 25–40.

40 Kercher, *Outsiders*, 8–9; 171–9.

41 Anthony Trollope, *Australia and New Zealand*, in two volumes (London: Dawsons of Pall Mall, 1873), 381.

42 Trollope, *Australia and New Zealand*, 382–3.

43 'Vagrancy', *Hobarton Mercury*, 29 February 1856: 3; 'Police Court', *Launceston Examiner*, 9 August 1860: 3.

44 Shaunnagh Dorsett and John McLaren eds., *Legal Histories of the British Empire: Laws, Engagements and Legacies* (London and New York: Routledge, 2014), 3. Georgine Clarsen describes settler-colonial worlds as 'stridently mobile formations' in her introductory essay for a Special Section of *Transfers: Interdisciplinary Journal of Mobility Studies* focused on 'Settler-Colonial Mobilities', 5, no. 3 (December 2015): 2.

45 Paul Ocobock suggests these laws were essentially 'European' in his 'Introduction: Vagrancy and Homelessness in Global and Historical Perspective', in *Cast Out: Vagrancy and Homelessness in Global and Historical Perspective*, ed. A. L. Beier and Paul Ocobock (Ohio: Ohio University Press, 2009), 2.

46 The theme of vulnerability is further examined in Chapter 5 of this book.

47 Lauren Benton, *A Search for Sovereignty: Law and Geography in European Empires, 1400–1900* (New York: Cambridge University Press, 2010), 3, 23.

48 Alan Atkinson, *The Europeans in Australia, Volume Two: Democracy* (Melbourne and New York: Oxford University Press, 2004).

49 Catharine Coleborne, 'Consorting with Others: Vagrancy Laws and Unauthorized Mobility across Colonial Borders in New Zealand from 1877 to 1900', in *Empire and Mobility in the Long Nineteenth Century*, ed. Peter Merriman and David Lambert (Manchester: Manchester University Press, 2020), 136–51. See also Susanne Davies, Vagrancy and the Victorians: The Social Construction of the Vagrant in Melbourne, 1880–1907, PhD Thesis, University of Melbourne, Australia. 1990: 20; 131–2; 137–55.

50 Curry, 'A Bundle of Vague Diverse Offences', 523–36.

51 Ocobock, 'Introduction', in *Cast Out*, 1–2.

52 Anne O'Brien, '"Homeless" Women and the Problem of Visibility: Australia 1900–1940', *Women's History Review* 27, no. 2 (2018): 144.

53 Kociumbus, 'Not Slaves, Not Citizens', 168.

54 Kociumbus, 'Not Slaves, Not Citizens', 280.

55 G. D. Woods, *A History of Criminal Law in New South Wales: The Colonial Period, 1788–1900* (Sydney: Federation Press, 2002), 137–8.

56 Woods, *A History of Criminal Law in New South Wales*, 137–8.

57 Meg Foster writes that laws regulating both vagrancy and bushranging contained 'exceptional' methods for police to control elements of the populations deemed dangerous by colonial authorities. See Meg Foster, 'Protecting the Colony from Its People: Bushranging, Vagrancy, and Social Control in Colonial New South Wales', *Law and History Review* 40 (2022): 656.

58 Kercher, *An Unruly Child*, 105.

59 See Byrne, *Criminal Law and Colonial Subject*, chapter 5, 129–51.

60 Carol Baxter, *Captain Thunderbolt and His Lady: The True Story of Bushrangers Frederick Ward and Mary Anne Bugg* (Sydney: Allen and Unwin, 2011), 27.

61 Kercher, *An Unruly Child*, 105; 108.

62 Another recent study of bushranging examines the life of Mary Ann Ward (also known as Bugg). See chapter 4 of Meg Foster, *Boundary Crossers: The Hidden History of Australian's Other Bushrangers* (Sydney: NewSouth Books, 2022).

63 Ward, *A Tramp to the Diggings*, 229; 245–6.

64 Emma McPherson, *My Experiences in Australia* (London: J. F. Hope, 1860), 126–7.

65 McPherson, *My Experiences in Australia*, 63.

66 Ward, *A Tramp to the Diggings*, 230.

67 For an account of the ways this 1835 law operated – based on secondary research interpretations – see Kimber, 'Poor Laws', 539–42.

68 This is explained further below in this chapter but also by Davies, 'Vagrancy and the Victorians', 131–2.

69 Finnane, 'Law and Regulation', 405.

70 Kimber, 'Poor Law', 538.

71 An Act to Regulate the Police in Certain Towns and Ports within the Island of Van Diemen's Land and to Make More Effectual Provision for The Preservation of the Peace and Good Order Throughout the Said Island and Its Dependencies Generally (2 Vic, No 22), *Hobart Town Gazette*, 28 December 1838, pp. 1209–33. See http://classic.austlii.edu.au/au/legis/tas/num_act/aatrtpictapwtiovdlatmmepftpotpagottsiaidg2vn222076/. The relevant section is LXI, which appears on pp. 1229–30. The summary in the margin states, 'Vagabonds, beggars, prostitutes, &c., or persons found with implements of housebreaking upon them, liable to three months' imprisonment'.

72 'Vagrancy', *Hobarton Guardian*, 23 February 1848: 3.

73 *Colonial Times*, 26 October 1849: 2, 'THE MERCURY', *Hobart Town Daily Mercury*, 14 January 1858: 2.

74 Convict Department, Tasmania, *Rules and Regulations for the Constabulary*, Tasman's Peninsula (Hobart. W. Fletcher, 1868).

75 Kociumbus, 'All That Glitters', 314.

76 'The Thirty Thousand Vagabonds' *Argus*, 26 December 1851: 2.

77 Coleborne, *Insanity, Identity and Empire*, 29–32; 53–68. Michael Cannon, *Melbourne after the Goldrush* (Main Ridge: Loch Haven Books, 1993), 43–50.

78 David Goodman, *Gold Seeking: Victoria and California in the 1850s* (Sydney: Allen & Unwin, 1994), 76–7.

79 A description of the evolution of vagrancy in law forms part of Susanne Davies' thesis about vagrancy in Victoria; see Davies, 'Vagrancy and the Victorians', 129–41.

80 Davies, 'Vagrancy and the Victorians', 135.

81 Sarah Carr, 'Regulating Sexuality in Early Otago, 1848–1867', *New Zealand Journal of History* 50, no. 1 (2016): 41.

82 Carr, 'Regulating Sexuality', 41–2.

83 'Editorial', *The Inangahua Times* (14 January 1885): 2. See also Coleborne, 'Consorting with Others', 141.

84 For more on the way New Zealand parliamentary debates about the legislation were reported, see Catharine Coleborne, 'Law's Mobility: Vagrancy and Imperial Legality in the Trans-Tasman Colonial World', in *New Zealand's Empire*, ed. Katie Pickles and Catharine Coleborne (Manchester UK: Manchester University Press, 2015), 94–5.

85 On vagrancy laws of empire, see Coleborne and O'Connor, 'Vagrancy, Mobility and Colonialism', 375–82.

86 Christina Twomey, 'Vagrancy, Indolence and Ignorance: Race, Class and the Idea of Civilization in the Era of Aboriginal "Protection", Port Phillip 1835–49', in *Writing Colonial Histories: Perspectives on Race, Place and Identity*, ed. Tracey Banivanua Mar and Julie Evans (Basingstoke: Palgrave Macmillan, 2010); Miles Fairburn,

'Vagrants, "Folk Devils" and Nineteenth-Century New Zealand as a Bondless Society', *Historical Studies* 21 (1985): 495–514.

87 Hitchcock, *Vagrancy in English Culture and Society, 1650–1750*, 56.

88 'Police News', *Hobarton Mercury*, 19 March 1855: 2; see this case is also found in Libraries Tasmania Open Repository: https://stors.tas.gov.au/LC247-1-24$init=LC247-1-24P421 where the surname of the defendant is spelt 'Spowage' and he is described as FS (free by servitude). However, he received a conditional pardon in July 1845 (see https://stors.tas.gov.au/CON31-1-39$init=CON31-1-39P204) and could therefore not technically have been free by servitude.

89 See https://stors.tas.gov.au/CON18-1-10$init=CON18-1-10P49 for a record of his arrival as a convict aged 19.

90 See https://stors.tas.gov.au/RGD37-1-3$init=RGD37-1-3P185.

91 See https://stors.tas.gov.au/RGD33-1-1$init=RGD33-1-1-P425; https://stors.tas.gov.au/RGD33-1-2$init=RGD33-1-2-P519; https://stors.tas.gov.au/RGD33-1-2$init=RGD33-1-2-P025 and https://stors.tas.gov.au/RGD35-1-2$init=RGD35-1-2P198.

92 'Police Court', *Hobart Town Advertiser*, 13 June 1855: 3.

93 See https://stors.tas.gov.au/SC32-1-9$init=SC32-1-9P045; https://stors.tas.gov.au/SC32-1-9$init=SC32-1-9P042; also Digital History Tasmania Convict Database record.

94 Digital History Tasmania Convict Database record.

95 See https://stors.tas.gov.au/HAJ1871-63$init=HAJ1871-63_057.

96 See https://stors.tas.gov.au/RGD35-1-15$init=RGD35-1-15P55.

97 Fairburn, *The Ideal Society and Its Enemies*, 249.

98 See Coleborne, 'Consorting with Others'.

99 'The Vagrant Act', *Evening Post*, 5 March 1903: 6.

100 Coleborne, 'Consorting with others'.

101 Davies, 'Vagrancy and the Victorians', 131–2; Davies also cites Michael Sturma's work here. See also Foster, 'Protecting the Colony from Its People', 670.

102 Amanda Nettelbeck, 'Creating the Aboriginal Vagrant: Protective Governance and Indigenous Mobility in Colonial Australia', *Pacific Historical Review* 87, no. 1 (2018): 90–1; Twomey, 'Vagrancy, Indolence and Ignorance'. See also Penny Edmonds, 'The Intimate, Urbanising Frontier: Native Camps and Settler Colonialism's Violent Array of Spaces around Early Melbourne', in *Making Settler Colonial Space: Perspectives on Race, Place and Identity*, ed. Penelope Edmonds and Tracy Banivanua-Mar (Basingstoke: Palgrave Macmillan, 2010), 44.

103 Lynette Russell, '"Tickpen", "Boro Boro": Aboriginal Economic Engagements in Early Melbourne', in *Settler Colonial Governance in Nineteenth-Century Victoria*, ed. Leigh Boucher and Lynette Russell (Canberra: ANU Press and Aboriginal History, 2015), 37–8.

104 Edmonds, 'The Intimate, Urbanising Frontier', 37–8.
105 Nettelbeck, 'Creating the Aboriginal Vagrant', 83.
106 Twomey, 'Vagrancy, Indolence and Ignorance', 99–100. See also Nan Seuffert, 'Civilisation, Settlers and Wanderers: Law, Politics and Mobility in Nineteenth-Century New Zealand and Australia', *Law Text Culture* 15 (2011): 10–44.
107 Nettelbeck, 'Creating the Aboriginal Vagrant', 94.
108 Charley Ambert, *NSW Police Gazette,* 22 June 1878, Kiama Police Station.
109 'Local news: Police Court', *Illawarra Mercury*, 12 May 1876: 2.
110 'Saturday, June 22', *Kiama Independent* and *Shoalhaven Advertiser*, Tuesday 25 June 1878: 2.
111 John Johnson, 11 April 1876, Goulburn Police Station; Eliza White, 23 March 1878, Cowra Police Station; Thomas Rowe, 20 May 1879, Dubbo Police Station: *NSW Police Gazette.*
112 Nettelbeck, 'Creating the Aboriginal Vagrant', 90–1.
113 Nettelbeck, 'Creating the Aboriginal Vagrant', 98–9.
114 27 January 1879, Hone Paika, *Police Gazette.*
115 7 October 1879, *Police Gazette*; *New Zealand Herald,* 29 October 1879. On Māori insane, see: Lorelle Burke and Catharine Coleborne, 'Insanity and Ethnicity in New Zealand: Māori Encounters with the Auckland Mental Hospital, 1860–1900', *History of Psychiatry* 22, no. 3 (September 2011): 285–301.
116 Sarah Downes, alias Rahena Taone, 15 January 1881; 22 March 1881, *NZPG.*
117 *Evening Post,* 11 August 1881.
118 Foster examines the question of Mary Ann's ethnicity and identity in *Boundary Crossers*, chapter 4.
119 Mary Anne first came to my attention in *Bignold's Police Offences and Vagrancy Acts* (1951), where the judicial opinion about her case was reproduced. She also appears in the data set for NSW vagrants as Mary Anne Ward in the account of her arrest and charge in the *NSW Police Gazette.*
120 As I uncovered more about Mary Ann, I discovered that she has been written about several times: in book chapters by David Roberts and Carol Baxter about her association with Thunderbolt, in extended research about the pair by Carol Baxter, in an Honours thesis about her life as Mary Ann Bugg by Kali Bierens at the University of Tasmania in 2008, and as a character in a play by Julie Janson called 'Black Mary' first performed in at the Sydney Street Theatre Space in 1996. Artworks featuring Mary Anne were shown as part of an exhibition: 'Female Drivers' Maitland Regional Art Gallery, NSW, 28 May–28 August 2022: https://mrag.org.au/exhibition/female-drivers/. Mary Anne is depicted as a woman outlaw heroine by artist Bern Emmerichs, and in poetry by Joe Pascoe.
121 David Andrew Roberts and Carol Baxter, '"Mrs Thunderbolt": Setting the Record Straight on the Life and Times of Mary Ann Bugg', *Journal of the Royal Australian Historical Society* 99, Part 1 (2013): 55–7.

122 Roberts and Baxter, 'Mrs Thunderbolt', 58.

123 See, for instance, Kali Bierens, The Captain's Lady: Mary Ann Bugg, Unpublished Honours Thesis in Aboriginal Studies, University of Tasmania, 2008, 21; 24.

124 William Monckton, *Three Years with Thunderbolt*, ed. Ambrose Pratt (Melbourne: Cassell and Co., 1907), 70.

125 Baxter, *Thunderbolt and His Lady*, 252–3.

126 Bierens, *The Captain's Lady*, 25–6.

127 Bierens, *The Captain's Lady*, 26–7; see also David Buchanan, https://adb.anu.edu.au/biography/buchanan-david-3099 URL accessed 24 July 2023.

128 Bierens, *The Captain's Lady*, 27.

129 This point is also made by Bierens, who shows that the case was still cited in legal texts in the late twentieth century; see *The Captain's Lady*, 28, n. 11.

130 *Bignold's Police Offences and Vagrancy Acts*, 167–8.

131 'Paterson Justice', Original correspondence, *Maitland Mercury and Hunter River General Advertiser*, 14 February 1867: 3.

132 Coleborne and O'Connor, 'Vagrancy, Mobility and Colonialism', 374–89. See also Foster, *Boundary Crossers*, chapter 4.

133 Places of origin/birthplaces and ethnicity as categories are not analysed in this book but offer enormous potential for future data analysis.

134 M. B. Schedvin and C. B. Schedvin, 'The Nomadic Tribes of Urban Britain: A Prelude to Botany Bay', *Historical Studies* 18, no. 71 (1978): 260.

135 Schedvin and Schedvin, 'The Nomadic Tribes of Urban Britain', 260; 264.

136 Chapters in *Law, History, Colonialism: The Reach of Empire*, ed. Diane Kirkby and Catharine Coleborne (Manchester: Manchester University Press, 2001; 2010) show the vast collaborative aspect to lawmaking across empire.

137 Lauren Benton, *Law and Colonial Cultures: Legal Regimes in World History, 1400–1900* (Cambridge and New York: Cambridge University Press, 2002), 3. See also Alannah Tomkins and Catharine Coleborne, 'Professional Migration, Occupational Challenge, and Mental Health: Medical Practitioners in New Zealand, 1850s–1890s', *Social History of Medicine* 34, no. 3 (2021); D. Lambert and A. Lester eds., *Colonial Lives across the British Empire: Imperial Careering in the Long Nineteenth Century* (New York: Cambridge University Press, 2006).

138 Paul Ocobock suggests these laws were essentially 'European' in his 'Introduction: Vagrancy and Homelessness in Global and Historical Perspective', 2.

139 Ocobock, *Cast Out*, 13.

140 Occupational categories are not analysed in this book but offer enormous potential for future data analysis.

141 Philippa Levine, *Prostitution, Race and Politics: Policing Venereal Disease in the British Empire* (New York and London: Routledge, 2003), 187.

142 Penny Edmonds, *Urbanizing Frontiers: Indigenous Peoples and Settlers in 19th-Century Pacific Rim Cities* (Toronto: UBC Press, 2010), 244.

143 Fairburn, *The Ideal Society and Its Enemies*, 195–6.

144 John Pratt, 'The Dark Side of Paradise: Explaining New Zealand's History of High Imprisonment', *British Journal of criminology* 46, no. 4 (2006): 541–60.

145 Fairburn, *The Ideal Society and Its Enemies*, 134–5.

Chapter 3

1 Peter Cunningham, *Two Years in New South Wales* (London: Henry Colburn, 1827), 66.

2 James Boyce, *Van Diemen's Land* (Melbourne: Black Inc., 2008), 218.

3 Paula Jane Byrne, 'Mapping Power: Yass and the Law in the 1850s', *Law & History* 9, no. 1 (2022).

4 Mark Finnane and Stephen Garton, 'The Work of Policing: Social Relations and the Criminal Justice System in Queensland 1880–1914, Part One', *Labour History* 62 (May 1992): 64.

5 Boyce, *Van Diemen's Land*, 217.

6 Finnane and Garton, 'The Work of Policing', 59.

7 John Shaw, *A Tramp to the Diggings* (London: Richard Bentley, 1852), 299.

8 Mark Finnane, '"Absolutely Free"? Freedom of Movement and "The Police Power" in Federation Australia', *Australian Historical Studies* 54, no. 1 (2023): 6.

9 Boyce, *Van Diemen's Land*, 219.

10 Miles Fairburn, 'Vagrants, "Folk Devils" and Nineteenth-Century New Zealand as a Bondless Society', *Historical Studies* 21, no. 85 (October 1985): 50.

11 Tony Ballantyne, 'Mobility, Empire, Colonisation', *History Australia* 11, no. 2 (2014): 23.

12 Fairburn, 'Vagrants, "Folk Devils" and Nineteenth-Century New Zealand', 50.

13 Susanne Davies, Vagrancy and the Victorians: The Social Construction of the Vagrant in Melbourne, 1880–1907, Unpublished PhD Thesis in History, University of Melbourne, 1990, 145.

14 Finnane and Garton, 'The Work of Policing', 64; 68–9.

15 Finnane and Garton, 'The Work of Policing', 68–9.

16 Finnane and Garton, 'The Work of Policing', 64.

17 Finnane and Garton, 'The Work of Policing', 65; see also S. K. Mukerjee et al., *Crime and Punishment in the Colonies: A Statistical Profile* (Kensington, NSW: History project Inc., 1986).

18 Mark Finnane, 'The Politics of Police Powers: The Making of the Police Offences Acts', in *Policing in Australia: Historical Perspectives*, ed. M. Finnane (Kensington: UNSW Press, 1987), 88–113.

19 Alana Piper and Lisa Durnian, 'Theft on Trial: Prosecution, Conviction and Sentencing Patterns in Colonial Victoria and Western Australia', *Australia and New*

Zealand Journal of Criminology 50, no. 1 (2017): 5–22; John Pratt, 'The Dark Side of Paradise: Explaining New Zealand's History of High Imprisonment', *British Journal of Criminology* 46, no. 4 (2006): 541–60.

20 Byrne, 'Mapping Power: Yass and the Law in the 1850s', 131.

21 Catharine Coleborne, 'Passage to the Asylum: The Role of Police in Committals of the Insane in Victoria, Australia, 1848–1900', in *The Confinement of the Insane, 1800–1965: International Perspectives,* ed. Roy Porter and David Wright (Cambridge, UK: Cambridge University Press, 2003), 129–48; Richard Hill, *The History of Policing in New Zealand, Volume One. Policing the Colonial Frontier* (Wellington: Historical Publications Branch, Department of Internal Affairs, 1986).

22 Histories of policing before 1850 include Michael Sturma's account in *Vice in a Vicious Society: Crime and Convicts in Mid-nineteenth Century New South Wales* (St Lucia: University of Queensland Press, 1983), 163–73.

23 Grace Karskens, *The Rocks: Life in Early Sydney* (Carlton: Melbourne University Press, 1997), 197.

24 Karskens, *The Rocks*, 197.

25 New South Wales Police, *Rules and Regulations for the Government and Guidance of the Metropolitan Police Force of New South Wales* (Sydney: W. W. Davies, Government Printing Office, 1853). SLNSW 352.2/14A1.

26 New South Wales Police, *Rules and Regulations for the Government and Guidance of the Metropolitan Police Force of New South Wales,* 9.

27 Sturma, *Vice in a Vicious Society*, 166.

28 New South Wales Police, *Rules and Regulations for the Government and Guidance of the Metropolitan Police Force of New South Wales,* 67–8.

29 New South Wales Police, *Rules and Regulations for the Government and Guidance of the Metropolitan Police Force of New South Wales,* 69–70.

30 New South Wales Police, *Rules and Regulations for the Government and Guidance of the Metropolitan Police Force of New South Wales,* 71–2. See Caroline Daley, 'A Gendered Domain: Leisure in Auckland, 1890–1940', in *The Gendered Kiwi,* ed. Caroline Daley and Deborah Montgomerie (Auckland: Auckland University Press, 1999), 87–112.

31 Archives New Zealand, Christchurch. CAAR 19946/ R8417798. Police to Provincial Secretary; CAAR 19936/R17560619.

32 *Rules for the Management of the Police Force of NSW*, Thomas Richards, Government Printer 1862; *General Instructions for the Guidance of the Police Force,* Issued by the Inspector General, Sydney, 1862; *Manual for Members of the Police Force of Enactments Affecting Their Duties,* Thomas Richards, Government Printer Sydney 1862.

33 *Rules for the Management of the Police Force of NSW,* 44–5.

34 *Rules for the Management of the Police Force of NSW*, 50–3.

35 New South Wales Police, *Rules and Regulations for the Government and Guidance of the Metropolitan Police Force of New South Wales,* 6.

36 New South Wales Police, *Rules and Regulations for the Government and Guidance of the Metropolitan Police Force of New South Wales*, 7.
37 Public Record Office of Victoria (PROV), Victoria Police, VA724.
38 *Manual of Police Regulations for the Guidance of the Constabulary of Victoria* (Melbourne: John Ferres, 1856). RARELT 351.74 V66M Victoria, 1856, 9–10
39 *Manual of Police Regulations*, Victoria, 1856, 10–1
40 *Manual of Police Regulations*, Victoria, 1856, 74–81.
41 Coleborne, 'Passage to the asylum', 137–40.
42 Coleborne, 'Passage to the Asylum', 138.
43 Peter Adams, 'History of Policing in Tasmania', *Tasmania Police Journal* (March 1979): 30.
44 Stefan Petrow, 'Policing in a Penal Colony: Governor Arthur's Police System in Van Diemen's Land, 1826–1836', *Law and History Review*, 18, no. 2 (2000): 351–95. See also 'Creating an Orderly Society: The Hobart Municipal Police 1880–1898' *Labour History* 78 (1998): 175–94.
45 NSW Police Department, 'Rules for the Management of the Police Force of New South Wales', 1864, 16–18. SLNSW 363.23/1.
46 See 'NSW Police Uniforms 1863–1918', Justice & Police Museum Collection, JP99/0442.
47 *Manual of Police Regulations*, Victoria, 1856, 19.
48 'The vagrant act', *Evening Post*, 5 March 1903: 6.
49 Davies, 'Vagrancy and the Victorians', 155; Coleborne, 'Passage to the asylum', 133–48.
50 'Bigamy Case at Dunedin', *Globe*, 5 July 1875: 3.
51 R. V. Charlotte Schmid, Supreme Court Dunedin, New Zealand's Lost Cases; Constable Bevan's name is spelt as 'Bevan' in the entry and in the newspapers, but as Bevin's in a description of his career here: https://otagotaphophile.blogspot.com/2018/02/honour-600-1060-sergeant-major-john.html
52 For more about travel writing, see Chapter 6.
53 *Manual of Police Regulations*, Victoria 1856, 75–6.
54 General Instructions for the Guidance of the Police Force, issued by the Inspector General, Sydney, 1862. SLNSW MF 1 Q 20, 46. See also *Manual for Members of the Police Force of Enactments Affecting their Duties*, Thomas Richards, Government Printer, Sydney, 1862, SLNSW MF 1 Q 20.
55 *Regulations for the Guidance of the Constabulary* (Victoria, 1873), p. 79.
56 Coleborne, 'Passage to the asylum', 129–48.
57 https://www.familysearch.org/en/wiki/Use_of_Aliases_-_an_Overview, URL accessed 13 September 2022.
58 https://mortimerhistory.com/the-origin-of-alias-names/, URL accessed 13 September 2022; https://www.familysearch.org/en/wiki/Use_of_Aliases_-_an_Overview, URL accessed 13 September 2022.

59 'Photography and Crime', *Australasian Photographic Review*, 21 July 1903: 240.
60 AAAC, Box 15, Photographs of Prisoners, 1902–6, P27 3.
61 Historical Publications Branch, Police Records. Woodville Jail Book, 1882–96 W3539, Wellington, 140.
62 N. J. Crowson, 'Tramps' Tales: Discovering the Life-Stories of Late Victorian and Edwardian Vagrants', *English Historical Review* 125, no. 577 (2020): 1490–1.
63 Crowson, 'Tramps' Tales', 1490. See also Alistair Robinson, *Vagrancy in the Victorian Age: Representing the Wandering Poor in Nineteenth-Century Literature and Culture* (Cambridge: Cambridge University Press, 2022), 12.
64 *New South Wales Police Gazette*, 27 April 1876, Hay PS; see also Jane Maxwell, 8 November 1882.
65 Nancy Cushing, *A History of Crime in Australia: Australian Underworlds* (London and New York: Routledge, 2023), 110.
66 Finnane, '"Absolutely Free"? Freedom of Movement and "The Police Power" in Federation Australia', 4.
67 See https://www.police.govt.nz/about-us/history/museum/exhibitions/suspicious-looking-19th-century-mug-shots/introduction-mug-shots-new-zealand, URL accessed 14 September 2022.
68 Archives New Zealand Factsheet, *Police Gazettes*.
69 Collections of mugshots exhibited in virtual museums include https://vagrantsandmurderesses.com/; https://dictionaryofsydney.org/blog/mugshots_1920s_style
70 Tim Cresswell, *The Tramp in America* (London: Reaktion Books, 2001), 214.
71 Mark Finnane, 'Law and Regulation', in *The Cambridge History of Australia: Volume 1: Indigenous and Colonial Australia*, ed. Alison Bashford and Stuart McIntyre (Cambridge: Cambridge University Press, 2013), 404–5.
72 See Angela Hawk, 'Going "Mad" in Gold Country: Migrant Populations and the Problem of Containment in Pacific Mining Boom Regions', *Pacific Historical Review* 80, no. 1 (2011): 64–96; Heather Holst, 'Equal Before the Law? The Chinese in the Nineteenth-Century Castlemaine Police Courts', *Journal of Australian Colonial History* 6 [special issue: Active Voices, Hidden Histories: the Chinese in Colonial Australia] (2004): 113–36; and Coleborne, 'Passage to the asylum', 143–5.
73 Robinson, *Vagrancy in the Victorian Age*, 103.
74 Sturma, *Vice in a Vicious Society*, 173.
75 'Offences Not Otherwise Described', *New South Wales Police Gazette and Weekly Record of Crime*, no. 37 (15 September 1875): 270.
76 On the bodies of women vagrants, see Charlotte Macdonald, 'Crime and Punishment in New Zealand, 1840–1913: A Gendered History', *New Zealand Journal of History* 23, no. 1 (1989): 15.
77 13 September 1899, *New Zealand Police Gazette*.
78 Macdonald, 'Crime and Punishment in New Zealand, 1840–1913', 15.

79 'An Appeal for "Vagrants"', *Argus*, 22 October 1863: 7.

80 The entry for Rosa Lake appears in the *New Zealand Police Gazette*, 14 January 1880. Lake was also arrested on 17 February 1879.

81 https://www.sciencedirect.com/science/article/pii/S1388245721005654 Charcot was observing twitching faces and bodies.

82 *The Cambridge History of the English Language*, 309; the example is used in relation to writer James Hardy Vaux. See also 'old lag', Ken Gelder and Rachael Weaver, *Colonial Australian Fiction: Character Types, Social Formations and the Colonial Economy* (Sydney: Sydney University Press, 2017), 15.

83 William Burrows, *Adventures of a Mounted Trooper* (London: Routledge, Warne and Routledge, 1859), 28–9.

84 John Buckley Castieau, 1 September 1874, *The Difficulties of My Position: The Diaries of Prison Governor John Buckley Castieau 1855–1884*, ed. with an introduction by Mark Finnane (Canberra: National Library of Australia, 2004), 264.

85 Anon, 'IX. Prisoner Discharged Free', *New South Wales Police Gazette and Weekly Record of Crime*, no. 51 (23 December 1863): 393.

86 Castieau, 15 January 1874: *The Difficulties of My Position*, 225.

87 Castieau, 15 November 1874: *The Difficulties of My Position*, 266.

88 Castieau, 6 August 1855: *The Difficulties of My Position*, 15.

89 'POLICE COURT', *Cornwall Chronicle*, 13 May 1863: 5.

90 'POLICE COURT', *Mercury*, 24 October 1863: 2.

91 New South Wales, *Rules and Regulations for Police* 1853, 86.

92 Dean Wilson, 'Police Poverty: Destitution and Police Work in Melbourne, 1880–1910', *Australian Historical Studies* 125 (2009): 99.

93 Report of the Committee of Inquiry into Female Convict Prison Discipline, April 1841, Evidence 248, 182.

94 See NSW State Archives collection, Museums of History NSW, NRS 906 Colonial Secretary's Special Bundles: Persons out of employment in Sydney, 1866 [4/581.2], https://mhnsw.au/indexes/unemployment/unemployed-in-sydney/.

95 'The Unemployed in Sydney', *Sydney Mail*, 20 October 1866: 3.

96 John Stanley James, 'The Outcasts of Melbourne', 1876.

97 Robinson, *Vagrancy in the Victorian Age*, 13. In London the police courts were staffed by amateur magistrates, 13.

98 John Freeman, *Lights and Shadows of Melbourne Life* (London: Sampson Low, Marston, Searle, and Rivington Ltd, 1888), 42.

99 Robinson, *Vagrancy in the Victorian Age*, 102.

100 *NSW Rules and Regulations* 1864, 12–3.

101 Byrne, 'Yass and the law in the 1850s', 156.

102 Byrne, 'Yass and the law in the 1850s', 156.

103 'The Definition of Vagrancy: A Legal Point', *Star*, 10 August 1900: 3.

104 AAAC, Box 15, Photographs of Prisoners, 1902–6, P27 3.

105 *New Zealand Police Gazette,* 10 June 1896, 103.

106 Historical Publications Branch, Police Records. Woodville Jail Book, 1882–96 W3539, Wellington, 29; 102; 134; 142; 177.

107 Catharine Coleborne, *Insanity, Identity and Empire: Colonial Institutional Confinement in Australia and New Zealand, 1870–1910* (Manchester UK: Manchester University Press, 2015); Coleborne, 'Mobility Stopped in Its Tracks: Narratives of the Failures of the Mobile in the Trans-Tasman World of the Nineteenth Century', *Transfers: Interdisciplinary Journal of Mobility Studies* 5, no. 3 (Winter 2015): 87–103; and Coleborne, 'Regulating "Mobility" and Masculinity through Institutions in Colonial Victoria, 1870s–1890s', *Law, Text, Culture* 15 (December 2011): 45–71.

108 'LOCAL AND GENERAL', *Daily Telegraph* (Launceston), 7 February 1906: 5.

109 Julie Kimber, '"A Nuisance to the Community": Policing the Vagrant Woman', *Journal of Australian Studies* 34, no. 3 (2010): 275–93; Alana Piper and Victoria Nagy, 'Versatile Offending: Criminal Careers of Female Prisoners in Australia, 1860–1920', *Journal of Interdisciplinary History* 48, no. 2 (2017): 187–210.

110 Victoria Nagy and Alana Piper, 'Imprisonment of Female Urban and Rural Offenders in Victoria, 1860–1920', *International Journal for Crime, Justice and Social Democracy* 8, no. 1 (2019): 100–115.

111 John Kelly, alias Kelly the Rake, age sixty-four, was convicted of vagrancy and drunkenness in December 1899 at Reefton and had numerous prior convictions. He was described as 'The Famous Kelly the Rake, a man who has visited every lock-up in New Zealand almost' (*Otago Daily Times*, 9 October 1911), and he had 107 convictions by 1914. He was a labourer who also used the alias James McCarthy. He appears in the data set for vagrancy prosecutions in New Zealand: 5 July 1900.

112 Several entries appear in the data set for New Zealand for Margaret Williams.

113 'Ashburton - Monday', *Ashburton Guardian,* 23 November 1891: 2.

114 A police mugshot of Lawson taken 12 July 1890 is found at: https://www.police.govt.nz/about-us/history-museum/museum/exhibitions/suspicious-looking-mug-shots.

115 Christina Lawson appears in the data sampled for New Zealand from the New Zealand Police Gazettes (1877–1900).

116 'The Management of Dunedin Gaol', *Appendices to the Journal of the House of Representatives AJHR*, 1883 H-31, 1–2.

117 *New Zealand Police Gazette* record in database; Year 1881.

118 'The Courts To-day', *Evening Star*, 21 February 1881: 2; 'City Police Court', *Otago Daily Times*, 19 April 1881: 3.

119 Macdonald, 'Crime and Punishment in New Zealand', 13.

120 Macdonald, 'Crime and Punishment in New Zealand', 15.

121 'City Police Court: Larceny', *Otago Daily Times*, 6 August 1883: 3.

122 'City Police Court: Breach of the Peace; Prostitution', *Otago Daily Times*, 6 February 1884: 4.

123 'Magistrate's Court, THIS DAY: Drunkenness', *Evening Post*, 12 May 1886: 3.

124 The annual reports of the Armed Constabulary of the Police Force in New Zealand in the *AJHR* contain lists of apprehensions and convictions; this evidence was presented to the Select Committee established to investigate the 'social evil' of prostitution in 1869. They also reported on the number of brothels in cities and their inhabitants. See Charlotte MacDonald, 'The "Social Evil": Prostitution and the Passage of the Contagious Diseases Act (1869)', in *Women in History: Essays on European Women in New Zealand*, ed. Barbara Brookes, Charlotte MacDonald and Margaret Tennant (Wellington: Allen & Unwin/Port Nicholson Press, 1986), 17; 30–3.

125 'Magistrate's Court, THIS DAY: Drunkenness', *Evening Post*, 6 December 1886: 2.

126 'Been in All Dominion Gaols: Over 120 Convictions', *Dominion*, 5 February 1912: 4.

127 'The Police Force of the Colony', *AJHR*, 1895, H-28, 2.

128 https://teara.govt.nz/en/prisons/page-2, URL accessed 29 August 2022.

129 'The Management of Dunedin Gaol', *AJHR*, 1883 H-31, 1–2.

130 'Been in All Dominion Gaols: Over 120 Convictions', *Dominion*, 5 February 1912: 4.

131 'Magisterial', *Star*, 1 August 1895: 3; 'Police Court: Drunkenness', *Press*, 25 March 1904: 2; 'Magistrate's Court: Drunkenness', *Press*, 2 October 1905: 3; 'Magisterial: This Day', *Star*, 15 April 1893: 3; 'Magistrate's Court, *Evening Post*, 15 November 1911: 8.

132 'A dash for liberty', *New Zealand Truth*, 9 May 1908: 5. The Samaritan Home was opened in the former Addington Gaol in 1896 and was operated by the Anglican Church and the Charitable Aid Board until in 1911, functioning as a 'half-way house' for both women and men. In 1911, women were transferred to the female refuge and the building was taken over by the government; see National Archives New Zealand record at https://www.archives.govt.nz/research-guidance/research-guides/welfare/charitable-aid-and-welfare-records-christchurch URL accessed 31 July 2023. See also Margaret Tennant, 'Elderly Indigents and Old Men's Homes 1880–1920', *New Zealand Journal of History* 17, no. 1 (1983): 5.

133 Historian Margaret Tennant has outlined the different organizations that emerged in New Zealand between the 1880s and 1910 to support women and men released from prisons; see *The Fabric of Welfare: Voluntary Organisations, Government and Welfare in New Zealand, 1840–2005* (Wellington: Bridget Williams Books, 2007), 54–5.

134 Ernest M. Pollock and A. M. Latter, 'Legislation on Inebriates in England and the Colonies', *British Institute of International and Comparative Law* 2, no. 2 (1900): 289–93.

135 Bronwyn Morrison, 'Controlling the "Hopeless": Re-visioning the History of Female Inebriate Institutions c. 1870–1920', in *Punishment and Control in Historical Perspective,* ed. Helen Johnston (London: Palgrave Macmillan, 2008), 138.
136 See https://archives.salvationarmy.org.nz/article/island-retreats-inebriates, URL accessed 31 August 2022.
137 'Magisterial: An incorrigible', *Lyttelton Times,* 14 August 1907: 5.
138 'A dash for liberty', *New Zealand Truth*, 9 May 1908: 5.
139 'A Social Canker', *New Zealand Truth*, 11 September 1909: 6.
140 'A Social Canker', *New Zealand Truth*, 11 September 1909: 6.
141 'An Old Offender', *Star,* 24 June 1910: 3.
142 On inebriate retreats, see: https://prov.vic.gov.au/about-us/our-blog/inebriate-retreats.
143 MacDonald, 'The "Social Evil"': 21.
144 'One hundred and eighty-three convictions', *Lyttelton Times*, 5 June 1916: 9.
145 'One hundred and eighty-three convictions', *Lyttelton Times*, 5 June 1916: 9.
146 Contemporaries noticed that this was how policing functioned in relation to people who had disability and illness; see 'An appeal for "vagrants"', *Argus*, 22 October 1863: 7.
147 'An Old Offender', *Star,* 24 June 1910: 3.
148 Magistrate's Court, 'Today's cases', *Sun*, 17 April 1920: 7.
149 Tanya Evans, *Fractured Families: Life on the Margins in Colonial New South Wales* (Sydney: UNSW Press, 2015), 178–9.
150 Anne O'Brien, '"Homeless" Women and the Problem of Visibility: Australia 1900–1940', *Women's History Review* 27, no. 2 (2018): 144.

Chapter 4

1 Historians examining institutional records, such as those of the English workhouse, find evidence of agency as expressed by 'inmates'; see Carol Beardmore, '"This Man Really Is an Intolerable Pest": Perceptions and Treatment of the Disabled in the Workhouse, 1834–1900', *Family & Community History* 25, no. 2 (2022): 132. My own work has also examined the idea of 'resistance' in the hospitals for the insane, as well as expressions of selfhood in that context; see Coleborne, *Reading 'Madness': Gender and Difference in the Colonial Asylum in Victoria, Australia, 1848–1880s* (Perth: API Network and Curtin University Australia Research Centre, 2007). Tim Cresswell interprets mobility itself as a form of resistance in his 'The Production of Mobilities', *New Formations* 43 (2001): 15.
2 See, for instance, Anthony Giddens, *Sociology: A Brief but Critical Introduction* (London: Macmillan, 1982), 97–119.

3 Lynette Russell, '"Tickpen", "Boro Boro": Aboriginal Economic Engagements in Early Melbourne', in *Settler Colonial Governance in Nineteenth-Century Victoria*, ed. Leigh Boucher and Lynette Russell (Canberra: ANU Press and Aboriginal History, 2015), 33, 36, 44.
4 Georg Simmel, 'The Stranger', in *Georg Simmel: On Individuality and Social Forms*, ed. Donald Levine (Chicago: University of Chicago Press, 1971), 143–50.
5 John Ward, *A Tramp on the Diggings* (London: Richard Bentley, 1852), 230.
6 Mark Freeman, '"Journeys into Poverty Kingdom": Complete Participation and the British Vagrant', *History Workshop Journal* 52 (2001): 99–121; see also Susanne Davies, Vagrancy and the Victorians: The Social Construction of the Vagrant in Melbourne, 1880–1907. PhD Thesis, University of Melbourne, Australia, 1990, 60, 62–3.
7 Graeme Davison and David Dunstan, '"This Moral Pandemonium": Images of Low Life', in *The Outcasts of Melbourne: Essays in Social History*, ed. Graeme Davison, David Dunstan and Chris McConville (Sydney: Allen & Unwin, 1985), 29–31.
8 John Stanley James, 'The Outcasts of Melbourne', in *The Vagabond Papers*, First published in 5 v. by George Robertson 1877–8, ed. Michael Cannon (Melbourne: Melbourne University Press, 1969); John Freeman, *Lights and Shadows of Melbourne Life* (London: Sampson Low, Marston, Searle, and Rivington Ltd, 1888). See also the 'female vagabond', Catherine Hay Thomson, who wrote about colonial women and children in the social and welfare institutions she observed, as well as about the Melbourne Hospital, in her different essays.
9 Mary Higgs, *Five Days and Five Nights as a Tramp among Tramps* (London: Heywood, 1904); see Simon Featherstone, 'Tramping: The Cult of the Vagabond in Early Twentieth-Century England', in *Idleness, Indolence and Leisure in English Literature*, ed. Monika Fludernik and Miriam Nandi (Basingstoke: Palgrave Macmillan, 2014), 245–6.
10 Catherine Hay Thompson, 'The Female Side of Kew Asylum', *The Argus*, 26 March 1886, 6.
11 James, 'The Outcasts of Melbourne', 30.
12 James, 'The Outcasts of Melbourne', 30.
13 James, 'The Outcasts of Melbourne', 31.
14 James, 'The Outcasts of Melbourne', 34.
15 Freeman, *Lights and Shadows of Melbourne Life*.
16 Freeman, *Lights and Shadows of Melbourne Life*, 14; 10; 17; 206–12.
17 Freeman, *Lights and Shadows of Melbourne Life*, 111, 122.
18 Freeman, *Lights and Shadows of Melbourne Life*, 38–9.
19 David Hitchcock, 'A Typology of Travellers: Migration, Justice and Vagrancy in Warwickshire, 1670–1730', *Rural History* 23, no. 1 (2012): 21–39.
20 Freeman also refers to the Romany, see *Lights and Shadows of Melbourne Life*, 209.
21 See Melissa Bellanta, *Larrikins: A History* (St Lucia, Queensland: University of Queensland Press, 2012).

22 Victoria Nagy and Alana Piper, 'Imprisonment of Female Urban and Rural Offenders in Victoria, 1860–1920', *International Journal for Crime, Justice and Social Democracy* 8, no. 1 (2019): 106.
23 Colin G. Pooley and Jean Turnbull, *Migration and Mobility in Britain since the Eighteenth Century* (London: UCL Press, 1998); Colin G. Pooley, 'The Mobility of Criminals in North-West England, c 1880s–1910', *Local Population Studies* 53 (1994): 14–28.
24 Shirley Fisher, 'The Family and the Sydney Economy in the Late Nineteenth Century', in *Families in Colonial Australia*, ed. Patricia Grimshaw, Chris McConville and Ellen McEwen (Sydney: Allen & Unwin, 1985), 156.
25 Fisher, 'The Family and the Sydney Economy', 156.
26 Fisher, 'The Family and the Sydney Economy', 155.
27 Fisher, 'The Family and the Sydney Economy', 155.
28 Fisher, 'The Family and the Sydney Economy', 154–6.
29 Davison, Dunstan and McConville eds., *The Outcasts of Melbourne*: 15.
30 James Boyce, *Van Diemen's Land* (Melbourne: Black Inc., 2008), 228.
31 'POLICE COURT', *Mercury*, 10 October 1863: 2.
32 'POLICE COURT', *Mercury*, 10 October 1863: 2.
33 Frances Steel, *Oceania under Steam: Sea Transport and the Cultures of Colonialism, c. 1870–1914* (Manchester: Manchester University Press, 2011), 88.
34 Steel, *Oceania under Steam*, 88.
35 *New Zealand Police Gazette*, 9 November 1881, William Robertson.
36 Steel, *Oceania under Steam*, 89.
37 Andrew Brown-May, *Melbourne Street Life* (Melbourne: Australian Scholarly Publishing, 2017), 72–3; 75–6.
38 F. B. Smith, 'Disputes about Typhoid Fever in Victoria in the 1870s', *Health & History* 4, no. 2 (2002): 1–2.
39 Lloyd Robson, *A Short History of Tasmania*, updated by Michael Roe (Melbourne: Oxford University Press, 1997), 46–7; 48–9.
40 Dean Wilson, 'Community and Gender in Victorian Auckland', *New Zealand Journal of History* 30, no. 1 (1996): 24–42.
41 Brown-May, *Melbourne Street Life*, 56–7.
42 Alana Jayne Piper and Victoria Nagy, 'Versatile Offending: Criminal Careers of Female Prisoners in Australia, 1860–1920', *Journal of Interdisciplinary History* 48, no. 2 (2017): 205–6.
43 City of Sydney Archives, Letters received – Municipal Council, 18 June 1863, vol 62, 26/62/540, https://archives.cityofsydney.nsw.gov.au/nodes/view/1083736.
44 City of Sydney Archives, Letters received – Municipal Council of Sydney, 11 September 1877, vol 146, A-00302322, https://archives.cityofsydney.nsw.gov.au/nodes/view/1104242#idx1564174.

45 City of Sydney Archives, Letters received – Municipal Council, 15 October 1879, vol 160, 26/160/1230, ID A-00303896, https://archives.cityofsydney.nsw.gov.au/nodes/view/1105815.
46 Davies, 'Vagrancy and the Victorians', 102–4.
47 See Miles Fairburn, *The Ideal Society: The Foundations of Modern New Zealand Society, 1850–1900* (Auckland: Auckland University Press, 1989), 249.
48 Freeman, *Lights and Shadows of Melbourne Life*, 37–8.
49 Boyce, *Van Diemen's Land*, 119–20.
50 Grace Karskens, *The Rocks: Life in Early Sydney* (Carlton: Melbourne University Press, 1997), 72–4; 152–3. See also Grace Karskens, 'Revisiting the Worldview: The Archaeology of Convict Households in Sydney's Rocks Neighbourhood', *Historical Archaeology* 37, no. 1 (2003): 34–55.
51 Victoria Nagy, 'The Health and Medical Needs of Victoria's Older Female Prisoners, 1860–1920', Prison Medicine: Health and Incarceration in History Conference, University of Wollongong, May 2019, 4.
52 John Singleton, *A Narrative of Incidents in the Eventful Life of a Physician* (Melbourne: M.L. Hutchinson, 1891), 223.
53 Inspector for the Insane, Report on the Lunatics Asylums of New Zealand for 1881, *Appendices to the Journal of the House of Representatives* (*AJHR*), 6.
54 PROV, VPRS7400 Yarra Bend Asylum, Patient casebooks, /P1/Unit 14, 14 March 1906.
55 National Archives, Auckland, YCAA Auckland Asylum, 1048/9 29, 15 July 1900.
56 David Roth, Life, Death and Deliverance at Callan Park Hospital for the Insane 1877 to 1923, Unpublished PhD Thesis in History, Australian National University, 2020, 152–6.
57 Michael Lever, 'When Absence Is the Artifact: Unmarked Graves in the Jewish Section, Melbourne General Cemetery', *International Journal of Historical Archaeology* 13, no. 4 (2009).
58 'The Death of Mrs Fell' was reported in the *Maitland Mercury*, 6 March 1850, and included in a compilation of New South Wales Inquests, 1850. See The Ohio State University collection.
59 Inquests Book 1, 1 July 1842, Number 14, Johnson: in Laurie Gluckman, *Touching on Deaths: A Medical History of Early Auckland Based on the First 384 Inquests*, ed. Ann Gluckman and Mike Wagg (Auckland: Doppelganger, 2000), 124–5.
60 Inquests Book 1, 1 July 1842, Gluckman, *Touching on Deaths*, 124.
61 Tim Cresswell, 'Towards a Politics of Mobility', *Environment and Planning D: Society and Space* 28 (2010): 20.
62 Hamish Maxwell-Stewart and Rebecca Kippen, '"What is a man that is a bolter to do? I would steal the Governor's axe rather than starve": Old lags and recidivism in the Tasmanian Penal Colony', in *Transnational Penal Cultures: New Perspectives*

on Discipline, Punishment and Desistance*, ed. Vivien Miller and James Campbell (London and New York: Routledge, 2015), 172.

63 Boyce, *Van Diemen's Land*, 216.

64 Jessica Gerrard, 'The Interconnected Histories of Labour and Homelessness', *Labour History*, no. 112 (May 2017): 170.

65 'LAW', *Mercury*, 30 November 1865: 2. See also the Libraries Tasmania record: https://stors.tas.gov.au/LC247-1-32$init=LC247-1-32-P0395

66 https://stors.tas.gov.au/CON19-1-2$init=CON19-1-2p180

67 See Boylan's offences at https://trove.nla.gov.au/newspaper/article/3335741; https://trove.nla.gov.au/newspaper/article/203384454 and https://trove.nla.gov.au/newspaper/article/3340058

68 https://trove.nla.gov.au/newspaper/article/232856753; https://trove.nla.gov.au/newspaper/article/197427897

69 See https://stors.tas.gov.au/HAJ1871-63$init=HAJ1871-63_058 and https://stors.tas.gov.au/RGD35-1-8$init=RGD35-1-8P41.

70 'POLICE OFFICE', *Mercury*, 30 October 1860: 2.

71 Libraries Tasmania, https://stors.tas.gov.au/CON33-1-87$init=CON33-1-87P39

72 https://stors.tas.gov.au/CON37-1-10$init=CON37-1-10P283. There are a few more records about him in the Tasmanian Names Index, including a gaol record showing he was convicted of being idle and disorderly again in March 1892 (see https://stors.tas.gov.au/GD63-2-1$init=GD63-2-1P197JPG). He died in May 1901 aged ninety-two in the New Town Charitable Institution (see https://stors.tas.gov.au/AF35-1-2$init=AF35-1-2P94) and was buried as a pauper (see https://stors.tas.gov.au/AF70-1-26$init=AF70-1-26P117JPG).

73 Note that this case appears on https://stors.tas.gov.au/LC346-3-9$init=LC346-3-9P200JPG.

74 See the Hobart Gaol record for Maurice Jeffrey, 30 September 1899 which includes two photographs: https://stors.tas.gov.au/GD128-2-1$init=GD128-2-1_050.

75 'Destitution', *Cornwall Chronicle*, 8 May 1844: 3; 'Vagrancy', *Hobarton Guardian*, 23 February 1848: 3; 'Police court', *Launceston Examiner*, 9 August 1860: 3.

76 'CURRENT TOPICS', *Examiner*, 18 February 1901: 5.

77 'Vagrancy', James Sullivan, 3 July 1879, *Wanganui Herald:* 3.

78 City of Sydney Archives, Letters received – Municipal Council, Sydney, 5 March 1883, vol 190, ID 29/190/368, https://archives.cityofsydney.nsw.gov.au/nodes/view/1084021#idx1529493

79 Davies, 'Vagrancy and the Victorians', 101–2.

80 VPRS7399/P1, Unit 9, 18 July 1891.

81 Gerrard, 'The Interconnected Histories of Labour and Homelessness': 170.

82 'LOCAL AND GENERAL', *Daily Telegraph* (Launceston), 7 February 1906: 5.

83 Roslyn Otzen, *Dr John Singleton 1808–1891: Christian, Doctor, Philanthropist* (Melbourne: Melbourne City Mission, 2008), 47.

84 Singleton, *A Narrative of Incidents in the Eventful Life of a Physician*, 322.
85 'Living in the Domain', *New Zealand Herald*, 18 October 1915: 5.
86 Davison, Dunstan and McConville eds., *The Outcasts of Melbourne*, 10–11.
87 'To the Editor', *West Coast Times*, 7 December 1882: 3.
88 Fairburn writes about the food eaten by labouring men in *The Ideal Society*, 249.
89 Judith A. Allen, *Sex and Secrets: Crimes Involving Australian Women since 1880* (Melbourne and Oxford: Oxford University Press, 1990), 60.
90 'Intercolonial News: New South Wales', *The Illustrated Australian News*, 23 January 1884: 11.
91 'Accidents and offences', *Illustrated Australian News*, 22 March 1876: 38.
92 Karskens, *The Rocks: Life in Early Sydney*, 47.
93 Nagy and Piper, 'Imprisonment of Female Urban and Rural Offenders',106.
94 Nagy and Piper, 'Imprisonment of Female Urban and Rural Offenders', 106.
95 Wilson, 'Community and Gender in Victorian Auckland', 24–42.
96 Wilson, 'Community and Gender in Victorian Auckland', 26.
97 Wilson, 'Community and Gender in Victorian Auckland', 34.
98 The database for 'discharged prisoners' in New South Wales derived from the *Police Gazette* includes entries for Sarah Jones when she was charged with the crime of vagrancy starting in 1868 with the final entry in 1876. All but one of these resulted in a six-month gaol sentence at Darlinghurst Gaol, with the 1872 charge outcome a three-month prison sentence in Bathurst Gaol.
99 Additional research for this story was conducted by Dr Rachel Franks, who found several later criminal entries for Sarah Jones (aka The Cockroach) in the 1880s.
100 Interestingly, the *Police Gazette* list her as 'Cockroach' first, then Sarah Jones.
101 'Central Police Court', *The Australian Star*, 31 August 1888: 5.
102 *Evening News*, 10 December 1887: 5.
103 'At the central', *The Australian Star*, 28 May 1897: 5.
104 See SRNSW, NRS2027, 5/1425, 238.
105 See https://dictionaryofsydney.org/building/central_police_station_and_court_house.
106 See https://dictionaryofsydney.org/blog/the_last_public_hanging_at_darlinghurst_gaol, URL accessed 7 November 2022. See also:https://www.sydneybarani.com.au/sites/darlinghurst-gaol/.
107 New South Wales Gaol Description and Entrance Books, 1818–1930, NSW State Records. See also data set for New South Wales entries for Sarah Jones, with the earliest record 1869. Some prison sentences may be missing from the archival record.
108 'Home, sweet home', *The Australian Star*, 28 June 1889: 5.
109 Miles Fairburn, *Nearly out of Heart and Hope: The Puzzle of a Colonial Labourer's Diary* (Auckland: Auckland University Press, 1995).

Chapter 5

1 Stephen Garton, *Out of Luck: Poor Australians and Social Welfare 1788–1899* (Sydney, Wellington, London and Boston: Allen & Unwin, Sydney, Wellington, London and Boston, 1990), 3.

2 Garton, *Out of Luck*, 3.

3 N. J. Crowson, 'Tramps' Tales: Discovering the Life-Stories of Late Victorian and Edwardian Vagrants', *English Historical Review* 125, no. 577 (2020): 1490.

4 Crowson, 'Tramps' Tales', 1489–90.

5 'Offences Heard and Determined at Magistrates' Courts, Australia 1860–1980', in *Australians, Historical Statistics*, ed. Wray Vamplew (Broadway: Fairfax, 1987), 308.

6 Miles Fairburn, 'Vagrants, "Folk Devils" and Nineteenth-Century New Zealand', *Historical Studies* 21, no. 85 (1985): 506.

7 See 'How He May Be Treated in Future', *The Star*, 26 April 1906: 2.

8 Martha Albert Fineman, 'The Vulnerable Subject: Anchoring Equality in the Human Condition', *Yale Journal of Law and Feminism* 20, no. 1 (2008): 1–23.

9 'Sent to Gaol for Being Poor and Helpless', *Guardian*, 25 August 1877; *North Otago Times*, 27 August 1877: 2.

10 Tony Ballantyne, 'Mobility, Empire, Colonisation', *History Australia* 11, no. 2 (2014): 33.

11 Alan Atkinson, *The Europeans in Australia, Volume Two: Democracy* (Melbourne and New York: Oxford University Press, 2004), 282; 279–86; see also Catharine Coleborne, *Madness in the Family: Insanity and Institutions in the Australasian Colonial World 1860s–1914* (Basingstoke and New York: Palgrave Macmillan, 2010), 248–54.

12 Current scholarship in the social sciences reframes vulnerability as 'precarity', and sees connections between these terms and states: see Clara Han, 'Precarity, Precariousness, and Vulnerability', *Annual Review of Anthropology* 47 (2018): 331–43; Julie McLeod, 'Vulnerability and the Neo-liberal Youth Citizen: A View from Australia', *Comparative Education* 48, no. 1 (2012): 11–26.

13 'The Crime of Poverty', *Nelson Evening Mail*, 12 July 1900: 2.

14 See Anthea Maree Sutton's research about Beechworth asylum and gaol in the nineteenth century: Delineating the fine line between the mad and the bad: Victorian prisons and insane asylums, 1856–1914, PhD Thesis, University of New England, Armidale, New South Wales, 2022: 207–8; 222–3; 227.

15 Heather Shore, 'Crime, Criminal Networks and the Survival Strategies of the Poor in Early Eighteenth-Century London', in *The Poor in England 1700–1850: An Economy of Makeshifts*, ed. Alannah Tomkins and Steve King (Manchester: Manchester University Press, 2003), 138; and borrowing idea of survival from historian Olwen Hufton, 140.

16 Ballantyne, 'Mobility, Empire, Colonisation', 33.

17 Aparna Nair, '"They Shall See His Face": Blindness in British India, 1850–1950', *Medical History* 61, no. 2 (2017): 185.

18 Erik Olssen, 'Towards a New Society', in *The Oxford History of New Zealand*, 2nd edition, ed. Geoffrey W. Rice (Auckland: Oxford University Press, 1992), 282.

19 Julie-Marie Strange, 'Tramp: Sentiment and the Homeless Man in the Late-Victorian and Edwardian City', *Journal of Victorian Culture* 16, no. 2 (2011): 248.

20 Ballantyne, 'Mobility, Empire, Colonisation', 34.

21 Michael Lever, 'When Absence Is the Artifact: Unmarked Graves in the Jewish Section, Melbourne General Cemetery', *International Journal of Historical Archaeology* 13, no. 4 (2009): 474; 481.

22 See Lever, 'When Absence Is the Artifact', 481.

23 Alana Jayne Piper and Victoria Nagy, 'Versatile Offending: Criminal Careers of Female Prisoners in Australia, 1860–1920', *Journal of Interdisciplinary History* 48, no. 2 (2017): 205.

24 Victoria Nagy, 'The Health and Medical Needs of Victoria's Older Female Prisoners, 1860–1920', Prison Medicine: Health and Incarceration in History Conference, University of Wollongong, May 2019, 3.

25 'City Police Court', *Tasmanian News*, 13 March 1890: 2. Note that a record of this case also appears in Tasmanian Archives, LC247/1/36, https://stors.tas.gov.au/LC247-1-36$init=LC247-1-36-P796. Ann's surname was recorded there as McAvady, and she was described as FS (free by servitude).

26 'City Police Court', *Tasmanian News*, 13 March 1890: 2.

27 Summary of sources found in Tasmanian archives, using these links: See https://stors.tas.gov.au/CON41-1-33$init=CON41-1-33P101; https://stors.tas.gov.au/RGD37-1-12$init=RGD37-1-12P271; https://stors.tas.gov.au/CON33-1-101$init=CON33-1-101P175; https://stors.tas.gov.au/RGD35-1-7$init=RGD35-1-7P041; https://stors.tas.gov.au/HSD146-1-1$init=HSD146-1-1_0003.

28 Summary of sources in Tasmanian archives, found at these links: https://stors.tas.gov.au/POL709-1-19$init=POL709-1-19_1882P175; https://stors.tas.gov.au/POL709-1-21$init=POL709-1-21_1886P18; https://stors.tas.gov.au/POL709-1-21$init=POL709-1-21_1886P83; https://stors.tas.gov.au/POL709-1-21$init=POL709-1-21_1886P163; https://stors.tas.gov.au/POL709-1-21$init=POL709-1-21_1886P214; https://stors.tas.gov.au/POL709-1-21$init=POL709-1-21_1887P157; https://stors.tas.gov.au/POL709-1-22$init=POL709-1-22_1888P209; https://stors.tas.gov.au/POL709-1-22$init=POL709-1-22_1889P151; https://stors.tas.gov.au/POL709-1-23$init=POL709-1-23_1890P225; https://stors.tas.gov.au/POL709-1-24$init=POL709-1-24_1892P161.

29 Tasmanian Archives, GD63/2/1, p. 400, https://stors.tas.gov.au/GD63-2-1$init=GD63-2-1P403JPG.

30 See https://stors.tas.gov.au/RGD35-1-14$init=RGD35-1-14P160.

31 Margaret Tennant, 'Elderly Indigents and Old Men's Homes 1880–1920', *New Zealand Journal of History* 17, no. 1 (1983): 5–6, Table 1.

32 Tennant, 'Elderly Indigents', 5–7; 11.

33 Tennant, 'Elderly Indigents', 13.

34 Catharine Coleborne and Maree O'Connor, 'Vagrancy, Mobility and Colonialism', in *Handbook of Historical Geography*, ed. Mona Domosh, Michael Heffernan and Charles W. J. Withers (London: SAGE, 2020), 382–4. See also A. Gordon Darroch, 'Migrants in the Nineteenth Century: Fugitives or Families in Motion?' *Journal of Family History* 6, no. 3 (1981): 257–77.

35 Susanne Davies, Vagrancy and the Victorians: The Social Construction of the Vagrant in Melbourne, 1880–1907, PhD Thesis, University of Melbourne, Australia, 1990, 355. See also Shurlee Swain, 'The Poor People of Melbourne', in *The Outcasts of Melbourne: Essays in Social History*, ed. Graeme Davison, David Dunstan and Chris McConville (Sydney: Allen & Unwin, 1985), 91–112.

36 Davies, 'Vagrancy and the Victorians', 356–7.

37 Coleborne and O'Connor, 'Vagrancy, Mobility and Colonialism': 383; see also Annabel Cooper, 'Poor Men in the Land of Promises: Settler Masculinity and the Male Breadwinner Economy in Late Nineteenth-Century New Zealand', *Australian Historical Studies* 39 (2008): 245–61.

38 Bruce Scates, 'A Struggle for Survival: Unemployment and the Unemployed Agitation in Late Nineteenth-Century Melbourne', *Australian Historical Studies* 24, no. 94 (1990): 50.

39 'POLICE OFFICE', *Cornwall Chronicle*, 14 March 1860: 5.

40 Coleborne and O'Connor, 'Vagrancy, Mobility and Colonialism': 383; original newspaper report, *New Zealand Herald*, 4 August 1882: 5.

41 Case: BDM shows no record of a William Clarke born *c.*1854–8 to any Johanna.

42 Coleborne and O'Connor, 'Vagrancy, Mobility and Colonialism', 383. See also Darroch, 'Migrants in the Nineteenth Century', 257–77.

43 Margaret Tennant, *Paupers and Providers: Charitable Aid in New Zealand* (Wellington: Allen and Unwin New Zealand Ltd and Historical Branch, Dept of Internal Affairs, 1989), 127.

44 *Daily Southern Cross* 1872, 3; Tennant, *Paupers and Providers*, 128.

45 Davies, 'Vagrancy and the Victorians': 271.

46 Christina Twomey, *Deserted and Destitute: Motherhood, Wife Desertion and Colonial Welfare* (Melbourne: Australian Scholarly Publishing, 2002).

47 'POLICE COURT', *Cornwall Chronicle*, 16 May 1866: 4.

48 *Launceston Examiner*, 1 June 1881: 2.

49 Charlotte MacDonald, 'Crime and Punishment in New Zealand, 1840–1913: A Gendered History', *New Zealand Journal of History* 23, no. 1 (1989): 5–21.

50 'Nobody's Daughters', *Christchurch Star*, 26 November 1896: 3.
51 Nair, 'They Shall See His Face', 193.
52 Jan Kociumbas, *The Oxford History of Australia. Volume 2, 1770–1860: Possessions* (Melbourne: Oxford University Press, 1992), 292.
53 'An appeal for "vagrants"', *Argus*, 22 October 1863: 7.
54 Catharine Coleborne, 'Disability in Colonial Institutional Records', in *Handbook of Disability History*, ed. Michael A. Rembis, Kim Nielsen and Catherine Kudlick (Oxford: OUP, 2018).
55 Cases reported mentioning James Sullivan: 30 September 1871, *The Star:* 3; 13 August 1873, *The Star:* 3; 3 July 1879, *Wanganui Herald:* 3; 4 November 1879, *New Zealand Herald:* 6; 15 September 1880, *The Star:* 3; 16 September 1880, *The Star*: 3; 17 September 1880, *The Star*: 3; 8 October 1880, *The Star*: 3.
56 *New Zealand Police Gazette* entries: 7 March 1879, three months hard labour; 5 April 1881, three months hard labour. Both entries show Sullivan came from a gaol (Timaru and Addington).
57 Each of these vagrants appears in the NSW data set.
58 Coleborne, 'Disability in Colonial Institutional Records'.
59 John Williams, *New Zealand Police Gazette*, 17 July 1877: 19; sentenced to one month in gaol.
60 'Sent to Gaol for Being Poor and Helpless', *North Otago Times*, 27 August 1877: 2.
61 *Press*, 14 April 1904: 5; 'The Crime of Poverty', *Nelson Evening Mail*, 12 July 1900: 2.
62 Thomas Dobeson, *Out of Work Again: The Autobiographical Narrative of Thomas Dobeson 1885–1891*, ed. Graeme Davison and Shirley Constantine (Clayton: Monash Publications in History, 1990), 90.
63 Cooper, 'Poor Men in the Land of Promises', 258–9.
64 John A. Lee, *Roughnecks, Rolling Stones and Rouseabouts, With an Anthology of Early Swagger Literature* (Auckland: Penguin, [1977] 1989), 22.
65 Scates, 'A Struggle for Survival', 50.
66 Lee, *Roughnecks*, 22.
67 Lee, *Roughnecks,* 24.
68 Jessica Gerrard, 'The Interconnected Histories of Labour and Homelessness', *Labour History*, no. 112 (May 2017): 174.
69 Angela Hawk, 'Going "Mad" in Gold Country: Migrant Populations and the Problem of Containment in Pacific Mining Boom Regions', *Pacific Historical Review* 80, no. 1 (2011): 68.
70 Sidney L. Harring, 'Class Conflict and the Suppression of Tramps in Buffalo, 1892–1894', *Law and Society Review* 11 (1977): 873–912.
71 Harring, 'Class Conflict and the Enforcement of the Tramp Acts in Buffalo', 875; 878–9.
72 Olssen, 'Towards a New Society', 274–5.
73 Dobeson, *Out of Work Again*, p. 91.

74 Scates, 'A Struggle for Survival', cites the William Farrell Papers in the La Trobe Library MS 10029, 47.

75 Lee, *Roughnecks*, 35.

76 Margaret Tennant, *The Fabric of Welfare: Voluntary Organisations, Government and Welfare in New Zealand, 1840–2005* (Wellington: Bridget Williams Books, 2007), 62.

77 Miles Fairburn, *The Ideal Society and Its Enemies: The Foundations of Modern New Zealand Society, 1850–1900* (Auckland: Auckland University Press, 1989), 248–9.

78 Fairburn, *The Ideal Society*, 249.

79 Tennant, *The Fabric of Welfare*, 62.

80 'Looking for work', *Evening Post*, 19 June 1909: 9.

81 Fairburn, *The Ideal Society*, 250.

82 Miles Fairburn, 'Cox, James' Dictionary of New Zealand Biography, first published in 1996, updated February, 2019. Te Ara – the Encyclopedia of New Zealand, https://teara.govt.nz/en/biographies/3c39/cox-james (accessed 24 February 2023).

83 Fairburn's edited book, *Nearly Out of Heart and Hope: The Puzzle of a Colonial Labourer's Diary* (Auckland: Auckland University Press, 1995), offers a reading of Cox in his times. See also Coleborne, *Insanity, Identity and Empire*, 131.

84 Fairburn tends to see Cox as somewhat hopeless in his interpretation of Cox's problems and failures. By reading Cox's life story and episodes of hardship framed by a larger story of vagrancy and prosecutions of men like him, we can reinterpret his doggedness and see some of his successes. See Fairburn, 'Cox, James', *Dictionary of New Zealand Biography* (*DNZB*), first published in 1996, updated February, 2019. Te Ara – the Encyclopedia of New Zealand, https://teara.govt.nz/en/biographies/3c39/cox-james (accessed 24 February 2023).

85 Erik Olssen, *A History of Otago* (Dunedin: John McIndoe, 1984), 90–1.

86 Fairburn, 'Cox, James', DNZB; Cooper, 'Poor Men in the Land of Promises', 254.

87 Fairburn, *Nearly out of Heart and Hope*, 57.

88 Fairburn, *Nearly out of Heart and Hope*, 61.

89 Fairburn, *Nearly out of Heart and Hope*, 63.

90 Fairburn, *Nearly out of Heart and Hope*, 60; 64; 69.

91 Fairburn, *Nearly out of Heart and Hope*, 66–7.

92 Fairburn, *Nearly out of Heart and Hope*, 72–3.

93 Lee, *Roughnecks*: 39. See also: https://culturewaitaki.org.nz/epitaph/remembering-robert-winter-barney-whiterats, URL accessed 28 April 2023.

94 http://jamesfaganhistoryblog.blogspot.com/2013/06/tinkers-swagmen-rovers-or-travellers.html, URL accessed 28 April 2023.

95 Garton's book *Out of Luck* includes a photograph of an elderly man who was photographed around 1900; he looks just like Robert Winter; see Garton, *Out of Luck*, 35.

96 Scates, 'A Struggle for Survival', comments that William Farrell also provides a 'rare insight into the psychology of the unskilled employee', 47.

97 Miles Fairburn, 'Cox, James', *DNZB*, Te Ara, Encyclopedia of New Zealand, February 2019: see https://teara.govt.nz/en/biographies/3c39/cox-james, URL accessed 24 February 2023.

98 'Vagrancy, British and Colonial', *Hobart Mercury*, 8 March 1906: 4.

99 'Wanderer' (1841–95) was known to be an Englishman with Jewish heritage who was a civil engineer who travelled and wrote fiction. He was also associated with magazine publishing. See Cherry A. Hankin ed., *Life in a Young Colony: Selections from Early New Zealand Writing* (Christchurch, Sydney and London: Whitcoulls Publishers, 1981), 213–9.

100 'Topics of the day', *Marlborough Express*, 22 April 1904: 1; 'England's Unemployed', *Press*, 23 April 1904: 8.

101 'The unfortunate pauper', *The Star*, 18 July 1901: 2.

102 William Pember Reeves, *State Experiments in Australia and New Zealand*, Volume II (Melbourne: Macmillan Australia, 1969 [Grant Richards, 1902]), 218–9.

103 Reeves, *State Experiments*, 219.

104 'How He May Be Treated in Future', *The Star*, 26 April 1906: 2.

105 See Featherstone, 'Tramping', 244–5.

106 Paul Ocobock, 'Introduction: Vagrancy and Homelessness in Global and Historical Perspective', in *Cast Out: Vagrancy and Homelessness in Global and Historical Perspective*, ed. A. L. Beier and Paul Ocobock (Ohio: Ohio University Press, 2009), 2.

107 Shurlee Swain, 'The Value of the Vignette in the Writing of Welfare History', *Australian Historical Studies* 39, no. 2 (2008): 207–8.

108 M. B. Schedvin, M. B. and C. B. Schedvin, 'The Nomadic Tribes of Urban Britain: A Prelude to Botany Bay', *Historical Studies* 20, no. 78 (1978): 264–5.

109 Fairburn, *Nearly out of Heart and Hope*, 58.

110 Fairburn, *The Ideal Society*, 204.

111 Fineman, 'The Vulnerable Subject', 1151–2.

Chapter 6

1 Simon Featherstone, 'Tramping: The Cult of the Vagabond in Early Twentieth-Century England', in *Idleness, Indolence and Leisure in English Literature* ed. Monika Fludernik and Miriam Nandi (Basingstoke: Palgrave Macmillan, 2014), 247.

2 On colonial 'types' in Australian fiction, and especially their relationship to the economy, see Ken Gelder and Rachael Weaver, *Colonial Australian Fiction* (Sydney: Sydney University Press, 2017), 1; 14.

3 Frank Tobias Higbie, 'Between Romance and Degradation: Navigating the Meanings of Vagrancy in North America, 1870–1940', in *Cast Out: Vagrancy and*

Homelessness in Global and Historical Perspective ed. A. L. Beier and Paul Ocobock (Ohio: Ohio University Press, 2009), 253.

4 I have written elsewhere about the concept of 'wanderers' and also about travellers who wrote descriptions of colonial life in relation to poverty and vagrancy; see Catharine Coleborne, *Insanity, Identity and Empire: Immigrants and Institutional Confinement in Australia and New Zealand, 1873–1910* (Manchester: Manchester University Press, 2015), 27; 53; 75; 102; Catharine Coleborne, 'Consorting with "others": Vagrancy Laws and Unauthorised Mobility across Colonial Borders in New Zealand from 1877 to 1900', in *Empire and Mobility in the Long Nineteenth Century* ed. Peter Merriman and David Lambert (Manchester: Manchester University Press, 2020), 141–4; and Catharine Coleborne and Maree O'Connor, 'Vagrancy, Mobility and Colonialism', in *Handbook of Historical Geography* ed. Mona Domosh, Michael Heffernan and Charles W. J. Withers (London: SAGE, 2020), 374–89.

5 David Hitchcock, *Vagrancy in English Culture and Society, 1650–1750* (London: Bloomsbury Academic, 2016), 19.

6 See, for instance, Gareth Stedman Jones, *Outcast London: A Study in the Relationship between Classes in Victorian Society* (Oxford: Clarendon Press, 1971).

7 David Hitchcock, *Vagrancy in English Culture and Society*, 1. See also Simon Featherstone, 'Tramping: The Cult of the Vagabond in Early Twentieth-Century England', 235–7.

8 Featherstone, 'Tramping', 244.

9 John Hunter Kerr, *Glimpses of Life in Victoria: By 'A Resident'* ed. with an introduction by Marguerite Hancock (Melbourne: Miegunyah Press, [1872] 1996), 164.

10 Owen Suffolk, *Days of Crime and Years of Suffering*, ed. with an introduction by David Dunstan (Kew: Australian Scholarly Publishing, 2000), 12–3.

11 Suffolk, *Days of Crime and Years of Suffering*, 19.

12 M. A. Crowther, 'The Tramp', *Myths of the English* ed. Roy Porter (Cambridge UK: Polity, 1992), 103.

13 Crowther, 'The Tramp', 118.

14 Alistair Robinson, *Vagrancy in the Victorian Age: Representing the Wandering Poor in Nineteenth-Century Literature and Culture* (Cambridge: Cambridge University Press, 2022), 167.

15 Kerr, *Glimpses of Life in Victoria: By 'A Resident'*, 164.

16 William Howitt, *Land, Labour and Gold or Two Years in Victoria. With Visits to Sydney and Van Diemen's Land* (London: Longman, 1855 [Kilmore: Lowden, 1972]), 196–7.

17 See Coleborne, *Insanity, Identity and Empire*, 114–38.

18 Howitt, *Land, Labour and Gold*, 198.

19 John A. Lee, *Roughnecks, Rolling Stones and Rouseabouts, With an Anthology of Early Swagger Literature* (Auckland: Penguin [1977] 1989).

20 Lee, *Roughnecks*, 25.

21 Lee, *Roughnecks*, 25.

22 'From a Swagger's Point of View' cited in Lee, *Roughnecks*.

23 Lydia Wevers, *Country of Writing: Travel Writing and New Zealand 1809–1900* (Auckland: Auckland University Press, 2002), 64.

24 Wevers, *Country of Writing*, 65–73. Titles include Hume Nisbet, *A Colonial Tramp* and Charles Money, *Knocking about in New Zealand*.

25 Gelder and Weaver, *Colonial Australian Fiction*, 1. On colonial social identities, see Coleborne, *Insanity, Identity and Empire*.

26 Gelder and Weaver, *Colonial Australian Fiction*, 21–5.

27 See Catharine Coleborne and Maree O'Connor, 'Vagrancy, Mobility and Colonialism', 386.

28 Sarah Courage, in *The Adventures of Pioneer Women: From Their Letters, Diaries and Reminiscences*, ed. Sarah Ell (Auckland: Bush Press, 1992), 199, 53–6.

29 These ideas are also discussed in Coleborne and O'Connor, 'Vagrancy, Mobility and Colonialism', 386.

30 Kerr, *Glimpses of Life in Victoria: By 'A Resident'*, 164.

31 Miles Fairburn, *Nearly Out of Heart and Hope: The Puzzle of a Colonial Labourer's Diary* (Auckland: Auckland University Press, 1995).

32 Higbie, 'Between Romance and Degradation', 265.

33 Kerr, *Glimpses of Life in Victoria: By 'A Resident'*.

34 James Mills, *Madness, Cannabis and Colonialism: The 'Native Only' Lunatic Asylums of British India, 1857 to 1900* (Basingstoke: Palgrave, 2000), 68–9.

35 David Lambert and Peter Merriman eds., *Empire and Mobility in the Long Nineteenth Century* (Manchester: Manchester University Press, 2020), 8–12.

36 Tim Cresswell, *On the Move: Mobility in the Western World* (London and New York: Routledge, 2006), 12–3.

37 Cresswell, 'The Production of Mobilities', *New Formations: A Journal of Culture/Theory/Politics*, 43, (2001): 20.

38 Cresswell, 'The Production of Mobilities', 20.

39 Cresswell, *On the Move*, 21.

40 Durba Ghosh and Dane Kennedy eds., *Decentring Empire: Britain, India and the Transcolonial World* (Hyderabad: Orient Longman, 2006), 3.

41 See Edward Said, *Culture and Imperialism* (London: Vintage,1994), 332.

42 Ghosh and Kennedy eds., *Decentring Empire*, 2.

43 Marilyn Lake and Henry Reynolds, *Drawing the Global Colour Line: White Men's Countries and the International Challenge of Racial Equality* (Cambridge: Cambridge University Press, 2008), 23; Louis Knafla, *Crime, Gender and Sexuality*

in *Criminal Prosecutions: Criminal Justice History* (Westport, CT: Greenwood Press, 2002).

44 Lauren Benton, *Law and Colonial Cultures: Legal Regimes in World History, 1400–1900* (Cambridge and New York: Cambridge University Press, 2002), 3.

45 In Victoria, example of 1966 legislation.

46 David Hitchcock, 'A Typology of Travellers: Migration, Justice, and Vagrancy in Warwickshire, 1670–1730', *Rural History*, 23, no. 1 (2012): 35.

47 David Hitchcock, 'A Typology of Travellers', 29.

48 David Goodman, *Gold Seeking: Victoria and California in the 1850s* (St Leonards NSW: Allen & Unwin, 1994).

49 Tim Cresswell, *The Tramp in America* (London: Reaktion, 2001), 87–109.

50 Philippa Levine, *Prostitution, Race and Politics: Policing Venereal Disease in the British Empire* (New York and London: Routledge, 2003), 187.

51 Beier and Ocobock, *Cast Out,* 20.

52 Philippa Levine, 2004; see also Coleborne and O'Connor, 'Vagrancy, Mobility and Colonialism', 384.

53 On mobility regulation across the British world, see Coleborne and O'Connor, 'Vagrancy, Mobility and Colonialism', 375–82.

54 N. J. Crowson, 'Tramps' Tales: Discovering the Life-Stories of Late Victorian and Edwardian Vagrants', *English Historical Review*, 135, no. 577 (2020): 1493; 1490.

55 Robinson, *Vagrancy in the Victorian Age*, 12.

56 Robinson, *Vagrancy in the Victorian Age*, 12.

57 Cresswell, 'Towards a politics of mobility', 22–6.

58 Tony Ballantyne, 'Mobility, Empire, Colonisation', *History Australia*, 11, no. 2 (2014): 7–37. See also Tony Ballantyne and Antoinette Burton eds., *Moving Subjects: Gender, Mobility and Intimacy in an Age of Global Empire* (Chicago: University of Illinois Press, 2009). On the 'mobility turn' and humanities scholarship see Peter Merriman and Lynne Pearce, 'Mobility and the Humanities', *Mobilities*, 12, no. 4 (2017): 493–508.

59 On immigration restriction, see Jennifer S. Kain, *Insanity and Immigration Control in New Zealand and Australia, 1860–1930* (Basingstoke: Palgrave/Springer, 2019).

60 Sally Engle Merry and Donald Brenneis eds., *Law and Empire in the Pacific: Fiji and Hawai'i* (Santa Fe: SAR Press, 2004).

61 Higbie, 'Between Romance and Degradation', 252.

Epilogue

1 Jackie Stacey and Janet Wolff eds., *Writing Otherwise: Experiments in Cultural Criticism* (Manchester and New York: Manchester University Press, 2013).

2 Tim Cresswell, 'Towards a Politics of Mobility', *Environment and Planning D: Society and Space*, 28, (2010): 29.

3 This audience member mentioned the documentary film 'Riding the Rails' which screened on PBS in 2010 about American teen 'hobos' during the 1930s economic Depression. These young people were highly mobile as they hopped from freight train to freight train to both avoid poverty and seek opportunity. See http://thegoodsoldier.com/ridingtherails/index.html, URL accessed 24 July 2023.

4 Tim Cresswell, *Place: An Introduction* (Oxford: Wiley Blackwell, 2015), 175.

Annotated guide

1 For more detail on how these data sets can yield insights, see K. Inwood, H. Maxwell-Stewart, D. Oxley and J. Stankovich, 'Growing Incomes, Growing People in Nineteenth-Century Tasmania', *Australian Economic History Review*, 55, no. 2 (2015): 191–203.

2 Catharine Coleborne and Hamish Maxwell-Stewart, 'Former Convicts Prosecuted as Vagrants in Tasmania: Plotting a Shadowy History Using Tasmanian Police Gazette data, 1865–c. 1900', Unpublished paper, ANZLHS Conference: 'Tenuous Histories and Provable Pasts', UTS, 1–3 December 2022.

Bibliography

Archives and repositories

Archives New Zealand

Historical Publications Branch, Police Records. Woodville Jail Book, 1882–96 W3539. Archives New Zealand Te Rua Mahara o te Kāwanatanga, Wellington.

AAAc, Box 15, Photographs of Prisoners, 1902–6, P27 3. Archives New Zealand Te Rua Mahara o te Kāwanatanga, Wellington.

CAAR 19946/ R8417798. Police to Provincial Secretary; CAAR 19936/R17560619, Archives New Zealand Te Rua Mahara o te Kāwanatanga, Christchurch.

New Zealand Police Gazette, 1877–1900, BBAN 5803/50a-5803/63a. Archives New Zealand Te Rua Mahara o te Kāwanatanga, Auckland.

YCAA Auckland Asylum, 1048/9 29, Patient case files. Archives New Zealand Te Rua Mahara o te Kāwanatanga, Auckland.

City of Sydney Archives, New South Wales, Australia

Letters received - Municipal Council, 18 June 1863, vol 62, 26/62/540

Letters received - Municipal Council of Sydney, 11 September 1877, vol 146, A-00302322

Letters received - Municipal Council, 15 October 1879, vol 160, 26/160/1230, ID A-00303896

Letters received - Municipal Council, Sydney, 5 March 1883, vol 190, ID 29/190/368

Parliament of Tasmania

Tasmanian Parliamentary Papers, 1856–1901, https://www.parliament.tas.gov.au/tpl/PPWeb/

Public Record Office, Victoria (PROV)

PROV, VPRS 677/P0000, Victoria Police (including Officer of the Chief Commission of Police), 1853 - the present, Letter books, VA724.

PROV, VPRS7400 Yarra Bend Asylum, Casebooks of female patients, 1862–1912.

PROV, VPRS 5481, *Victorian Police Gazette*, 1856–1970.

State Library New South Wales (SLNSW)

Rules and Regulations for the Government and Guidance of the Metropolitan Police Force of New South Wales, NSW Police, Sydney: W.W. Davies, Government Printer, 1853, SLNSW 352.2/14A1.

General Instructions for the Guidance of the Police Force, issued by the Inspector General, Sydney, 1862. SLNSW MF 1 Q 20.

Manual for Members of the Police Force of Enactments Affecting their Duties, Thomas Richards, Government Printer, Sydney, 1862, SLNSW MF 1 Q 20.

Rules for the Management of the Police Force of New South Wales, NSW Police Department, 1864, SLNSW 363.23/1.

State Records New South Wales

New South Wales Criminal Depositions

New South Wales Criminal Court Records Index

New South Wales Bench of Magistrates Index, 1788–1820

New South Wales Gaol Descriptions and Entrance Books, 1818–1930

New South Wales Gaol Inmates/Prisoner Photos Index 1870–1930

New South Wales Police Gazette, 1854–1930, Series NRS-10958 (1862–1982)

State Library of Victoria (SLV)

Manual of Police Regulations for the Guidance of the Constabulary of Victoria. 1856. Melbourne: John Ferres. RARELT 351.74 V66M.

Regulations for the Guidance of the Constabulary of Victoria. 1877. Melbourne: John Ferres.

Convict Department, Tasmania, *Rules and Regulations for the Constabulary*, Tasman's Peninsula, Hobart. W. Fletcher, 1868. SLV, MS BOX 134/12(e).

Tasmanian Archives

Note: Tasmanian libraries and archives are all linked by a common digital domain and website. Links provided to records cited in this book correspond with materials held in the Tasmanian Archives and share the common subdomain 'stors'.

Convict Department; Conduct Registers of Male Convicts arriving in the Period of the Assignment System, CON31-1-39, 1 January 1803–31 December 1843.

Convict Department; Description Lists of Male Convicts, CON18-1-10, 10 January 1830–30 June 1840.

Convict Department; Conduct Registers of Male Convicts arriving in the Period of the Probation System, CON33-1-5, 11 September 1840–5 February 1841.

Convict Department; Conduct Registers of Male Convicts arriving in the Period of the Probation System, CON33/1/101, 20 December 1850–19 March 1851.

Convict Department; Conduct Registers of Male Convicts arriving on Non-Convict Ships or Locally convicted, CON37/1/10, 1 January 1863–31 May 1877.

Convict Department; Description Lists of Male Convicts, CON18/1/8, 18 April 1828–22 January 1839.

Convict Department; Conduct Registers of Male Convicts arriving in the Period of the Assignment System, CON31-1-45, 1 January 1803–26 January 1830.

Convict Department; Conduct Registers of Female Convicts arriving in the Period of the Assignment System, CON40/1/2, 1 January 1836–31 December 1843.

Convict Department; Description Lists of Female Convicts, CON19/1/2, 15 December 1842–25 December 1843.

Gaol Branch; Prisoners Record Books, GD63/2/1, 1 January 1890–31 December 1892.

Gaol Branch; Prisoners Record Books, GD63/1/1, 1 January 1892–31 December 1894.

Gaol Branch; Photographic Record and Description of Prisoners, GD128/1/2, 1 July 1895–31 December 1897.

Hobart Lower Court; Record of Cases, LC247/1/16 - LC247/1/39, 1848–1900.

Hobart Public Cemetery; Registers of Burials and Cremations Cornelian Bay Cemetery, AF35/1/2, 30 June 1893–31 August 1915.

Hobart Public Cemetery; Orders of Burials and Cremations Cornelian Bay Cemetery, AF70/1/26, 1 January 1901–31 December 1902.

Launceston Magistrates Court; Record of Cases Heard in Petty sessions, LC346/3/9, 2 April 1900–5 May 1902.

Police Department; Tasmania Police Gazettes, POL709/1/19 - POL709/1/29, 1882–1900.

Registrar-General's Department; Registers of Marriages in all Districts, RGD37/1/3, 1 January 1842–16 October 1843.

Registrar-General's Department; Register of births in Hobart, RGD37/1/3, 10 December 1838–15 January 1844.

Registrar-General's Department; Register of births in Hobart, RGD33/1/2, 1 January 1844–17 May 1847.

Registrar-General's Department; Register of deaths in Hobart, RGD35/1/2, 2 January 1844–2 April 1850.

Registrar-General's Department; Register of deaths in Hobart, RGD35/1/15, 16 March 1895–19 November 1897.

Registrar-General's Department; Register of Deaths in Hobart, RGD35/1/8, 2 August 1870–2 October 1876.

Registrar-General's Department; Register of Deaths in Hobart, RGD35/1/14, 3 October 1892–14 March 1895.

Registrar-General's Department; Register of Marriages in all districts, RGD37-1-12, 1 January 1853–31 December 1853.

Registrar-General's Department; Register of Deaths in Hobart, RGD35/1/7, 18 December 1863–2 August 1870.

Royal Hobart Hospital; Requisitions for Coffins for Pauper Interments, HSD146/1/1, 11 February 1864–21 January 1876.

Supreme Court; Hobart – minutes of proceedings, SC32/1/9, 24 January 1865–5 April 1887.

Tasmania House of Assembly; Report of Royal Commission, Charitable Institutions, HAJ1871/63, 1871.

Tasmania House of Assembly; Report of Royal Commission, Charitable Institutions, HAJ1871/63, 1871.

Supreme Court; minutes of Proceedings in Criminal Cases, Various Centres, SC32/1/8, 25 January 1859–7 December 1864.

Legislation (in order of enactment)

Vagrancy Act, Britain, 1824.

Police Ordinance, Van Diemen's Land, 1824.

Malicious Trespassing Act, New South Wales, 1827.

Metropolitan Police Act, New South Wales, 1829.

Police Act, New South Wales, 1833.

An Act for the prevention of Vagrancy and for the punishment of idle and disorderly Persons Rogues and Vagabonds and incorrigible Rogues in the Colony of New South Wales, 1835.

Bushranging Act, New South Wales, 1835.

An Act to Regulate The Police in Certain Towns and Ports within the Island of Van Diemen's Land and to make more effectual provision for the preservation of peace and good order throughout the said Island and its dependencies generally, 1838.

Vagrancy Act, New South Wales, 1851.

Vagrancy Act, Victoria, 1852.

Vagrant Ordinance, Province of Otago, New Zealand, 1861.

Police Act, Tasmania, 1865.

An Act to amend the law related to the Police Force in Victoria,1873.

Police Act, Tasmania, 1879.

Police Act, Tasmania, 1905.

An Act to define and restrain Vagrancy, New Zealand (Vagrant Act), 1866.

Contagious Diseases Act, New Zealand, 1869.

Aborigines Protection Act, Victoria, 1869.

Police Offences Act, New Zealand, 1884.

Public Health Act, Tasmania, 1885.

Police Regulation Act, Tasmania, 1898.

Newspapers

Age
Argus
Auckland Weekly News
Cornwall Chronicle
Daily Telegraph
Dominion
Examiner
Evening Post
Evening Star
Guardian
Illawarra Mercury
Hobarton Guardian
Hobart Town Advertiser
Hobart Town Daily Mercury
Launceston Examiner
Lyttleton Times
Maitland Mercury and Hunter River General Advertiser,
New Zealand Herald
New Zealand Truth
Otago Daily Times
Press
The Star
Tasmanian News
The Australian Star
The Inangahua Times

Contemporary journals

'Photography and Crime.' *Australasian Photographic Review*, July 21, 1903.

Contemporary publications

Bignold, H.B. *The Police Offences Acts and The Vagrancy Acts, Together with Notes of English and Australasian Cases, Forms and Index, Also Complete Cross-References to Local Government Acts and Ordinances.* 3rd edn. Sydney: The Law Book Company, 1915.

Cunningham, Peter. *Two Years in New South Wales Comprising Sketches of the Actual State of Society in that Colony, of its Peculiar Advantages to Emigrants, of its Topography, Natural History, &c. &c.* London: Henry Colburn, 1827.

Freeman, John. *Lights and Shadows of Melbourne Life.* London: Sampson Low, Marston, Searle & Rivington, Ltd, 1888.

Harris, Alexander. *Settlers and Convicts: Recollections of Sixteen Years' Labour in the Australian Backwoods, by an Emigrant Mechanic.* London: Cox, 1847.

Higgs, Mary. *Five Days and Five Nights as a Tramp among Tramps.* London: Heywood, 1904.

Howitt, William. *Land, Labour and Gold, or Two Years in Victoria. With Visits to Sydney and Van Diemen's Land.* London: Longman, 1855 [Kilmore: Lowden, 1972].

James, John Stanley. 'The Outcasts of Melbourne.' Part 1, *Gippsland Times*, May 23, 1876. Part 2, *Gippsland Times*, May 27, 1876. Syndicated to the *Argus* (Melbourne), May 27, 1876.

Kerr, John Hunter. *Glimpses of Life in Victoria: By 'A Resident'*, 1872. Edited and with an introduction by Marguerite Hancock. Melbourne: Miegunyah Press, 1996.

Lee, John A. *Roughnecks, Rolling Stones and Rouseabouts, With an Anthology of Early Swagger Literature.* Auckland: Penguin, 1989 (1977).

McPherson, Emma. *My Experiences in Australia: Being Recollections of a Visit to the Australian Colonies in 1856–7.* London: J.F. Hope, 1860.

Monckton, William. *Three Years with Thunderbolt*, edited by Ambrose Pratt. Melbourne: Cassell and Co., 1907.

Money, Charles L. *Knocking about in New Zealand.* Melbourne: Samuel Mullen, 1871.

Ribton-Turner, C.J. *A History of Vagrants and Vagrancy, and Beggars and Begging.* London: Chapman and Hall, 1887. Reprint, Montclair, New Jersey: Patterson Smith, 1972.

Shaw, John. *A Tramp to the Diggings, Being Notes of a Ramble in Australia and New Zealand in 1852.* London: Richard Bentley, 1852.

Singleton, John. *A narrative of incidents in the eventful life of a physician.* Melbourne: M.L. Hutchinson, 1891.

Suffolk, Owen. *Days of Crime and Years of Suffering*, 1867. Edited and with an introduction by David Dunstan. Kew, Vic.: Australian Scholarly Publishing, 2000.

Trollope, Anthony. *Australia and New Zealand* (two volumes). London: Dawsons of Pall Mall, 1873.

Ward, John. *A Tramp to the Diggings Being Notes of a Ramble in Australia and New Zealand in 1852.* London: Richard Bentley, 1852.

Books

Allen, Judith A. *Sex and Secrets: Crimes Involving Australian Women since 1880.* Melbourne and Oxford: Oxford University Press, 1990.

Althammer, Beate, Lutz Raphael and Tamara Stazic-Wendt, eds. *Rescuing the Vulnerable: Poverty, Welfare and Social Ties in Modern Europe*. New York: Berghahn Books, 2016.

Atkinson, Alan. *The Europeans in Australia, Volume Two: Democracy*. Melbourne and New York: Oxford University Press, 2004.

Ballantyne, Tony. *Orientalism and Race: Aryanism in the British Empire*. New York: Palgrave, 2002.

Ballantyne, Tony and Antoinette Burton, eds. *Moving Subjects: Gender, Mobility and Intimacy in an Age of Global Empire*. Chicago: University of Illinois Press, 2009.

Ballhatchet, Kenneth. *Race, Sex and Class under the Raj: Imperial Attitudes and Policies Their Critics, 1793–1905*. London: Weidenfeld and Nicholson, 1980.

Baxter, Carol. *Thunderbolt and His Lady: The True Story of Bushrangers Frederick Ward and Mary Anne Bugg*. Sydney: Allen and Unwin, 2011.

Bear, Laura. *Lines of the Nation: Indian Railway Workers, Bureaucracy, and the Intimate Historical Self*. New York: Columbia University Press, 2007.

Beier, A.L. *Masterless Men: The Vagrancy Problem in England 1560–1640*. London and New York: Methuen, 1985.

Beier, A.L. and Paul Ocobock, eds. *Cast Out: Vagrancy and Homelessness in Global and Historical Perspective*. Ohio: Ohio University Press, 2009.

Bellanta, Melissa. *Larrikins: A History*. St Lucia, Queensland: University of Queensland Press, 2012.

Benton, Lauren. *A Search for Sovereignty: Law and Geography in European Empires, 1400–1900*. New York: Cambridge University Press, 2010.

Benton, Lauren. *Law and Colonial Cultures: Legal Regimes in World History, 1400–1900*. Cambridge and New York: Cambridge University Press, 2002.

Boyce, James. *Van Diemen's Land*. Melbourne: Black Inc., 2008.

Bradbury, Bettina and Tamara Myers. *Negotiating Identities in Nineteenth and Twentieth-Century Montreal*. Vancouver and Toronto: University of British Columbia Press, 2005.

Brown-May, Andrew. *Melbourne Street Life*. Melbourne: Australian Scholarly Publishing, 1998.

Byrne, Paula J. *Criminal Law and Colonial Subject: New South Wales 1810–1830*. Cambridge: Cambridge University Press, 1993.

Cannon, Michael, ed. *The Vagabond Papers*. by John Stanley James. Melbourne: Melbourne University Press, 1969. First published in 5 v. by George Robertson 1877–8.

Cannon, Michael. *Melbourne after the Goldrush*. Main Ridge: Loch Haven Books, 1993.

Castles, Alex. *An Australian Legal History*. Sydney: The Law Book Company, 1982.

Chatterjee, Indrani. *Gender, Slavery and the Law in Colonial India*. New Delhi: Oxford University Press, 2002.

Coleborne, Catharine. *Insanity, Identity and Empire: Immigrants and Institutional Confinement in Australia and New Zealand, 1873–1910*. Manchester: Manchester University Press, 2015.

Coleborne, Catharine. *Madness in the Family: Insanity and Institutions in the Australasian Colonial World 1860s–1914*. Basingstoke and New York: Palgrave Macmillan, 2010.

Collingwood, Elizabeth. *Imperial Bodies: The Physical Experience of the Raj, c.1800–1947*. Cambridge: Polity Press, 2001.

Crace, Jim. *Harvest*. London: Picador, 2013.

Cresswell, Tim. *On the Move: Mobility in the Western World*. London and New York: Routledge, 2006.

Cresswell, Tim. *The Tramp in America*. London: Reaktion, 2001.

Cresswell, Tim and Peter Merriman, eds. *Geographies of Mobilities: Practices, Spaces, Subjects*. Surry: Ashgate, 2011.

Daniels, Kay. *So Much Hard Work: Women and Prostitution in Australian History*. Sydney: Fontana/Collins, 1984.

Darian-Smith, Kate, Patricia Grimshaw, Kiera Lindsey and Stuart Mcintyre, eds. *Exploring the British World: Identity, Cultural Production, Institutions*. Melbourne: RMIT Publishing, 2004.

Davison, Graeme, David Dunstan and Chris McConville. *The Outcasts of Melbourne: Essays in Social History*. Sydney: Allen & Unwin, 1985.

Davison, Graeme, J.W. McCarty and Ailsa McLeary, eds. *Australians 1888*. Sydney: Fairfax, Syme and Weldon, 1987.

Dorsett, Shaunnagh and Ian Hunter, eds. *Law and Politics in British Colonial Thought: Transpositions of Empire*. Basingstoke and New York: Palgrave Macmillan, 2010.

Dorsett, Shaunnagh and John McLaren, eds. *Legal Histories of the British Empire: Laws, Engagements and Legacies*. London and New York: Routledge, 2014.

Edmonds, Penelope. *Urbanizing Frontiers: Indigenous Peoples and Settlers in Nineteenth-Century Pacific Rim Cities*. Vancouver and Toronto: University of British Columbia Press, 2010.

Ell, Sarah, ed. *The Adventures of Pioneer Women: From Their Letters, Diaries and Reminiscences*. Auckland: Bush Press, 1992.

Evans, Tanya. *Fractured Families: Life on the Margins in Colonial New South Wales*. Sydney: UNSW Press, 2015.

Fairburn, Miles. *Nearly out of Heart and Hope: The Puzzle of a Colonial Labourer's Diary*. Auckland: Auckland University Press, 1995.

Fairburn, Miles. *The Ideal Society and Its Enemies: The Foundations of Modern New Zealand Society, 1850–1900*. Auckland: Auckland University Press, 1989.

Finnane, Mark, ed. *Policing in Australia: Historical Perspectives*. Sydney: New South Wales University Press, 1987.

Foster, Meg. *Boundary Crossers: The Hidden History of Australian's Other Bushrangers*. Sydney: NewSouth Books, 2022.

Frances, Raelene. *The Politics of Work: Gender and Labour in Victoria, 1880–1939*. Melbourne and Cambridge: Cambridge University Press, 1993.

Freeman, Mark and Gillian Nelson, eds. Vicarious Vagrants: Incognito Social Explorers and the Homeless in England, 1860–1910. Glasgow: The True Bill Press, 2008.

Garton, Stephen. *Out of Luck: Poor Australians and Social Welfare 1788–1988*. Sydney: Allen & Unwin, 1990.

Ghosh, Durba and Dane Kennedy, eds. *Decentring Empire: Britain, India and the Transcolonial World*. Hyderabad: Orient Longman, 2006.

Gluckman, Laurie. *Touching on Deaths: A Medical History of Early Auckland Based on the First 384 Inquests*, edited by Ann Gluckman and Mike Wagg. Auckland: Doppelganger, 2000.

Godfrey, Barry S. and Graeme Dunstall, eds. *Crime and Empire 1840–1940: Criminal Justice in Local and Global Context*. Cullompton: Willan Publishing, 2005.

Goodman, David. *Gold Seeking: Victoria and California in the 1850s*. Sydney: Allen & Unwin, 1994.

Hankin, Cherry A., ed. *Life in a Young Colony: Selections from Early New Zealand Writing*. Christchurch, Sydney and London: Whitcoulls Publishers, 1981.

Heney, Helen, ed. *Dear Fanny: Women's Letters to and from New South Wales, 1788–1857*. Canberra: Australian National University Press, 1985.

Hill, Richard. *The History of Policing in New Zealand, Volume One. Policing the Colonial Frontier*. Wellington: Historical Publications Branch, Department of Internal Affairs, 1986.

Hitchcock, David. *Vagrancy in English Culture and Society, 1650–1750*. London: Bloomsbury Academic, 2016.

Howell, Philip. *Geographies of Regulation: Policing Prostitution in Nineteenth-Century Britain and the Empire*. Cambridge UK: Cambridge University Press, 2009.

Humphreys, Robert. *No Fixed Abode: A History of Responses to the Roofless and the Rootless in Britain*. Basingstoke: Palgrave Macmillan, 1999.

Kain, Jennifer S. *Insanity and Immigration Control in New Zealand and Australia, 1860–1930*. Basingstoke: Palgrave/Springer, 2019.

Karskens, Grace. *The Rocks: Life in Early Sydney*. Carlton: Melbourne University Press, 1997.

Kercher, Bruce. *An Unruly Child: A History of Law in Australia*. St Leonards: Allen & Unwin, 1995.

Kercher, Bruce. *Outsiders: Tales from the Supreme Court of NSW, 1824–1836*. Melbourne: Australian Scholarly Publishing, 2006.

Kingston, Beverley. *The Oxford History of Australia. Volume 3, 1860–1900: Glad, Confident Morning*. Melbourne: Oxford University Press, 1993.

Kirkby, Diane and Catharine Coleborne, eds. *Law, History, Colonialism: The Reach of Empire*. Manchester: Manchester University Press, 2001.

Knafla, Louis, ed. *Crime, Gender and Sexuality in Criminal Prosecutions: Criminal Justice History*. Westport, CT: Greenwood Press, 2002.

Kociumbas, Jan. *The Oxford History of Australia. Volume 2, 1770–1860: Possessions*. Melbourne: Oxford University Press, 1992.

Lake, Marilyn and Henry Reynolds. *Drawing the Global Colour Line: White Men's Countries and the International Challenge of Racial Equality*. Cambridge: Cambridge University Press, 2008.

Lambert, D. and A. Lester, eds. *Colonial Lives across the British Empire: Imperial Careering in the Long Nineteenth Century*. New York: Cambridge University Press, 2006.

Levine, Phillipa. *Prostitution, Race and Politics: Policing Venereal Disease in the British Empire*. New York and London: Routledge, 2003.

Levine, Phillipa. *The British Empire: Sunrise to Sunset*. Harlow: Pearson Education, 2013.

McCalman, Janet. *Vandemonians: The Repressed History of Colonial Victoria*. Carlton: Miegunyah Press, 2021.

MacKinnon, Dolly. *Earls Colne's Early Modern Landscapes*. Burlington: Ashgate, 2014.

Mawani, Renisa. *Colonial Proximities: Crossracial Encounters and Judicial Truths in British Columbia, 1871–1921*. Vancouver: UBC Press, 2009.

Merriman, Peter and Lynne Pearce, eds. *Mobility and the Humanities*. London and New York: Routledge, 2018.

Merry, Sally Engle and Donald Brenneis, eds. *Law and Empire in the Pacific: Fiji and Hawai'i*. Santa Fe: SAR Press, 2004.

Mills, James. *Madness, Cannabis and Colonialism: The 'Native Only' Lunatic Asylums of British India, 1857 to 1900*. Basingstoke: Palgrave, 2000.

Morgan, Cecilia. *Building Better Britains? Settler Societies in the British World, 1783–1920*. Toronto: University of Toronto Press, 2016.

Mukerjee, S. K. et al., eds. *Crime and Punishment in the Colonies: A Statistical Profile*. Kensington, NSW: History project Inc., 1986.

O'Brassill-Kulfan, Kristin. *Vagrants and Vagabonds: Poverty and Mobility in the Early American Republic*. New York: New York University Press, 2019.

Olssen, Erik, Clyde Griffen and Frank Jones. *An Accidental Utopia? Social Mobility and the Foundations of an Egalitarian Society, 1880–1940*. Dunedin: Otago University Press, 2011.

Orwell, George. *Down and Out in Paris and London*. Harmondsworth: Penguin, 1933.

Otzen, Roslyn. *Dr John Singleton 1808–1891: Christian, Doctor, Philanthropist*. Melbourne: Melbourne City Mission, 2008.

Pooley, Colin G. and Jean Turnbull. *Migration and Mobility in Britain since the Eighteenth Century*. London: UCL Press, 1998.

Prest, Wilfred. *William Blackstone: Law and Letters in the Eighteenth Century*. Oxford: Oxford University Press, 2008.

Reid, Kirsty. *Gender, Crime and Empire: Convicts, Settlers and the State in Early Colonial Australia*. Manchester: Manchester University Press, 2007.

Robinson, Alistair. *Vagrancy in the Victorian Age: Representing the Wandering Poor in Nineteenth-Century Literature and Culture*. Cambridge: Cambridge University Press, 2022.

Robson, Lloyd. *A Short History of Tasmania*. Melbourne and Oxford: Oxford University Press, 1985.

Rose, Lionel. *'Rogues and Vagabonds': Vagrant Underworld in Britain 1815–1985*. London and New York: Routledge, 1988.

Seabrook, Jeremy. *Pauperland: Poverty and the Poor in Britain*. London: C. Hurst & Co., 2013.

Spiller, Peter, Jeremy Finn and Richard Boast. *A New Zealand Legal History*. Wellington: Brookers, 1995.

Stacey, Jackie and Janet Wolff, eds. *Writing Otherwise: Experiments in Cultural Criticism*. Manchester and New York: Manchester University Press, 2013.

Stedman Jones, Gareth. *Outcast London: A Study in the Relationship between Classes in Victorian Society*. London and New York: Verso, 1971.

Steel, Frances. *Oceania under Steam: Sea Transport and the Cultures of Colonialism, c. 1870–1914*. Manchester: Manchester University Press, 2011.

Stoler, Anna Laura. *Along the Archival Grain: Epistemic Anxieties and Colonial Common Sense*. Princeton and Oxford: Princeton University Press, 2009.

Stoler, Ann Laura. *Carnal Knowledge and Imperial Power: Race and the Intimate in Colonial Rule*. Berkeley: University of California Press, 2004.

Stoler, Ann Laura. *Race and the Education of Desire: Foucault's History of Sexuality and the Colonial Order of Things*. Durham and London: Duke University Press, 1995.

Stoler, Ann Laura, ed. *Haunted by Empire: Geographies of Intimacy in North American History*. Durham and London: Duke University Press, 2006.

Sturma, Michael. *Vice in a Vicious Society: Crime and Convicts in Mid-Nineteenth Century New South Wales*. St Lucia: University of Queensland Press, 1983.

Swanton, Bruce. *The Police of Sydney: 1788–1862*. Canberra: Australian Institute of Criminology and NSW Police Historical Society, 1984.

Tennant, Margaret. *The Fabric of Welfare: Voluntary Organisations, Government and Welfare in New Zealand, 1840–2005*. Wellington: Bridget Williams Books, 2007.

Tennant, Margaret. *Paupers and Providers: Charitable Aid in New Zealand*. Wellington: Allen and Unwin New Zealand Ltd and Historical Branch, Dept of Internal Affairs, 1989.

Twomey, Christina. *Deserted and Destitute: Motherhood, Wife Desertion and Colonial Welfare*. Melbourne: Australian Scholarly Publishing, 2002.

Urry, John. *Mobilities*. Malden: Polity, 2007.

Walsham, Alexandra. *The Reformation of the Landscape: Religion, Identity and Memory in Early Modern Britain and Ireland*. Oxford: Oxford University Press, 2011.

Wilson, Dean. *The Beat: Policing a Victorian City*. Beaconsfield, Vic.: Circa, 2006.

Woods, G. D. *A History of Criminal Law in New South Wales: The Colonial Period, 1788–1900*. Sydney: Federation Press, 2022.

Chapters in an edited collection

Arnold, David. 'Vagrant India: Famine, Poverty, and Welfare under Colonial Rule.' In *Cast Out: Vagrancy and Homelessness in Global and Historical Perspective*, edited by A. L. Beier and Paul Ocobock, 86–100. Ohio: Ohio University Press, 2009.

Barcharm, Manuhuia. 'The Politics of Māori Mobility.' In *Population Mobility and Indigenous Peoples in Australasia and North America*, edited by John Taylor and Martin Bell, 163–83. London and New York: Routledge, 2004.

Barman, Jean. 'Race, Greed and Something More: The Erasure of Urban Indigenous Space in Early Twentieth-Century British Columbia.' In *Making Settler Colonial Space: Perspectives on Race, Place and Identity*, edited by Tracey Banivanua Mar and Penelope Edmonds, 156–8. New York: Palgrave Macmillan, 2010.

Black, Edwin R. 'British Columbia: The Spoilt Child of Confederation.' In *Politics, Policy, and Government in British Columbia*, edited by R. K. Carty, 32–44. Vancouver: UBC Press, 1996.

Coleborne, Catharine. 'Consorting with "Others": Vagrancy Laws and Unauthorised Mobility across Colonial Borders in New Zealand from 1877 to 1900.' In *Empire and Mobility in the Long Nineteenth Century*, edited by Peter Merriman and David Lambert, 136–51. Manchester: Manchester University Press, 2020.

Coleborne, Catharine and Maree O'Connor. 'Vagrancy, Mobility and Colonialism.' In *Handbook of Historical Geography*, edited by Mona Domosh, Michael Heffernan and Charles W.J. Withers, 374–89. London: SAGE, 2020.

Coleborne, Catharine. 'Disability in Colonial Institutional Records.' In *Handbook of Disability History*, edited by Michael A. Rembis, Kim Nielsen and Catherine Kudlick, 281–92. Oxford: Oxford University Press, 2018.

Coleborne, Catharine. 'Law's Mobility: Vagrancy and Imperial Legality in the Trans-Tasman Colonial World.' In *New Zealand's Empire*, edited by Katie Pickles and Catharine Coleborne, 89–101. Manchester: Manchester University Press, 2016.

Coleborne, Catharine. 'Crime, the Legal Archive and Postcolonial Histories.' In *Crime and Empire 1840–1940: Criminal Justice in Local and Global Context*, edited by Graeme Dunstall and Barry Godfrey, 92–105. Devon: Willan Publishing, 2005.

Coleborne, Catharine. 'Passage to the Asylum: The Role of Police in Committals of the Insane in Victoria, Australia, 1848–1900.' In *The Confinement of the Insane, 1800–1965: International Perspectives*, edited by Roy Porter and David Wright, 129–48. Cambridge, UK: Cambridge University Press, 2003.

Cresswell, Tim. 'The Vagrant/Vagabond: The Curious Career of a Mobile Subject.' In *Geographies of Mobilities: Practices, Spaces, Subjects*, edited by Tim Cresswell and Peter Merriman, 239–54. London: Ashgate, 2011.

Crowther, Margaret. 'The Tramp.' In *Myths of the English*, edited by Roy Porter, 91–113. Cambridge: Polity Press, 1992.

Daley, Caroline. 'A Gendered Domain: Leisure in Auckland, 1890–1940.' In *The Gendered Kiwi*, edited by Caroline Daley and Deborah Montgomerie, 87–112. Auckland: Auckland University Press, 1999.

Davies, Susanne. '"Ragged, Dirty … Infamous and Obscene": The Vagrant in Late Nineteenth-Century Melbourne.' In *A Nation of Rogues? Crime, Law & Punishment in Colonial Australia*, edited by D. Philips and S. Davies, 141–65. Melbourne: Melbourne University Press, 1994.

Edmonds, Penelope. 'From Bedlam to Incorporation: Whiteness and the Racialisation of Colonial Urban Space in Victoria, British Columbia and Melbourne, Victoria, 1840s–1880s.' In *Exploring the British World: Identity, Cultural Production, Institutions*, 60–90. Melbourne: RMIT Publishing, 2004. Available online: https://search.informit.com.au/documentSummary;dn=872195844562722;res=IELHSS. ISBN: 0864593449. Accessed 31 October 2017.

Edmonds, Penelope. 'The Intimate, Urbanising Frontier: Native Camps and Settler Colonialism's Violent Array of Spaces around Early Melbourne.' In *Making Settler Colonial Space: Perspectives on Race, Place and Identity*, edited by Penelope Edmonds and Tracy Banivanua-Mar, 129–54. Basingstoke: Palgrave Macmillan, 2010.

Featherstone, Simon. 'Tramping: The Cult of the Vagabond in Early Twentieth-Century England.' In *Idleness, Indolence and Leisure in English Literature*, edited by Monika Fludernik and Miriam Nandi, 235–51. Basingstoke: Palgrave Macmillan, 2014.

Finnane, Mark. 'Law and Regulation.' In *The Cambridge History of Australia*, edited by Alison Bashford and Stuart Macintyre, 391–413. Cambridge: Cambridge University Press, 2013.

Finnane, Mark. 'The Limits of Jurisdiction: Law, Governance, and Indigenous Peoples in Colonized Australia.' In *Law and Politics in British Colonial Thought: Transpositions of Empire*, edited by Shaunnagh Dorsett and Ian Hunter, 149–68. Basingstoke and New York: Palgrave Macmillan, 2010.

Finnane, M. 'The Politics of Police Powers: The Making of the Police Offences Acts.' In *Policing in Australia: Historical Perspectives*, edited by M. Finnane, 88–113. Kensington: UNSW Press, 1987.

Fisher, Shirley. 'The Family and the Sydney Economy in the Late Nineteenth Century.' In *Families in Colonial Australia*, edited by Patricia Grimshaw, Chris McConville and Ellen McEwen, 153–62. Sydney: Allen & Unwin, 1985.

Garton, Stephen. 'Mad or Bad: Developments of Incarceration in NSW, 1880–1920.' In *What Rough Beast? The State and Social Order in Australian History*, edited by Sydney Labour History Group, 89–110. North Sydney: George Allen & Unwin, 1982.

Godfrey, Barry S. 'The English Model? Policing in Late Nineteenth-Century Tasmania.' In *Crime and Empire, 1840–1940: Criminal Justice in Local and Global Context*, edited by Barry Godfrey and Graeme Dunstall, 135–48. Cullompton: Willan, 2005.

Hammerton, A. James. 'Gender and Migration.' In *Gender and Empire*, edited by Philippa Levine, 156–80. Oxford: Oxford University Press, 2004.

Haskins, Victoria. 'Decolonizing the Archives: A Transnational Perspective.' In *Sources and Methods in the Histories of Colonialism: Approaching the Imperial Archive*, edited by Kirsty Reid and Fiona Paisley, 47–68. London and New York: Routledge, 2017.

Lee, Jenny Bol Jun. 'Eating Pork Bones and Puha with Chopsticks.' In *Unfolding History, Evolving Identity: The Chinese in New Zealand*, edited by Manying Ip, 94–112. Auckland: Auckland University Press, 2002.

Levine, Philippa. 'Sexuality, Gender and Empire.' In *Gender and Empire*, edited by Philippa Levine, 134–55. Oxford: Oxford University Press, 2004.

MacDonald, Charlotte. 'The "Social Evil": Prostitution and the Passage of the Contagious Diseases Act (1869).' In *Women in History: Essays on European Women in New Zealand*, edited by Barbara Brookes, Charlotte MacDonald and Margaret Tennant, 13–33. Wellington: Allen & Unwin/Port Nicholson Press, 1986.

Maxwell-Stewart, Hamish and Rebecca Kippen. '"What Is a Man That Is a Bolter to Do? I Would Steal the Governor's Axe Rather Than Starve": Old Lags and Recidivism in the Tasmanian Penal Colony.' In *Transnational Penal Cultures: New Perspectives on Discipline, Punishment and Desistance*, edited by Vivien Miller and James Campbell, 165–83. New York: Routledge, 2015.

May, A.J. 'Good Fences: Affective Sociability, Neighbourly Relations and Australian Municipalism.' In *Urban Emotions and the Making of the City: Interdisciplinary Perspectives*, edited by Katie Barclay and Jade Riddle, 107–23. London and New York: Routledge, 2021.

McLaren, John, Robert J. Menzies and Dorothy E. Chunn. 'Introduction.' In *Regulating Lives: Historical Essays on the State, Society, the Individual and the Law*, edited by John McLaren, Robert J. Menzies and Dorothy E. Chunn, 3–23. Vancouver: UBC Press, 2002.

Mongia, Radhika Viyas. 'Race, Nationality, Mobility: A History of the Passport.' In *After the Imperial Turn: Thinking with and through the Nation*, edited by Antoinette Burton, 196–214. Durham and London: Duke University Press, 2003.

Morrison, Bronwyn. 'Controlling the "Hopeless": Re-visioning the History of Female Inebriate Institutions c. 1870–1920.' In *Punishment and Control in Historical Perspective*, edited by H. Johnston, 135–57. London: Palgrave Macmillan, 2008.

Russell, Lynette. '"Tickpen", "Boro Boro": Aboriginal Economic Engagements in Early Melbourne.' In *Settler Colonial Governance in Nineteenth-Century Victoria*, edited by Leigh Boucher and Lynette Russell, 27–46. Canberra: ANU Press and Aboriginal History, 2015.

Said, Edward. *Culture and Imperialism*. London: Vintage, 1994.

Shore, Heather. 'Crime, Criminal Networks and the Survival Strategies of the Poor in Early Eighteenth-Century London.' In *The Poor in England 1700–1850: An Economy of Makeshifts*, edited by Alannah Tomkins and Steve King, 137–65. Manchester: Manchester University Press, 2003.

Simmel, Georg. 'The Stranger.' In *Georg Simmel: On Individuality and Social Forms*, edited by Donald Levine, 143–50. Chicago: University of Chicago Press, 1971.

Simmonds, Alecia. 'Legal Records.' In *Sources for the History of Emotions: A Guide*, edited by Katie Barclay, Sharon Crozier-De Rosa and Peter N. Stearns, 79–91. London and New York: Routledge, 2020.

Suzuki, Akihito. 'Lunacy and Labouring Men: Narratives of Male Vulnerability in Mid-Victorian England.' In *Medicine, Madness and Social History: Essays in Honour of Roy Porter*, edited by Roberta Bivins and John V. Pickstone, 118–28. Basingstoke and New York: Palgrave Macmillan, 2007.

Twomey, Christina. 'Vagrancy, Indolence and Ignorance: Race, Class and the Idea of Civilization in the Era of Aboriginal "Protection", Port Phillip 1835–49.' In *Writing Colonial Histories: Perspectives on Race, Place and Identity*, edited by Tracey Banivanua Mar and Julie Evans, 93–113. Basingstoke: Palgrave Macmillan, 2010.

Translated book

Foucault, Michel. *Discipline and Punish*. Translated by Alan Sheridan. London: Penguin, 1977.

Journal articles

Adams, Peter. 'History of Policing in Tasmania.' *Tasmania Police Journal* 54, no. 2 (March 1979).

Althammer, Beate. 'Roaming Men, Sedentary Women? The Gendering of Vagrancy Offenses in Nineteenth-Century Europe.' *Journal of Social History* 51, no. 4 (2018): 736–59.

Arnold, David. 'European Orphans and Vagrants in India in the Nineteenth Century.' *Journal of Imperial and Commonwealth History* 7, no. 2 (1979): 104–27.

Ballantyne, Tony. 'Mobility, Empire, Colonisation.' *History Australia* 11, no. 2 (2014): 7–37.

Beardmore, Carol. '"This Man Really Is an Intolerable Pest": Perceptions and Treatment of the Disabled in the Workhouse, 1834–1900.' *Family & Community History* 25, no. 2 (2022): 121–39.

Blackie, Daniel and Alexia Moncrieff. 'State of the Feld: Disability History.' *History* 107, no. 377 (2022): 789–811.

Breathnach, Ciara. 'Even "Wilder Workhouse Girls": The Problem of Institutionalisation among Irish Immigrants to New Zealand.' *Journal of Imperial and Commonwealth History* 39, no. 5 (2011): 771–94.

Bright, David. 'Loafers Are Not Going to Subsist upon Public Credulence: Vagrancy and the Law in Calgary, 1900–1914.' *Labour/Le Travail* 36 (1995): 37–58.

Burke, Lorelle and Catharine Coleborne. 'Insanity and Ethnicity in New Zealand: Māori Encounters with the Auckland Mental Hospital, 1860–1900.' *History of Psychiatry* 22, no. 3 (2011): 285–301.

Byrne, Paula Jane. 'Freedom in a Bonded Society: The Administrative Mind and the "Lower Classes" in Colonial New South Wales.' *Journal of Australian Studies* 21, no. 53 (1997): 51–8.

Byrne, Paula Jane. 'Mapping Power: Yass and the Law in the 1850s.' *Law & History* 9, no. 1 (2022): 125–57.

Carr, Sarah. 'Regulating Sexuality in Early Otago, 1848–1867.' *New Zealand Journal of History* 50, no. 1 (2016): 30–46.

Coleborne, Catharine. 'Regulating "Mobility" and Masculinity through Institutions in Colonial Victoria, 1870s–1890s.' *Law Text Culture* 15 (2011): 45–71.

Coleborne, Catharine. 'Mobility Stopped in Its Tracks: Narratives of the Failures of the Mobile in the Trans-Tasman World of the Nineteenth Century.' *Transfers: Interdisciplinary Journal of Mobility Studies* 5 (2015): 87–103.

Cooper, Annabel. 'Poor Men in the Land of Promises: Settler Masculinity and the Male Breadwinner Economy in Late Nineteenth-Century New Zealand.' *Australian Historical Studies* 39 (2008): 245–61.

Cresswell, Tim. 'The Production of Mobilities.' *New Formations: A Journal of Culture/Theory/Politics* 43 (2001): 11–25.

Cresswell, Tim. 'Towards a Politics of Mobility.' *Environment and Planning D: Society and Space* 28 (2010): 17–31.

Cresswell, Tim. 'Embodiment, Power and the Politics of Mobility: The Case of Female Tramps and Hobos.' *Transactions of the Institute of British Geographers* NS 24 (1999): 175–92.

Crowson, N.J. 'Tramps' Tales: Discovering the Life-Stories of Late Victorian and Edwardian Vagrants.' *English Historical Review* 125, no. 577 (2020): 1488–526.

Curry, Gerard. 'A Bundle of Vague Diverse Offences: The Vagrancy Laws with Special Reference to the New Zealand Experience.' *Anglo-American Law Review* 1 (1972): 523–36.

Darroch, A. Gordon. 'Migrants in the Nineteenth Century: Fugitives or Families in Motion?' *Journal of Family History* 6, no. 3 (1981): 257–77.

Davies, Sue. 'Working Their Way to Respectability: Women, Vagrancy and Reform in Late Nineteenth-Century Melbourne.' *Lilith* 6 (1989): 50–63.

Dickey, Brian. 'Why Were There No Poor Laws in Australia?' *Journal of Policy History* 4, no. 2 (1992): 111–33.

Eccles, Audrey. '"Furiously Mad": Vagrancy Law and a Sub-group of the Disorderly Poor.' *Rural History* 24, no. 1 (2013): 25–40.

Ernst, Waltraud. 'European Madness and Gender in Nineteenth-Century British India.' *Social History of Medicine* 9, no. 3 (1996): 357–82.

Fairburn, Miles. 'Vagrants, "Folk Devils" and Nineteenth-Century New Zealand as a Bondless Society.' *Historical Studies* 21 (1985): 495–514.

Fineman, Martha Albertson. 'The Vulnerable Subject: Anchoring Equality in the Human Condition.' *Yale Journal of Law and Feminism* 20, no. 1 (2008): 1–23.

Finnane, Mark. '"Absolutely Free"? Freedom of Movement and "The Police Power" in Federation Australia.' *Australian Historical Studies* 54, no. 1 (2023): 6–23.

Finnane, Mark. '"They Were Subject to Our Laws": Aboriginal Defendants in NSW Courts 1850–1914.' *History Australia* 17, no. 3 (2020): 448–70.

Finnane, Mark. 'The Origins of Criminology in Australia.' *Australian and New Zealand Journal of Criminology* 45, no. 2 (2012): 157–78.

Finnane, Mark and Stephen Garton. 'The Work of Policing: Social Relations and the Criminal Justice System in Queensland 1880–1914: Part 1.' *Labour History* 62 (1992): 52–70.

Fischer-Tiné, Harald. 'Britain's Other Civilizing Mission: Class Prejudice, European "Loaferism" and the Workhouse-System and Colonial India.' *Indian Economic and Social History Review* 42 (2005): 295–338.

Foster, Meg. 'Protecting the Colony from Its People: Bushranging, Vagrancy, and Social Control in Colonial New South Wales.' *Law and History Review* 40 (2022): 655–77.

Foster, Meg. 'The Forgotten War of 1900: Jimmy Governor and the Aboriginal People of Wollar.' *Australian Historical Studies* 50, no. 3 (2019): 305–20.

Freeman, Mark. 'Journeys into Poverty Kingdom: Complete Participation and the British Vagrant, 1866–1914.' *History Workshop Journal* 52, no. 1 (2001): 99–121.

Ganachari, Aravind. '"White Man's Embarrassment": European Vagrancy in Nineteenth-Century Bombay.' *Economic and Political Weekly* 37, no. 25 (2002): 22–8.

Garton, Stephen. '"Once a Drunkard Always a Drunkard": Social Reform and the Problem of "Habitual Drunkenness" in Australia, 1880–1914.' *Labour History* 53 (1987): 38–53.

Gerrard, Jessica. 'The Interconnected Histories of Labour and Homelessness.' *Labour History* 112 (2017): 155–74.

Han, Clara. 'Precarity, Precariousness, and Vulnerability.' *Annual Review of Anthropology* 47 (2018): 331–43.

Harring, Sidney. 'Class Conflict and the Enforcement of the Tramp Acts in Buffalo during the Depression of 1893–94.' *Law and Society Review* 11 (1977): 873–912.

Hawk, Angela. 'Going "Mad" in Gold Country: Migrant Populations and the Problem of Containment in Pacific Mining Boom Regions.' *Pacific Historical Review* 80, no. 1 (2011): 64–96.

Helps, Lisa. 'Body, Power, Desire: Mapping Canadian Body History.' *Journal of Canadian Studies* 41 (2007): 126–50.

Hitchcock, David. 'A Typology of Travellers: Migration, Justice and Vagrancy in Warwickshire, 1670–1730.' *Rural History* 23, no. 1 (2012): 21–39.

Hitchcock, David. 'Editorial: Poverty and Mobility in England, 1600–1850.' *Rural History* 24, no. 1 (2013): 1–8.

Hitchcock, Tim. 'The London Vagrancy Crisis of the 1780s.' *Rural History* 24, no. 1 (2013): 59–72.

Holst, Heather. 'Equal before the Law? The Chinese in the Nineteenth-Century Castlemaine Police Courts.' *Journal of Australian Colonial History* 6 [special issue: Active Voices, Hidden Histories: the Chinese in Colonial Australia] (2004): 113–36.

Inwood, Kris, H. Maxwell-Stewart, D. Oxley. and J. Stankovich. 'Growing Incomes, Growing People in Nineteenth-Century Tasmania.' *Australian Economic History Review* 55, no. 2 (2015): 187–211.

Karskens, Grace. 'Revisiting the Worldview: The Archaeology of Convict Households in Sydney's Rocks Neighbourhood.' *Historical Archaeology* 37, no. 1 (2003): 34–55.

Karskens, Grace. '"This Spirit of Emigration": The Nature and Meanings of Escape in Early New South Wales.' *Journal of Australian Colonial History* 7 (2005): 1–34.

Kaufmann, Vincent, Manfred Max Bergman and Dominique Joye. 'Motility: Mobility as Capital.' *International Journal of Urban and Regional Research* 28, no. 4 (2004): 749–50.

Kimber, Julie. '"A Nuisance to the Community": Policing the Vagrant Woman.' *Journal of Australian Studies* 34, no. 3 (2010): 275–93.

Kimber, Julie. 'Poor Laws: A Historiography of Vagrancy in Australia.' *History Compass* 11 (2013): 537–50.

Leith, Sam. 'Jim Crace's Closed Communities.' *The Times Literary Supplement* no. 5734 (22 February, 2013): 20.

Lever, Michael. 'When Absence Is the Artifact: Unmarked Graves in the Jewish Section, Melbourne General Cemetery.' *International Journal of Historical Archaeology* 13, no. 4 (2009): 464–87.

Maxwell-Stewart, H., K. Inwood and J. Stankovich. 'The Prison and the Colonial Family.' *History of the Family* 20, no. 2 (2015): 231–48.

McCalman, Janet and Rebecca Kippen. 'The Life-Course Demography of Convict Transportation to Van Diemen's Land.' *History of the Family* 25, no. 3 (2020): 432–54.

McCausland, Ruth and Eileen Baldry. '"I feel Like I failed Him by Ringing the Police": Criminalising Disability in Australia.' *Punishment and Society* 19, no. 3 (2017): 290–309.

McConville, Chris. 'The Location of Melbourne's Prostitutes, 1870–1920.' *Australian Historical Studies* 19, no. 74 (1980): 86–97.

McLeod, Julie. 'Vulnerability and the Neo-liberal Youth Citizen: A View from Australia.' *Comparative Education* 48, no. 1 (2012): 11–26.

Macdonald, Charlotte. 'Crime and Punishment in New Zealand, 1840–1913: A Gendered History.' *New Zealand Journal of History* 23, no. 1 (1989): 5–21.

McLeod, Andrew. 'On the Origins of Consorting Laws.' *Melbourne University Law Review* 37, no. 1 (2013): 103–42.

Merriman, Peter and Lynne Pearce. 'Mobility and the Humanities.' *Mobilities* 12, no. 4 (2017): 493–508.

Moloughney, Brian and John Stenhouse. '"Drug-besotten, Sin-begotten, Fiends of filth": New Zealanders and the Oriental Other, 1850–1920.' *New Zealand Journal of History* 33, no. 1 (1999): 43–64.

Mullaly, Sasha. 'Marginally Relevant? The "Fathers of Confederation" and Canadian History.' *Canadian Historical Review* 98 (2017): 728–33.

Murphy, John. *A Decent Provision: Australian Welfare Policy, 1870 to 1949*. Farnham, Surrey: Ashgate, 2011.

Nagy, Victoria. 'Women, Old Age and Imprisonment in Victoria, Australia 1860–1920.' *Women and Criminal Justice* 30, no. 3 (2020): 151–71.

Nagy, Victoria and Alana Piper. 'Imprisonment of Female Urban and Rural Offenders in Victoria, 1860–1920.' *International Journal for Crime, Justice and Social Democracy* 8, no. 1 (2019): 100–115.

Nair, Aparna. '"They Shall See His Face": Blindness in British India, 1850–1950.' *Medical History* 61, no. 2 (2017): 181–99.

Nettelbeck, Amanda. 'Creating the Aboriginal "Vagrant": Protective Governance and Indigenous Mobility in Colonial Australia.' *Pacific Historical Review* 87, no. 1 (2017): 79–100.

O'Brien, Anne. 'Pauperism Revisited.' *Australian Historical Studies* 42, no. 2 (2011): 212–29.

O'Brien, Anne. '"Homeless" Women and the Problem of Visibility: Australia 1900–1940.' *Women's History Review* 2, no. 2 (2018): 135–53.

Offer, Elizabeth. 'Police Use or Misuse? Police Agency and "The Neglected and Criminal Children's Act 1864".' *Victorian Historical Journal* 89, no. 1 (2019): 27–43.

Petrow, Stefan. 'Creating an Orderly Society: The Hobart Municipal Police 1880–1898.' *Labour History* 78 (1998): 175–94.

Petrow, Stefan. 'Juvenile Delinquents in Launceston: 1860 to 1896.' *University of Tasmania Law Review* 17, no. 2 (1998): 134–63.

Petrow, Stefan. 'Policing in a Penal Colony: Governor Arthur's Police System in Van Diemen's Land, 1826–1836.' *Law and History Review* 18, no. 2 (2000): 351–95.

Piper, Alana and Lisa Durnian. 'Theft on Trial: Prosecution, Conviction and Sentencing Patterns in Colonial Victoria and Western Australia.' *Australia and New Zealand Journal of Criminology* 50, no. 1 (2017): 5–22.

Piper, Alana and Victoria Nagy. 'Versatile Offending: Criminal Careers of Female Prisoners in Australia, 1860–1920.' *Journal of Interdisciplinary History* 48, no. 2 (2017): 187–210.

Piper, Alana and Victoria Nagy. 'Risk Factors and Pathways to Imprisonment among Incarcerated Women in Victoria, 1860–1920.' *Journal of Australian Studies* 42, no. 3 (2018): 268–84.

Pitsula, James. 'The Treatment of Tramps in Late Nineteenth-Century Toronto.' *Historical Papers* 15 (1980): 116–32.

Pooley, Colin. 'The Mobility of Criminals in North-West England, c 1880s–1910.' *Local Population Studies* 53 (1994): 14–28.

Pooley, Colin. 'On the Street in Nineteenth-Century London.' *Urban History* 48, no. 2 (2021): 211–26.

Poutanen, M.A. 'Regulating Public Space in Early Nineteenth-Century Montreal: Vagrancy Laws and Gender in a Colonial Context.' *Social History* 35 (2002): 35–58.

Pratt, John. 'The Dark Side of Paradise: Explaining New Zealand's History of High Imprisonment.' *British Journal of Criminology* 46, no. 4 (2006): 541–60.

Rhook, Nadia. 'Listen to Nodes of Empire: Speech and Whiteness in Victorian Hawker's License Courts.' *Journal of Colonialism and Colonial History* 15, no. 2 (2014): DOI: 10.1353/cch.2014.0022.

Roberts, David Andrew and Carol Baxter. '"Mrs Thunderbolt": Setting the Record Straight on the Life and Times of Mary Ann Bugg.' *Journal of the Royal Australian Historical Society* 99, no. 1 (2013): 55–76.

Roberts, M.J.D. 'Public and Private in Early Nineteenth-Century London: The Vagrant Act of 1822 and Its Enforcement.' *Social History* 13, no. 3 (1988): 273–94.

Rollison, David. 'Exploding England: The Dialectics of Mobility and Settlement in Early Modern England.' *Social History* 24, no. 1 (1999): 1–16.

Scates, Bruce. 'A Struggle for Survival: Unemployment and the Unemployed Agitation in Late Nineteenth-Century Melbourne.' *Australian Historical Studies* 24, no. 94 (1990): 41–63.

Schedvin, M.B. and C.B. Schedvin. 'The Nomadic Tribes of Urban Britain: A Prelude to Botany Bay.' *Historical Studies* 20, no. 78 (1978): 254–76.

Seuffert, Nan. 'Civilisation, Settlers and Wanderers: Law, Politics and Mobility in Nineteenth-Century New Zealand and Australia.' *Law Text Culture* 15 (2011): 10–44.

Sestanovich, Clare. 'Logs vs. Dead Donkeys: The Tweet That Helped Me Make Sense of Jim Crace.' *The Atlantic* (September 10, 2013). https://www.theatlantic.com/entertainment/archive/2013/09/logs-vs-dead-donkeys-the-tweet-that-helped-me-make-sense-of-jim-crace/279487/.

Smith, F.B. 'Curing Alcoholism in Australia, 1880s–1920s.' *Journalism of Australian Colonial History* 8 (2006): 137–58.

Southall, Humphrey. 'The Tramping Artisan Revisits: Labour Mobility and Economic Distress in Early Victorian England.' *Economic History Review* 44, no. 2 (1991): 272–96.

Strange, Julie Marie. 'Tramp: Sentiment and the Homeless Man in the Late-Victorian and Edwardian City.' *Journal of Victorian Culture* 16, no. 2 (2011): 242–58.

Straw, Leigh. '"The Worst Female Character": Criminal Underclass Women in Perth and Fremantle, 1900–1939.' *Journal of Australian Studies* 37, no. 2 (2013): 208–24.

Swain, Shurlee. 'Destitute and Dependent: Case Studies in Poverty in Melbourne, 1890–1900.' *Australian Historical Studies* 19, no. 74 (1990): 98–107.

Swain, Shurlee. 'The Value of the Vignette in the Writing of Welfare History.' *Australian Historical Studies* 39, no. 2 (2008): 199–212.

Taylor, David 'Melbourne, Middlesbrough and Morality: Policing Victorian "New Towns" in the Old World and the New.' *Social History* 31, no. 1 (2006): 15–38.

Tennant, Margaret. 'Elderly Indigents and Old Men's Homes 1880–1920.' *New Zealand Journal of History* 17, no. 1 (1983): 3–20.

Tomkins, Alannah and Catharine Coleborne. 'Professional Migration, Occupational Challenge and Mental Health: Medical Practitioners in New Zealand, 1850s–1890s.' *Social History of Medicine* 34, no. 3 (2021): 874–93.

Twomey, Christina. 'Courting Men: Mothers, Magistrates and Welfare in the Australian Colonies.' *Women's History Review* 8, no. 2 (1999): 231–46.

Wilson, Dean. 'Community and Gender in Victorian Auckland.' *New Zealand Journal of History* 30, no. 1 (1996): 24–42.

Wilson, Dean. 'Policing Poverty: Destitution and Police Work in Melbourne, 1880–1910.' *Australian Historical Studies* 36 (2005): 97–112.

Zelinsky, Wilbur. 'The Hypothesis of the Mobility Transition.' *Geographical Review* 61 (1971): 219–49.

Conference papers

Coleborne, Catharine and Hamish Maxwell-Stewart. 'Former Convicts Prosecuted as Vagrants in Tasmania: Plotting a Shadowy History Using Tasmanian Police Gazette Data, 1865–c. 1900.' Paper presented at ANZLHS Conference: 'Tenuous Histories and Provable Pasts', UTS, 1–3 December 2022.

Nagy, Victoria. 'The Health and Medical Needs of Victoria's Older Female Prisoners, 1860–1920.' Paper presented at Prison Medicine: Health and Incarceration in History Conference, University of Wollongong. 2019.

Thesis or dissertation

Bierens, Kali. 'The Captain's Lady: Mary Ann Bugg.' Honours thesis, University of Tasmania, Australia. 2008.

Davies, Susanne. 'Vagrancy and the Victorians: The Social Construction of the Vagrant in Melbourne, 1880–1907.' PhD Thesis, University of Melbourne, Australia. 1990.

Helps, Lisa. 'Bodies Public, City Spaces: Becoming Modern Victoria, British Columbia, 1871–1901.' MA thesis, University of Victoria, British Columbia, Canada. 2005.

Law, Penelope. "'Too Much "Yellow" in the Melting Pot?": Perceptions of the New Zealand Chinese, 1930–1960.' Honours thesis, University of Otago, New Zealand. 1994.

Mitchell, Marjorie Anne. 'Central West New South Wales, 1891–1893. A Regional History "from Below".' PhD Thesis, Australian National University, Canberra, Australia. 2018.

Powell, Debra. 'A History of Infanticide and Child-Homicide in New Zealand, 1870–1910.' PhD Thesis, University of Waikato, New Zealand. 2013.

Roth, David. 'Life, Death and Deliverance at Callan Park Hospital for the Insane 1877 to 1923.' PhD Thesis, Australian National University, Canberra, Australia. 2020.

Sutton, Anthea Maree. 'Delineating the Fine Line between the Mad and the Bad: Victorian Prisons and Insane Asylums, 1856–1914.' PhD Thesis, University of New England, Armidale, New South Wales. 2022.

Wilson, Dean. 'Community Violence in Auckland, 1850–1875.' MA thesis, University of Auckland, New Zealand. 1993.

Index

www.ingramcontent.com/pod-product-compliance
Lightning Source LLC
Chambersburg PA
CBHW062026270326
41929CB00014B/2338

* 9 7 8 1 3 5 0 2 5 2 7 2 1 *